WERTHEIM PUBLICATIONS IN INDUSTRIAL RELATIONS

Established in 1923 by the family of the late Jacob Wertheim "for the support of original research in the field of industrial cooperation . . ."

Workers Councils

A STUDY OF WORKPLACE ORGANIZATION ON BOTH SIDES OF THE IRON CURTAIN

ADOLF STURMTHAL

Harvard University Press
CAMBRIDGE, MASSACHUSETTS
1964

DISTRIBUTED IN GREAT BRITAIN BY OXFORD UNIVERSITY PRESS, LONDON
LIBRARY OF CONGRESS CATALOG CARD NUMBER 64-13429

PRINTED IN THE UNITED STATES OF AMERICA

Foreword

The plant or work level of the organization of workers is one of the most distinctive features of any national industrial relations system. Among advanced countries there is a wide assortment of plant-level bodies. The local union, or a unit of that local, in an industrial plant in the United States stands in marked contrast to the workers' councils in many countries of Europe. The place of the plant-level organization of workers in the larger industrial relations system is to be understood in terms of its interactions with labor organizations outside the plant, managements, and governmental officials.

Professor Sturmthal has provided us with a comparative study of workers councils in Germany and France in Western Europe, and Poland and Yugoslavia in Eastern Europe. He traces the historical and ideological development of these bodies in each country and details their functions and actual operations. The comparative method is particularly appropriate to this study; the experience of these continental countries is related to that of Great Britain and the United States.

There is keen interest in the plant level, in the relations among the worker, his supervisor, and labor representative, in both the advanced and the newly developing countries. Governments, managers, and labor organizations everywhere are concerned with ways of eliciting improved effort and performance; they are exploring new ways of training and supervising a workforce, and they seek new procedures to develop discipline and to settle complaints or dissipate protest. The range of experience with workers' councils provides a record of general interest to those shaping or modifying industrial relations and economic institutions.

Professor Sturmthal is one of the few scholars qualified to write this volume. He is thoroughly familiar with Western European experience from his early years in the Austrian labor movement and his extensive contacts, research, and writing since the end of World War II. Over the years he has closely followed developments in Eastern Europe. He also has a wide acquaintance and rich understanding of industrial relations in the United States. This volume thus reflects the research and experience of a mature scholar.

The work is a part of the Inter-University Study of Labor Problems in Economic Development under the direction of Clark Kerr, Frederick H. Harbison, Charles A. Myers, and John T. Dunlop, financed in part by the Ford Foundation.

John T. Dunlop

Contents

Author's Preface ix

Introduction 1

CHAPTER I The Evolution of the Councils 6

CHAPTER II France 25

CHAPTER III Germany 53

CHAPTER IV Yugoslavia 86

CHAPTER V Poland 119

CHAPTER VI The Councils and the Labor Movement 140

CHAPTER VII Problems of the Bargaining Councils 156

CHAPTER VIII Problems of the Managerial Councils 168

CHAPTER IX The Councils in Perspective 180

Notes 195

Index 211

Tables

1. Industrial Production Index between 1946 and 1950 in Yugoslavia 90
2. National income and investment between 1938 and 1948 in Yugoslavia 92
3. Election systems of works councils in the four countries 147
4. Council functions in the four countries 163

Author's Preface

This study was intended to be a worm's eye view of industrial relations. I soon realized that even from this lowly perspective the answer to many questions would have to be sought in the fundamentals of the social, economic, and political systems. The fact that a comparative study was made in four countries — two each in Western and Eastern Europe — accentuated the need to push the investigation ahead into the area of theory. An attempt was made to formulate hypotheses about whether and how ideology and even more the stage of industrialization in the four countries affect the industrial relations system in the plant.

The selection of the countries was determined primarily by the desire to examine the operation of workers' councils in different social systems, in the second place by the author's acquaintance with certain countries, their labor movements, language, and politics. Beyond this, United States and British experience and institutions served as a framework within which the comparative analysis was made.

The range of the problems into which this study was necessarily expanded is bounded by the Yugoslav council system at one end and the grievance procedure and the process of wage determination in France and Germany at the other end. In other words, this book deals with the attempt to establish a decentralized market economy on the basis of Socialist property arrangements — one of the most interesting social experiments which this century has produced — as well as with the status of the German and French unions in the plant. The significance of the Yugoslav council system as the cornerstone of non-Stalinist communism was underlined by Khrushchev's somewhat reluctantly approving remarks in 1963. At about the same time the Institute of German Industry referred to the then impending elections to the workers' councils as "a part of economic democracy in action."

The hypotheses outlined in the latter part of this study permit tentative forecasts regarding the development of the main forces likely to determine the evolution of the workers' councils in their function as bargaining agents:

rising prosperity tends to move the focus of union concern nearer to the plant; rapid technological change requires action outside the scope of collective bargaining, at the level of political, general economic, and social decision-making. It is difficult to foresee at this stage what the future status of the councils will be as the result of these contradictory trends. The future of the councils as special forms of management is, at least in the short run, contingent upon political far more than economic developments. It is tied up with the profound upheaval of the Communist world which has found its current expression in the China-Soviet dispute.

Since the manuscript of this book was completed by the middle of 1962, no reference could be made to material published since then. In particular, the interesting articles of Arthur Ross ("Prosperity and Labor Relations in Western Europe: Italy and France," *Industrial and Labor Relations Review,* 16.1 (October, 1962), and "Prosperity and Labor Relations in Europe: The Case of West Germany," *Quarterly Journal of Economics,* LXXVI.3 (August, 1962) can only be acknowledged in this place, along with the investigation of the shop stewards in Danish industry undertaken by the Danish National Institute of Social Research and reported in the *British Journal of Industrial Relations,* I.3 (1963).

Thanks are due to the following for permissions to quote from published material: Basil Blackwell; Carnegie Endowment for International Peace; Droit Social; Harvard University Press; Questions Actuelles du Socialisme; B. C. Roberts. The *Industrial and Labor Relations Review* of Cornell University permitted me to reprint material previously published in the *Review.*

Charles Myers of Massachusetts Institute of Technology and John Windmuller (Cornell University) have read an earlier version of the manuscript and offered a number of valuable suggestions for its improvement. The usual caveat must of course be added as regards the final product.

To June Hill of the Wertheim series and Barbara Dennis of the University of Illinois go my thanks for editorial assistance.

The Ford Foundation and the Graduate Research Board of the University of Illinois enabled me to do the field work necessary for this study. International comparative work tends to be particularly expensive in time and money. I am grateful to both institutions for their assistance. Needless to say they are not to be held responsible for my judgments and interpretations.

Adolf Sturmthal

Champaign, Illinois
December 1963

WORKERS COUNCILS: A Study of Workplace Organization on Both Sides of the Iron Curtain

Introduction

The drive for workplace organization of workers has had many sources in history, just as the forms and the purposes of the organization have varied from country to country and from period to period. The observer is thus confronted with a bewildering variety of motivations, objectives, and types of organizations, as well as of designations. The shop steward (grievance man in the United States), checkweigh man in British coal mining, the "father of the chapel" in the printing industry, the French *délégué du personnel,* the member of the "plant committee," the German works councillor, and the member of the *Commissione Interne* in Italy are only a few examples of the many appellations for representatives of the shop organization. Moreover, it would seem that not only the student of workers' organization in the shop, but also its participants and even its promoters were not always clear about what they were aiming at or about the nature of the organization in which they were involved. At times, there were sharp cleavages within the workers' councils — as we shall call the workplace organization for the sake of brevity — and the labor movements at large about the purposes of workshop groups and the methods to be used in their establishment. Some of these disputes took on historic significances: The slogan "all power to the Soviets" — Soviets being the Russian term for workers' councils — accompanied the rise of the Bolsheviks, and the issue of whether the German workers' councils were to be organs of legislation and public administration or supplementary bargaining agents in the plant divided German Communists and Social Democrats during a decisive phase of German history after World War I. In other situations, organizations at the workshop level performed two different functions at once or changed their character over the course of time. G. D. H. Cole[1] has shown how the British shop steward movement during World War I evolved from a simple workshop device in the system of industrial relations into a reform movement aiming at refashioning the trade unions and, finally, into a nucleus of revolutionary organization. Like the labor movement itself, the shop organization of the workers has been an instrument used for different purposes in different countries at different times.

Yet, in this diversity, certain similarities and patterns can be discerned. The simplest type of shop steward and the one which historically represents in all probability the first step toward shop organization is the "collector" ("card steward" or "ticket steward"), a union functionary in the shop entrusted with "the duty of trying to ensure that the skilled workers employed belonged to the Union and paid their contributions regularly."[2] These shop stewards are essentially agents of internal union administration and form a liaison between the union member and the lowest level of the union administration — the local branch — a function which is especially necessary when the branch has a geographic base and is not limited to one shop.

Another type of shop organization most familiar to the American reader has been developed as part and parcel of the collective bargaining process or as a supplement thereto. The union steward or the grievance man functions within the framework of a workplace organization in connection with the bargaining process. Third, the Syndicalists and the guild socialists regarded the shop organization as an instrument to enable the workers to play a role in the management of the enterprise.[3] They assigned managerial functions to the councils. In the fourth place, there is a tendency to use the workplace organization as a political device. This was the point of the Bolshevik slogans in 1917, but one should not infer from this example that the political intent of the workers' councils is necessarily communistic. During the Hungarian rebellion of 1956, for example, the Budapest workers' councils took the leadership of the anti-Communist rebellion. There have also been attempts to use the councils as tools to reform the trade union movement or sometimes as substitutes for the conventional trade unions. Examples of such attempts can be found in England and Germany, as well as in other countries.

Stewards need not operate as committees and in fact do not always do so. However, it is not sufficient to examine union statutes or laws to determine whether workshop committees exist, for such committees are often formed *de facto* without special statutory provisions. Moreover, certain types of councils can only perform their duties, in part or altogether, by convening in committees.

According to their objectives we can thus distinguish five main types of shop stewards or workers' councils which we may characterize in the following terms:

Organizing (membership) stewards
Bargaining councils
Managerial councils
Political councils
Union reform councils

This distinction refers to the tasks that the councils are supposed to perform or to the issues with which they are to deal. However, the difference is less clear-cut than the terminology might lead one to think. As we pointed out above, a council may perform more than one function. Union agents act as grievance handlers or otherwise as bargaining agents. The boundary between the purposes of bargaining and managerial councils is fluid. Collective bargaining gives labor a voice in determining policies in certain areas of plant administration, although no one has been able to define once and for all the limits of these areas. In fact, they have shown a long run tendency to expand, and it is difficult to predict whether and at what point this process will reach its end.[4] The further it progresses, the less significant becomes the distinction between bargaining and participation in management from the point of view of the subject matter involved, for bargaining represents a form of influencing management decisions, just as does participation in management. Traditionally, the term "collective bargaining" refers to negotiations about a limited range of subjects — issues directly relating to the wages and working conditions of the employees. But the range of these issues has tended to widen over the years, and if the process is to continue, a larger and larger part of managerial decision-making — technical, economic, and financial — will be directly affected by the bargaining process. For the time being, however, the difference between collective bargaining and the concept of worker participation in the management of the enterprise is still clearly felt, since at this time and in this country, at least, collective bargaining has an impact upon only a small part of the prism of managerial decision-making.

A second criterion upon which the distinction, particularly between bargaining and managerial councils, can be based relates to the methods by which the councils exert their influence. Bargaining councils tend to influence management, but the latter makes the decisions, except perhaps in cases where the impartial umpire settles a grievance in the last resort. Even then, strictly speaking, management must transmit or implement the umpire's decision. Managerial councils are themselves in some way directly responsible for the administration of the enterprise, forming a smaller or larger part of management itself. Their voices may carry different degrees of authority.

The variation in the form by which the councils act should not be translated into a difference in degree of power or influence. Managerial councils may simply serve as fig leaves for powerful director generals—as seems to have long been the case in some of the French nationalized enterprises which were supposedly run by boards on which workers are represented. On the contrary, anyone can name American unions which, while refusing to accept managerial responsibilities, have exerted tremendous influence upon the entire management of the enterprise. The obvious paraphernalia of managerial responsibility are not necessarily symptoms of real control over the decision-making process, just as the absence of the symbols of power is not conclusive evidence of a lack of effective control.

Both bargaining and managerial councils may first be distinguished from the political and the union reform councils by their purposes. Beyond this, the political and reform councils are characterized by a tendency to operate beyond the limits of a single enterprise, while the bargaining and managerial councils, though they may occasionally also expand their area of operation, frequently limit themselves to one enterprise or at most a group of enterprises. Political councils may originate in a plant but will usually acquire a territorial base. They are essentially what the Germans call *überbetrieblich* — operating on a level above the enterprise.

A typical example of the political council is the Russian Soviet — a "transmission belt" between the revolutionary leadership and the masses of workers in the plants during the revolutionary period, and an organ of public administration when the revolution succeeded.

The union reform council has rarely been more than a passing phase in the industrial relations system. When the union reform council begins, however, its appearance has often been a significant event. Great Britain, in particular, has had ample experience with it, especially in connection with policies of self-restraint which the unions pursued during both world wars and after World War II.

This multiplicity of purpose which councils may serve is increased by the fact that councils or the promoters of the councils may pursue more than one objective or may — voluntarily or by compulsion — change their purposes. The French plant committees, as we shall see, designed originally to provide for some measure of worker participation in the general affairs of the plant, have in fact in most cases been limited to the administration of welfare activities. The revolutionary movement after World War I which aimed at establishing political councils — Bolshevik style — changed its objective once the immediate revolutionary crisis was over, and substituted workers' participation in management as the goal to be attained by way of the councils. Thus we cannot always simply assign one type of a council to a particular country or period. The evolution of the councils over time, lack of clarity about their own objectives, or conscious changes on the part of the promoters of the council idea, produce a blurring of the picture and require a combination of historical and analytical study for a fuller understanding of the occurrence. While practice combines various aspects of the different types of councils in one historic phenomenon, it is indispensable for purposes of analysis to keep the different movements as far apart as possible. Such distinctions are all the more important as the different concepts of the council had different historical roots and form parts of different views of the role of labor in society.

This last fact finds its expression in the relationship between the councils and other organizations of the labor movement — primarily the unions and the political party. The issues raised by these different relationships will form an important part of this study.

Of the five council types we have distinguished, two will be of primary concern here: the bargaining and the managerial councils. Political councils will be referred to briefly in a few places, but in the main they are outside the industrial relations system with which we are concerned (though at times such councils have had considerable impact upon the system). Union reform councils, of great importance at different times in some countries, have rarely been permanent phenomena. The organizing steward, finally, is somewhat less of a problem, at least compared with the bargaining and managerial councils upon which we shall concentrate our attention. The term "bargaining" as used in this context will include grievance handling.

CHAPTER I

The Evolution of the Councils — Ideas and Facts

In the introductory pages an attempt was made to present a typology of councils. Although it was pointed out that no classification could be fully satisfactory, we shall for the sake of brevity employ the terminology developed in the introduction. We shall thus speak of a council acting as a union agent, of the bargaining council, the managerial council, the political, and the union reform council. Each type fits into a system of relations involving labor, management, and society at large, and, consequently, of the functions of the labor movement at a given stage of the social evolution corresponding to a pattern of the special tasks which various organs of the labor movement may have to perform.

From the point of view of the contemporary American trade union movement, collective bargaining represents the central task of the labor movement as a whole and in some respects of the shop organization as well. The same may be said of the Canadian and the British unions — the "industrial branch" of the British labor movement. In this view, the shop organization is primarily designed to assist the union in its bargaining task. Historically, however, the relationship between the shop organization and the union branch in the Western world was somewhat more complicated.

"Many of the earliest [British] Trade Unions," G. D. H. Cole reports, "began in effect as work clubs or companionships, formal or informal associations of the workers employed by a particular establishment. Then when Trade Unionism became a general movement, many local trade societies and many branches of larger bodies continued to consist of workers drawn either from a single works or factory, or from a group of neighboring and closely related works. Indeed, it may be said that Trade Unionism in its early stages was based on works organization to a larger extent than it is today."[1] Workshop organization thus often preceded the rise of the trade union as an effective bargaining agent.

The objectives of workers' organization in these early beginnings of the labor movement, however, far exceeded the limited scope of trade unionism. Early trade unionism was far more than a simple association for the improvement of wages and working conditions. The union was also a social community within which the members could find comradeship and associations which a class-society often denied them.

> The early Union was club and social center, the focus of recreation and fellowship, as well as — even more than — a mechanism for getting higher wages . . . The worker went to his Trade Union branch — which usually, in the early days, held its meetings in a public house — to chat and smoke with his friends, as well as to devise ways of improving his standard of life and work in an economic sense.[2]

Where and when these broader functions prevailed, the union organization in this early stage of social development was geographical in nature. "All kinds of social adjuncts quickly became attached to the organization which, significantly enough, was on a geographical basis, where a purely vocational function would have suggested an industrial basis." Economic and social development, however, as well as the growth of the movement, gradually produced differentiation and integration. Some of the functions of trade unions were taken over by the state — primary and secondary education and some welfare and social insurance activities. Specialized organizations arose in the fields of politics, sports, and recreation. With the breakdown of the sharp class divisions, social clubs and other associations opened their doors to manual workers. While this process is still going on, it has long reached a level at which the unions are primarily, but still not exclusively, an economic defense organization. In many countries on the continent, the Social Democratic Party rather than the unions originally played the part of the many-purpose organization of the workers. Any study of the German or Austrian Social Democratic parties during the first decades of their life will illustrate this point. It would be tempting to ascribe the still-existing geographic organization of the German unions to the same factors which Milne-Bailey emphasizes in the case of the British unions. This explanation, however, is hardly convincing, in the light of the role which the party played.

The center of gravity of the union movement was constantly being shifted. The rise of national markets, the progressive centralization of economic life, the accent placed on economic and social policies determined by the national government and — more clearly in the case of England than in the case of the United States — the evolution toward national collective agreements tended to transfer the power of decision within the unions to district or even to national headquarters. The unions, having consolidated the local groups into national organizations — the new "amalgamated" societies — became increasingly concerned with the establishment of uniform conditions throughout the trade. To attain the "common rule," as the Webbs called it, over larger areas, became the major objective of union policy. "The problem of the period," says Cole, "was for them the successful establishment of standard or minimum district conditions; the insistence was all on the uniformity of conditions throughout the trade, and not on diverse problems arising in particular establishments.[3]

As far as union organization was concerned, this trend led toward:

> the fusion, into larger local branches of the new national unions, of many of the local trade clubs which had previously centered round a single factory, so that all the organized workers belonging to a single craft or group of crafts in a particular town came to be organized in one branch of a single national union, or perhaps in rival branches of two or more overlapping national unions. Although in some cases local trade clubs survived, the works basis of organization generally disappeared in the majority of industries; for the new "amalgamated" societies did not, in most cases, preserve any special organization in the particular works in which their members were employed.

Residence rather than workplace became the main criterion for union organization.

Indeed, in some respects, "works trade unionism" came sometimes to be regarded as "the worst enemy of trade unionism, since it might become the instrument by means of which the employer would evade the recognition of the uniform conditions established by collective bargaining for all the workers in the trade and in the district concerned." In this observation are some remarkable parallels and interesting differences with current discussions in Germany regarding union-council relations.

Still, the workshop was not entirely lost in this development. It survived as the principal base of union organization in those industries in which residence and workplace naturally tend to coincide: coal mining is the obvious example. In some crafts, such as printing, branch organizations were never established so that the unit of the place of employment — the "chapel" — is the official union base. What often prevented the retention of effective workshop organization, however, were jurisdictional conflicts among various unions which weakened the bonds of solidarity among workers in the same shop. (The engineering industries before World War I are referred to by Cole as an example of union rivalries preventing effective workshop organization.)

The main impetus for revived and strengthened workshop organization came from changes in industrial technology. The rise of new industries led increasingly to a situation in which the general collective agreement set down merely a framework within which special arrangements of a workshop nature had to be made. Various schemes of piece rates and incentive pay systems made local or plant-wide bargains indispensable. The more the system of payment by results spread, the more it proved impossible to settle the payment completely by national negotiations.

> There are broadly three ways of regulating by national agreement the earnings of workers paid by results: a standard piecework price list can be negotiated for the industry as a whole (or by a segment of it) — this is only possible where the product and the work operations are not too varied; a level of earnings can be settled by agreement, bearing a specified relationship to time rates, which will be taken as the norm in determining actual piecework prices; or a minimum time rate is nationally agreed and the extra earnings gained from payment by results are settled entirely by individual or work bargaining. All of these methods have been adopted in various British industries, but none of them entirely eliminates wage bargaining below the national level. This is obvious with the second and the third methods, but even a standard list also raises complicated questions of interpretation (or disputes over conditions of work) which can only be settled locally by compromise.[4]

The workshop organization, as a result, was revived in many industries where it had declined, and fortified in those in which it had never ceased to function. Its main task was that of collective bargaining, including of course the handling of grievances under the agreement.

In addition, the councils functioned in many other capacities. "The shop steward," at least in the craft unions in the engineering industries, "began as a very minor functionary of the craft Union, with the duty of trying to ensure that the skilled workers employed belonged to the Union and paid their contributions regularly. He had at the outset no authority to negotiate, or even to deal with workshop grievances beyond reporting them to the trade Union branch or District Committee."[5] The wealth of functions performed by the shop representatives in Great Britain (most of which continue to this day) is illustrated in the following report:

Trade union workshop representatives go under a variety of descriptions of which "shop steward" is only the best known. In printing, the "father of the chapel" can be regarded as a rough equivalent of the steward; in coal mining, similar functions are often discharged by the "checkweighman," whose appointment, protected by statute, had originally a different purpose, namely that of checking on the weighing of the coal produced as coal-face miners are paid according to the amount of coal they produce. Many trade unions employ "collectors," "card stewards" or "ticket stewards" as their workshop representatives, but here the change of name corresponds to a limitation of function. Workshop representatives of this type are generally concerned with matters of internal union administration rather than with any form of negotiation. Thus they recruit new members, check membership cards for arrears of subscriptions and, very often, themselves collect the contribution of their members in their departments. They act, too, as "liaison officers" between the branch or the district committee and the rank-and-file members. They may be the means whereby the complaints of members, workshop grievances and incipient disputes are brought to the attention of the union officials whose responsibility it is to secure a settlement, and they may be required to report regularly to the branch or the district on the state of trade and of union organization in their particular establishments.[6]

These latter functions shade off from mere trade union representation to what we have called the bargaining functions of the councils. The combination of these two functions in one person is quite frequent.[7] This enhances the importance of the workshop organization, even though the majority of the British unions remain based on local branches, established on a geographical principle according to the member's residence.

As B. C. Roberts puts it: "The branch is . . . still the primary unit of trade union organization, and on it is based the whole pyramid of administrative and governmental structure."[8] But the functioning of modern unionism implies that "for the great majority of members, trade unionism begins and ends at the work place. Most workers probably become members of a union because a steward asks them to join, and to them the steward is the union." This applies perhaps even more to unions in the United States and Canada where the union local frequently — though not always — coincides with the workers' organization at the workplace. Where such coincidence is not practicable, the union local in these countries is nevertheless firmly based upon the organization of the members in the shop or other places of employment. It is true that the constitutions of relatively few American or British unions contain specific provision for workshop units. The auto workers, printing trades, and American Newspaper Guild are some of the American unions with specific provision for shop units. Even without constitutional authorization the shop organization is a vital part of the American and Canadian trade unions.

The union shop organization in the United States usually elects a shop chairman and some shop stewards. In small plants, it may just have an elected steward. The chairman and the shop stewards form the shop committee, and it is through this committee that the shop organization carries on its activities. The committee represents the union in the plant not only in many of the union's dealings with plant management, but also in the relations between the union and its members. The committee is the direct line of communication between the individual member and the higher union authorities; it also serves as one of the main steps in most grievance procedures. Under the principle of exclusive bargaining rights established by the Wagner Act, the union (the shop committee) represents all the workers in the bargaining unit if the majority of them have elected the union to be their spokesman.

The shop organization in Britain, Canada, and the United States thus combines two functions — those of union representation and of collective bargaining including grievance handling. It is obvious that such a combination is only possible when the union is recognized by management as the collective bargaining agent for all or part of the employees of the enterprise. Historically, therefore, open — or more often concealed — union representation in the plant would seem to precede the emergence of the bargaining council. There may be a kind of chicken-or-the-egg problem in determining whether unions were formed outside the shop because of fear of employers' retaliation or whether employers refused to recognize unions because they were formed outside the establishment. On the continent at least, but probably also in the Anglo-Saxon countries, the first of the alternatives seems the more typical. Roberts appears to hold the opposite view: "Because trade unions were organized outside their establishments," he says, "many employers, in the nineteenth century, refused for a long time to recognize the representatives of the unions in their workshops. They refused to have what they called 'outside interference,' and would negotiate only with their employees as individuals."

The Evolution in Germany

This sequence is especially noticeable in Germany where the internal evolution of the plant regime passed through several stages. The first period was that of unlimited control by the employer. He or his representatives were sovereign powers with regard to the life of their employees in the plant and often also outside. The workers had no representatives who could speak for them; the government, strongly influenced in industrial relations by laissez-faire ideas, did not intervene in the internal affairs of the plants.[9] This period lasted from the early beginnings of industrialization to the end of the sixties, about the time of the founding of the new German Empire.

This period was also one in which public authorities were generally hostile to industry, particularly where it threatened to eliminate, by its superior competition, old-established artisan shops. Yet the state intervened only when industry endangered public order or safety in a given place. Otherwise, the employer was free to deal with "his workers" as he saw fit.[10] This lack of public concern expressed not trust, but only the contempt in which the state and the social groups dominating it — aristocracy, army, and clergy — held the rising class of industrialists and businessmen. It is perhaps significant that King Friedrich Wilhelm IV of Prussia and Emperor Wilhelm I refused at that time to receive industrial employers at their courts.

In the seventies and eighties the absolutistic regime in the plants continued though with a different philosophy. Indeed, it grew in strength because gradually the status of industrial employers improved. Bismarck based the new German Empire upon a coalition of "steel and rye" — the Ruhr industrialists and the Prussian barons. Railroad construction and armaments production — both determined by strategic considerations — established close contact between the authorities and the new "barons of industry" of whom Alfred Krupp became a symbol. At the same time, while refusing to intervene in the internal affairs of the plant, the government demonstrated its concern with the social tensions accompanying the growth of modern industry: Bismarck's social insurance legislation was an attempt to channel the workers' protests away from the rising Socialist movement. It is significant, however, that this legislation was prepared with the advice of some leading industrialists. The advance of the Socialist movement, in spite of his legislation as well as of the anti-Socialist laws, indicated growing worker protest against "the system." Unions came into being in spite of the combined pressures of the employers and the state. Union organization, therefore, had to exist outside the plants, and only in a few exceptional cases was union recognition granted. In most plants union spokesmen ran the risk of immediate dismissal when found out.

This situation is, of course, not specifically German. A very similar state of affairs prevailed elsewhere in the West. The evolution followed a fairly general pattern also — though with differences in time in the different countries — when in the nineties, public intervention in industrial relations became an accepted procedure. The change of public attitudes in Germany was manifested in connection with a massive miners' strike in 1889. The following year the Emperor received, for the first time, a workers' delegation — a group of miners, and, subsequently, delegates of the mine owners. Strikes grew in frequency and intensity; employers' organizations came into being. World War I then rendered necessary the establishment of devices to avoid social conflicts. This was done by accepting the unions as equal partners with the employers in advising the government on matters concerning industry, and by the compulsory establishment of workers' committees in all essential plants. This occurred in connection with the enactment of the Auxiliary Service Law of 1916. In exchange for the sacrifices which this law imposed upon the workers, the government gave them the right to elect grievance committees in the plants.[11] In effect, this meant that the shop stewards were given legal protection. In most cases these were also union representatives.

The full implications of this step were barely realized at the time by most of the people involved, even though warning voices were raised by some of the union leaders. They feared that the committees might diminish the union's authority. But most of the union leaders were greatly relieved to be able to protect their men in the plants against the threat of dismissal or discrimination. Quite naturally, they regarded this as a great step forward in the process of union recognition by the employers. This was confirmed when at the time of the revolution of 1918 the two central organizations — the DGB and the employers' association — concluded an agreement of mutual recognition and of collaboration. Yet, this recognition referred far more to matters "above the plant level" (*überbetrieblich*), than to the internal management of the plant. In the plants, the workers' or complaint committees of World War I were at first continued and confirmed by government decree. In due course the committees were replaced by works councils whose authority was derived from the new Weimar Constitution. On the basis of the constitution the works council law of 1920 was enacted which was the model the post-World War II legislation followed in most essentials.

There was, at the beginning, considerable ambiguity about the councils' status in the Weimar Republic. This is the point at which the ideas of bargaining, managerial, political, and union reform councils simultaneously gained credence. From one point of view the councils were to be the extension of the unions into the plant in the bargaining process. For the revolutionary groups of the German labor movement, however, the councils were to "supersede what they regarded as the bureaucratic and official-ridden organization of the Trade Unions by a new type of organization based solely on the Councils System and imbued with the revolutionary spirit in contrast to the timid reformist socialism of which the government and the Trade Union leaders were adherents."[12] For others, the councils were to be the future managers of Socialist industry, and for still another group they were to be the cornerstones of the public administration of a future Socialist Germany. This ambiguity, furthered by the example of the Russian revolution, persisted throughout the writing of the constitution and the preparation of the legislation. One issue of particular concern to this study, which arose immediately, was "whether the Works Councils should be subordinated to the Trade Unions or whether, as the more radical members desired, the councils should constitute a separate organization distinct from the Trade Unions and destined, if successful, subsequently to supersede the latter." For the proponents of this idea the unions had become bureaucratic, conservative organizations, incapable of fulfilling their task of defending their members' interests. The councils, more immediately in contact with the rank and file, would be more effective organs of workers' representation. The employers sided with the unions for a bargaining council and against the advocates of the managerial council system, as well as against the political and the anti-union councils, all of which they regarded as instruments of a social revolution.

The relations between the unions and the councils at the present time will be the subject of extended discussion in a later part of this volume. In this brief survey it must be pointed out, however, that when the councils were given their permanent shape in the early days of the Weimar Republic, some of the unions were greatly concerned about their relationship to them. The Russian revolution served as a warning of what could happen if "the leadership of the industrial workers were wrested from the hands of the Trade Unions and transferred to an entirely different body of men." The unionists specified, therefore, in the legislation, that the "intention of the framers of the Act was that the Works Councils should act as subsidiary and subordinate organs of the Trade Unions, with distinct, if complementary, functions."

Even after the law with its built-in safeguards for the unions had been adopted, the struggle between the left wingers and the moderates continued. Attempts to substitute the councils for the unions in order to oust the old "bureaucratic" leadership of the workers continued. The councils were, in this view, to take over collective bargaining altogether, not merely to supplement the bargaining activities of the unions. Radical groups set up a works council bureau in Berlin to which some 26,000 councils affiliated. The Socialist-led unions responded by creating a bureau of their own consisting of four members of the ADGB, the Socialist-led trade union federation, and three members of the AFA, a central federation of salaried employees' unions. At a National Congress of Works Councils held in October 1920 and called by the ADGB and AFA, the struggle came to a head. It ended in a decisive victory for the old-line unionists. The resolution adopted by an overwhelming majority said:

> It is incumbent on Labor to develop the power, which lies in it as a class, to the maximum extent; to make use of this power in action; and to avail itself of all means which can serve this purpose. Important tasks are imposed on the Works Councils through their position in the productive process, and they have a great responsibility to shoulder. The Works Councils find their support in the Trade Unions, which remain, as before, the chief protagonists in the economic sphere, in the struggle between Capital and Labor. The Works Councils must base themselves on the Trade Unions because they can only accomplish their tasks if they are certain of the support of the Trade Unions. The development of the Trade Unions into powerful industrial unions is exclusively a matter for the Trade Unions themselves.
>
> The Works Councils are to be organised within the Trade Unions. A separate organisation of the Works Councils, whether local or central, is undesirable; apart from its effect in hindering the activity of the Trade Unions it would nullify the effective representation of the interests of the workers by the Works Councils. On the other hand, a local grouping of the Works Councils in conjunction with the local Committees of the ADGB and of the AFA, as well as the establishment of a Central Bureau jointly with the Central Bureau of the Trade Unions, is necessary. The Congress agrees to the local organisation of the Works Councils and the formation of a Central Bureau for the Reich, but only on the basis of the principles of the ADGB and of the AFA.

This, in effect, made the councils bargaining agents and instruments of the unions in the bargaining process. At the same time the influence of the current favoring "managerial councils" was broken. Yet it was not completely eliminated. A potential force for a development in this direction continued to exist in the principle of council representation on the governing boards of corporations and in the structure of joint economic councils provided for in legislation, but never realized.

In the main, the unions had asserted their control over the councils. But there was at least one consequence of the establishment of the works councils against which the unions could not protect themselves: the councils took the place of the unions in the plants. Trade union organization was not extended into the plant itself; the lowest level of union organization remained the local branch consisting of members of the same union according to their place of residence. The implications of this fact emerged in fuller significance mainly after World War II.

Throughout the life of the Weimar Republic the councils operated with some effectiveness, at least when measured against the background of traditional plant autocracy. The new institution introduced into the plants a modest element of democracy. The degree to which the councils had become a part of the German worker's life became manifest when, in 1933, the National Socialist dictatorship was established. It destroyed the unions and reintroduced the principle of autocracy into the industrial relations system of the country, modifying it only by superimposing upon management the Nazi dictatorship. The relationship between the two autocracies—that of the party and that of the employers—underwent some modifications during this period. The economic requirements of the war tended to give industrial management predominant influence toward the end of the regime. The party-imposed trustees of labor and the party representatives in the plant thus played less and less significant parts in shaping industrial relations at the plant level. But throughout these fluctuations in the relationship among the power centers of the new regime, many of the former works councillors continued informally to perform a number of services for the workers, particularly in connection with grievances. Their authority was purely personal, based upon their experience and the respect in which they were held by their colleagues and some of the managerial staff.

This informal authority was transformed into official status as soon as the end of the totalitarian regime made the change possible. The workers spontaneously proceeded to elect works councillors, instinctively following the basic pattern of industrial relations at the plant level in the First Republic. Unions resumed their activities, at first on a local and regional basis. The influence of the councillors and the unions was so strong, and that of the employers—often compromised by their cooperation with the Nazi regime—so weak, that in its first years the new system might well have been called a "laboristic" society. The issue of internal plant management, and thus of the status of the workers' representatives in the plant, soon became one of the major problems of the West German Republic. The work constitution law, to be discussed later, became the focus of public debate.

French Plant Committees

The evolution of French industrial relations from autocracy to some form of workers' representation in the plant in some respects followed the same pattern as the developments in Germany. The power of the Syndicalist current, however, is characteristically French. French syndicalism had of course its counterparts, not only in Italy, Spain, French Switzerland, and other Latin countries, but to some extent in Germany as well. But France was the center.

Syndicalism regarded the local "syndicat" as the future management of the plant, rather than as an agent of the employees in collective bargaining with management. Collective bargaining in general appeared to Syndicalists as a betrayal of the class struggle against capitalistic exploitation. The purpose of labor organizations, in this view, was to prepare to take over the management of all enterprises, after having ousted private employers in a revolutionary general strike. In a sharp conflict with Marxian Socialists, the Syndicalists obtained control of the organizations of labor in the nineties and retained it until World War I. Their influence then waned rapidly. Communists on the one hand and reform Socialists on the other took the lead. Yet the Syndicalist tradition did not vanish altogether. It remained alive not only in the emphasis on decentralization in the non-Communist unions, but also in the attempts to formulate a program of non-*etatistic* nationalization of industry. This term referred to decentralized forms of management of nationalized enterprises, with the government playing only a limited role in the administration of industry. Instead, the employees themselves and the consumers were to be given a voice in management. Under the name of "industrialized nationalization" this idea became part of the program of the non-Communist unions after World War I.[13]

On the level of actual developments, the weakness of French trade unionism — low and irregular membership, lack of unity, low economic power, and so forth — as well as the paternalistic attitude of French employers, delayed the development of effective workers' representation in the plant on a larger scale until 1936 just as effective collective bargaining for most of French industry did not win acceptance until then. The decisive event was the victory of the Popular Front government in 1936. Under its auspices (as a result primarily of political power changes), voluminous legislation was passed in the field of industrial relations. One of the laws then enacted by a parliament dominated by Socialists, Communists, and members of the Radical Party, was the law on workers' delegates in industrial and commercial establishments, voted on June 24, 1936.[14]

Prior to that date a few individual industrialists — among them Léon Harmel in 1885 — had established representative institutions permitting them to inform their workers of the state of business, and to listen to staff suggestions. During World War I, the Socialist Minister of Industrial Production, Albert Thomas — later the first director of the International Labour Office in Geneva — recommended the establishment of shop delegates in the plants. This was done in some 350 plants, but the shop delegates disappeared again when the war emergency was over.[15]

In the coal mines, shop representatives functioned as safety delegates; these were set up as a result of the demands of the miners in the Loire basin. Later, in 1890, a law extended this institution to all coal mines. There were also grievance men in the metal establishments of Le Creusot, set up as a result of an arbitration award by Prime Minister Waldeck-Rousseau in 1899, following a strike. A few other establishments followed this example. Still, most employers and a large part of the public saw in the shop delegates created in 1936 not an extension of these modest beginnings but rather an institution similar in spirit, if not in power, to the Soviets of the Russian revolution and to the German workers' and soldiers' councils. The shop delegates thus appeared to many Frenchmen as the spearhead of a great movement aiming at a social revolution.[16] This was the result not only of the semi-revolutionary circumstances in which the new legislation was introduced, but also of developments during the interwar period.

After 1918, the demand for workers' representation in the plant arose mainly in connection with movements in favor of some form of "workers' control." "Workers' control" meant different things to different people. At one extreme were the revolutionary ideas of the Communists — for whom this was a prelude to actual plant management by the workers and their unions. At the other extreme, the "reformist" union leaders aimed at a place for workers' representatives in the management of nationalized enterprises and at the establishment of grievance committees in all business establishments. These committees were to operate on the basis of collective agreements. In addition, the unions asked for the right to participate in discussions preparatory to the drafting of legislation in economic and social matters.[17] Our main concern, at this point, is with the demand for grievance committees.

The year 1936 marked the first great step forward in establishing plant grievance committees. Under the pressure of the great social upheaval in May and June of that year accompanying the election victory of the Popular Front, the Matignon agreement was concluded.[18] The contracting partners were the employers' federation on one hand and the trade unions on the other. One part of this agreement provided for the election of shop stewards (*délégués du personnel*). Shortly afterward, this was made part of the law on collective bargaining. According to the law, collective agreements could be "extended" (be given force of law) if they met certain requirements.[19] One of them was that the agreement had to provide for the establishment of shop stewards in all industrial and commercial enterprises with more than ten employees. The agreement was to specify in detail the organization and the tasks of the stewards.

As rapidly as collective bargaining had advanced after the victory of the Popular Front, so did it decline. Between 1936 and the outbreak of the war, the tide of unionism receded, and the newly established shop delegates went with the tide.

With the fall of France in 1940 and the advent of the Pétain government, new institutions emerged.

The so-called "Charter of Labor" enacted after the armistice of 1940 by the Pétain government (on October 4, 1941), established enterprise committees (*comités d'établissements*). They were to be organs of collaboration between management and the workers of the enterprise. This device was intended to reduce union influence, but the idea of using the enterprise committees in public affairs as representatives of the workers (to the exclusion of the unions) was abandoned. The new institutions proved, however, to be of only temporary significance. The liberation of the country brought with it a return to the ideas and institutions of the prewar period. New departures in the area of workers' representation in the plant were made just the same.

Participation in Management

The new institutions represented a return to the Syndicalist tradition which the reformist union leaders had diverted into the channel that led to the establishment of plant grievance committees. Now the issue of workers' management came again to the fore. Political and social circumstances at the end of World War II favored the re-emergence of some of the Syndicalist ideas.[20]

Syndicalism was never specifically an action program. Its supporters held a wide variety of views (and often no clear views at all) on how the workers were to manage the enterprises when a revolutionary general strike had ousted the previous management. Within this spectrum of ideas some main colors can be distinguished.

1) One principal issue on which variations in the scheme of workers' participation in management are based is that of the numerical degree of such participation. This may vary according to differences in the proportion of workers' representatives on the governing board of the enterprise. In that way three main solutions are obtained.[21]

(a) Full workers' control. This is the original position of French syndicalism, which was also popular among a number of British trade unions, particularly during the first two decades of this century. The Paris Commune of 1871 passed a decree which provided for the transformation of industrial enterprises into cooperatives to be administered by the workers. French syndicalism exerted a good deal of influence upon Daniel De Leon's Socialist Labor Party and its program of industrial unionism. The Syndicalist ideas spread to Australia, Canada, Mexico, and Great Britain. There, the Welsh miners' manifesto, "The Miners' Next Step" (1912) reflected Syndicalist influence. British guild socialism, though its popularity was enhanced by the prestige and propaganda of syndicalism, had its own roots, which can be traced back at least as far as William Morris and Robert Owen's Builders' Guild.

(b) Workers' share in management. This has many versions. An historically important variant is the one proposed by the Austrian Socialist leader, Otto Bauer.[22] He advocated that publicly owned enterprises be administered by governing boards composed of three groups of members—one third to represent the state, one third the consumers, and one third the employees in the enterprise. This formula was retained in the German socialization proposals drafted under Karl Kautsky's inspiration after World War I, and in the nationalization proposals of the French trade unions in 1919–1920. Under their influence this idea, implemented in a number of variations, became the basic scheme of the nationalization laws enacted in France after World War II.

(c) No official workers' representatives. Although trade unionists may become board members, they have to abandon their trade union positions upon appointment and are responsible solely to the government. The trade union viewpoint, but not the trade union, is represented. The competent minister alone has the power of appointment. This is the solution which the British unions ultimately adopted and which was carried out in the nationalization measures in Great Britain after World War II.

2) Other variations in the general scheme of workers' participation concern the subject matter, in the decisions on which workers' representatives participate, or the degree of influence they have on decisions. Subject matter variations may distinguish between personnel, technical, economic, or financial matters, and so forth. Collective bargaining on the plant level may be understood as a special form of joint decision-making, traditionally limited to certain areas of personnel administration and perhaps technical matters. Variations in the degree of influence may reach from full decision-making through consultation to mere information. Various shades in between can be thought of as well.

3) Finally, there are variations in the form by which participation in decision-making can be attained: workers' councils making agreements with management, employee delegates to the boards of directors, and joint employee-management plant committees are some types of arrangements that have been used in the recent past. Collective bargaining can be regarded as a special technique of workers' participation in decision-making.

German codetermination and the French system of administration of nationalized enterprises can be fitted into this classification: both are institutions in which workers' representatives join others in forming the governing boards of the enterprises with the workers' delegates forming less than half of the board membership. Their decision-making is to cover all aspects of plant management. In French private industry, the plant committees would be understood in terms of joint committees whose competencies vary according to the subject matter concerned. The German works council, on the other hand, operates as a committee representing only the employees with varying degrees of authority in different areas of management.

Managerial Councils

The workers' councils in Poland and Yugoslavia present a special puzzle. They consist exclusively of elected workers' representatives, but they share their power of decision on some subjects with other agencies such as the local administration and the plant director appointed by it. On other issues, the government or government-controlled institutions such as the banks exert decisive influence upon their decisions. Finally, there is the question of the degree and the form of party influence on the councils' activities. Our classification requires considerable modifications where the issue of "subterranean," invisible controls arises.

The official version of the ancestry of Polish and Yugoslavian councils commonly refers to the Russian revolution of 1905 which introduced factory councils. In May 1905, striking workers in Ivanovo-Voznesenk entrusted the leadership of their strike to an elected workers' council, and in the fall of that year:

> The printers' strike committee in St. Petersburg founded an over-all "Soviet of Workers' Deputies" which soon made political demands as well. With its 550 delegates representing 250,000 workers, it was a political mass organization of the workers so far unheard of in Russia; it was to become the prototype of the Soldiers' and Workers' Councils of 1917, the Soviets of Bolshevik Russia.[23]

It is interesting to point out that this first Soviet was under the political control of the Mensheviks; indeed the councils had come into being "with some opposition from the Bolsheviks."[24] The performance of the Soviets during the revolution, and their prestige in spite of their defeat, however, made a great impression upon Lenin who referred to them later as organs of "a new state power."[25]

As instruments of the revolution the councils again came into being in 1917. The slogan of "all power to the Workers' and Soldiers' Councils" was the formula by which Lenin assumed control of Russia. A decree of November 1917 turned the councils into managerial devices by giving them complete control of all enterprises. The next year, however, they were transformed into trade union branches, and as such they later became a part of the well-known "troika"—plant director, party cell secretary, secretary of the union branch—which was to control the industrial plants. Stalin then put an end to this last trace of the managerial council by abolishing the troika and giving the director alone full power.

This evolution may help explain why, much later, the anti-Stalinist Communist movements in Poland and Yugoslavia and perhaps even the rebellious workers of Hungary found a model in the early stages of the Russian revolution which they identified with Lenin and which Stalin was said, by his authoritarian and bureaucratic tendencies, to have deformed and betrayed.

In addition, there were incidents in Polish history, at the end of World War II, when workers' councils took over the management of enterprises abandoned by their previous owners or managers as a result of the German defeat. Just as in France, where experiments in workers' council management were undertaken for similar reasons, this was only a passing phase. But it was revived much later in 1950 when events put the idea once again on the agenda.

Less relevant, though also often quoted, is the example of the workers' commissions (*radnicki povjerenici*) established in Yugoslavia by law in 1945. These were, however, no more than consultative agencies which were to establish contact with management, government, and unions to defend the interests of the workers and help advance production. These commissions, not having any significant function, soon ceased to exist and were replaced by trade union branches just as had been done in the Soviet Union. Later, when the works councils were introduced as managerial devices, the reference to the workers' commission served to demonstrate the intrinsically national character of the new institution.

Nevertheless, from the ideological point of view, the workers' councils present a problem to the regimes in Poland and Yugoslavia. This is indicated by the background of the managerial council idea. Syndicalism, rather than Marxian communism, has been the origin of the movement to make self-governing workers the managers of their plant. The greater the authority of the councils, the sharper the contrast is likely to be between the Syndicalist aspects of the council system and the Communist version of Marxism.

Political Councils

Following the example set in Russia, some of the protagonists of the councils during the debates in Germany after World War I wanted to use them as instruments of a Socialist revolution. The attempt not only failed but turned against those who made it. In Germany as well as in Austria where the evolution proceeded in a somewhat similar fashion, the councils proved to be instruments of the anti-Communist groups in the labor movement.

Thus, the First Congress of Workers' and Soldiers' Councils of Germany, held in 1918, was so completely dominated by moderate groups that neither Rosa Luxemburg, nor Karl Liebknecht, the two outstanding leaders of the extreme left, were even permitted to address the congress. In Austria, Friedrich Adler, the chairman of the workers' and soldiers' councils, used Socialist control of the councils effectively to prevent a Communist revolution by using the authority of the councils to oppose, in behalf of the council idea, aggressive Communist moves.

Similarly, workers' councils were used in Hungary during the rebellion of October 1956, as leaders of the anti-Communist movement. Even though these events are outside the terms of reference of this study, they have some bearing upon the Polish developments. It may be useful to record the main facts as they occurred during the historical events in Hungary.

The first workers' councils were formed in Csepel, the industrial suburb of the Hungarian capital. This spontaneous process was acknowledged by the Central Committee of the Hungarian Workers' Party (the Communist Party) which stated in an appeal: "The Central Committee deems correct the election of workers' councils in the factories." However, by adding that this election should proceed "through the intermediary of the trade union organs," and by adding a reference to the need for wage increases, the party endeavored to channel the council movement into directions that were relatively harmless for the regime. A further attempt in the same direction, but making even greater concessions to the workers, was made[26] by the Central Council of Trade Unions, which stated: "The wish of the working class has been realized: the enterprises will be managed by workers' councils." Instructions issued at about the same time indicated that the Yugoslav pattern of workers' self-government was to be the main model to be followed.

The councils, however, proceeded to form regional associations. This fact made them inevitably political and potentially administrative devices.[27] They were recognized as such by the regime that took over after the Soviet troops had ousted the government of Imre Nagy. An article of Bela Hari, member of the secretariat of the Hungarian trade unions, published in April 1957,[28] states that the "counterrevolution" attempted to constitute "workers' councils in the counties, the districts, larger areas, in Budapest and finally on the national level" which would have been "a second power opposed to the government and which would have endeavored to assume full power later."

The article then refers to attempts of the works council federation of greater Budapest "to establish area councils in order to develop in this way into a national organ." As a result, the government established under the protection of the Red Army proceeded to dissolve the works council of greater Budapest.[29] Finally, works councils were forbidden to associate among themselves on a territorial basis in order to prevent their being used as political devices or as elements of public administration.

CHAPTER II

France

After the initial impetus given to the institution of workers' representatives in the plant by the Popular Front in 1936 a rapid decline set in. Plant representation shared the fate of French unionism which, after a sudden increase in power, membership, and financial means, suffered equally rapid losses in all three respects. But the idea of workers' representation on the plant level did not disappear altogether. It was revived — in a travesty — by the so-called Charter of Labor of the Vichy government, but also and far more significantly by the de Gaulle administration in the areas outside the control of Pétain. In these areas, primarily Algeria, the Free French government established joint production committees patterned after those existing at the same time in the United States, Canada, and Britain. While these were consultative committees limited to technical questions, the program of the resistance movement — the "underground" organizations opposing the German occupation forces as well as the French "collaborationists" — provided for later participation of the workers in management. This was one of the currents which was to lead to the establishment of plant committees. Another was the disappearance of managerial personnel at the time of the liberation. A number of plants were seized by Communist groups. Some managers fled; others were removed under the accusation of collaboration with the enemy. Managing committees (comités de gestion) selected by the staff took over. Old Anarcho-Syndicalist dreams were revived. As early as February 22, 1945, a decree of the de Gaulle government legalized the establishment of plant committees. The *exposé des motifs* (presentation of reasons) stated:

The great popular movement which has liberated France from its enemy was not only a movement of national liberation, but also one of social liberation. In the clandestine resistance as in London around General de Gaulle, projects for the economic and social reconstruction of France have been worked out. One of the ideas which one finds in almost all of these projects is the need for associating the workers with the direction of the economy and the administration of the enterprises. In this sense, right after the liberation of the country, production committees or management committees were formed spontaneously in many factories. The purpose of these committees was everywhere to set again in motion the industry necessary for the war and to increase its output. No doubt — as the experiences of the last four years in Great Britain, the United States and Canada have shown — the participation of the personnel in committees of this kind can have the happiest effect in this sense. The moment seems to have come to legalize and generalize the existence of these bodies.[1]

This decree legalized the committees to some extent without giving full satisfaction to the wishes of the unions as expressed in the Consultative Assembly.[2] The labor organizations particularly criticized the fact that the committees were restricted to enterprises with 100 employees or more; that they had no right to deal with wage problems; that they were merely to be informed about the general problems of the enterprise rather than consulted; and so forth.

Following a proposal by the Socialists, the Constituent Assembly revised the decree and replaced it by a law,[3] taking into account the wishes of the unions. The law provides in particular that plant committees be set up in all enterprises employing at least 50 workers and that even in smaller enterprises they could be organized by authorization of the minister. Under the law, workers who regularly perform work for a particular firm at home are to be counted as well. To provide for trade union influence upon the plant committees, the trade unions representing the workers are entitled to delegate one member each with consultative status to the committee. Nominations for committee members, moreover, are made by the "most representative unions." The election by secret ballot proceeds in two electoral colleges: one for the workers including the white-collar staff, the other for the upper ranks (engineers, superintendents, foremen, and so on). The distribution of the available seats between these two categories requires an agreement between management and unions with the labor inspector (a civil servant under the ministry of labor) as arbitrator. These and other clauses clearly indicate the concern of the unions over the possible loss of control over the plant committees.

For the nationalized enterprises — coal mining, electricity, gas, many banks and insurance companies, for instance — the revision had an unexpected result. At the time when the original decree had been issued, it was clear that it could probably not be uniformly applied to private and public enterprises. In the latter, the personnel is already represented in management through union representatives on the supervisory boards. In some public enterprises it was intended to regulate working conditions by a special law or decree (*Statut*). Some modifications of the general principle were, therefore, considered necessary in introducing plant committees into public enterprises. The original decree provided that further decrees would determine how and to what extent the general principle would be applied to public enterprises. When the original decree was replaced by the law of May 16, 1946, no other decrees had yet been issued. Through an oversight of the legislators, however, the law did not renew the authorization for the government to issue decrees on the formation of plant committees in public enterprises. Although a Socialist proposal was submitted to the assembly which would have corrected this mistake, no action was taken on it. As a result, a legal foundation was lacking for the operation of plant committees in public establishments.[4]

There are, however, special texts under which such committees operate in certain nationalized enterprises. Thus decrees of March 7 and April 14, 1945, established plant committees in the Renault plants, and other texts did so in the "Office National de l'Industrie de l'Azote" and in the Potash mines of Alsace.[5] In the coal mines similar committees were established by a decree of May 4, 1945, but they have narrower functions. Joint production committees were provided for in the arsenals and navy establishments, and generally in the technical enterprises of the ministry of armaments.[6] In other industries plant committees exist without legal basis; this is the case of the railroads (SNCF). Even before the decrees for the coal mines had been issued, an agreement between the unions and the coal mines of the Nord and Pas de Calais areas provided for the organization of plant committees.

In addition to the committees, the institution of shop stewards (*délégués du personnel*) was revived after World War II. The shop stewards, as will be remembered, had been created during the Popular Front period. But when the conservative tide set in, just prior to the outbreak of the war, the new institution declined. A new start was made after the liberation, and the shop stewards were given a legal base in 1946.

Shop stewards and plant committees are the main forms of workers' representation in the enterprise. They are, however, not the only forms. Safety delegates in the mines, health and safety committees in other industries, and disciplinary committees created under collective agreements exist and are often more effective than the shop stewards and plant committees. Moreover, under the managerial system of nationalized industries adopted in France after World War I and again after the 1944–45 period, the workers were given representation on the managing boards of the nationalized enterprises. We shall survey these various forms of plant representation in some detail.

The Shop Stewards

While the law (after the war a new law on the subject was enacted on April 16, 1946) prescribes certain rules about the election and the functions of the shop stewards, it also provides that collective agreements may substitute different arrangements. Shop stewards are to be elected in all industrial and commercial enterprises and public agencies as well as agricultural enterprises with at least ten employees. For plant committees, 50 employees are required, and agricultural enterprises are excluded. The number of shop stewards depends on the size of the plant. A plant with 11 to 25 employees has one shop steward and one deputy. The number grows less than proportionately with the number of employees: where there are 501 to 1000 employees, there are nine shop stewards and nine deputies, and one steward and one deputy are to be added for every additional 500 employees.

The candidates for the shop steward elections — as well as those for membership in the plant committee — are nominated by the "most representative unions." The latter also have the right to propose to the electorate the recall of those stewards or committee members who were nominated by them. These procedures were devised to give the unions influence over the workers' representatives. However, for the seats not filled in the first election round, a run-off election is held within two weeks. At this election new candidates can be nominated by any group, not merely the "most representative unions."

The conditions under which a candidate is elected in the first election round have undergone a significant change. The system in existence right after World War II provided for elections by majority. In 1947 — the year when a state of war began between the Communists and the government, and the non-Communist Force Ouvrière began to organize against Communist control of the trade unions — a system of proportional representation was introduced. Only in this way could a substantial representation of the non-Communist unions — a minority among the organized workers — be ensured. Proportional representation was combined with a two-round election system by stipulating[7] that a run-off election has to be held whenever the number of votes in the election is less than half that of the registered voters. (Invalid or blank votes are not to be counted as votes cast, according to a court decision. This makes for more frequent run-off elections.) Elections are by secret ballot. Any employee of French nationality, eighteen years old, having worked in the enterprise for six months and entitled to vote in political elections, has the right to vote for shop stewards and plant committee members. To be elected the candidate must be twenty-one years old, be able to read and write, and have worked in the enterprise for at least a year. The same person may be a shop steward and a member of the plant committee.

There must be at least two electoral colleges: one for workers and white-collar employees; another for engineers, superintendents, and foremen. In an enterprise with at least 500 salaried employees, the engineers and superintendents must have at least one full member on the plant committee, elected by the entire college of foremen, engineers, and superintendents.

Elections of the stewards are for one year, those of the plant committee members, for two years; representatives may be re-elected. No reason has ever been given for this difference in the term of office. The two laws were voted at different times. The term of office is ended prematurely by death, resignation, dismissal from the plant, or, in the case of shop stewards, by recall, upon proposal of the union which the steward represents and by secret decision of a majority of the appropriate electoral college.

The main function of the shop stewards is to act as grievance men in dealing with the plant management. Their jurisdiction, under the law, in the scope of the grievances they may handle, has grown since they came into being.

Originally a distinction was made between individual grievances—for the handling of which the shop stewards were responsible—and collective grievances; the latter, at the request of the employers, supported in this by the unions, were to be the exclusive province of the unions.[8] However, when the unions realized that they had a good deal of influence with the shop stewards, they changed their attitude on this point. In a number of cases shop stewards—who most frequently are union members or even union officers—were the object of disciplinary measures on the part of management because it regarded the grievances presented by the stewards as being of a collective nature. On the whole, however, management realized that it was preferable, from its own point of view, to discuss grievances, whatever their nature, with people on the payroll of the company rather than with "outsiders" such as union representatives.

By French law, the shop steward enters the process of grievance handling only after the worker has failed to settle his complaint to his satisfaction in dealings with his immediate superiors. This is in only apparent contradiction to Val Lorwin's statement that "the shop steward is normally the first resort of the worker with a grievance." What is meant is the first resort after the worker himself has unsuccessfully tried to solve his problem. Many French employers prefer that the worker, dissatisfied with the results of his appeal to his superior, appear before them before turning elsewhere. This "would seem to them a better protection of the worker's interests. It would guarantee that he would not be at the mercy of lower supervisory personnel, and that he would be able to present his case before the responsible head of the establishment."[9]

Ordinarily shop stewards present grievances to management individually. However, at least once a month or upon their request they appear collectively and, if they so wish, they can be accompanied by union representatives when going before the management representatives. Two days before the meeting, the shop stewards present a list of their grievances to management. Management must answer within six days. Both the grievances and the answers are recorded on a register which is open to inspection by the workers and by the official labor inspector.

Shop stewards are to be given fifteen hours a month of company time for their functions.[10] By mutual agreement and with the consent of the company, they may combine their time and allot it to one of their number who then becomes a specialist in grievance handling. Such an arrangement usually takes place only among shop stewards who belong to the same union.

Union division introduces special problems: a worker may prefer to have his grievance handled by a shop steward of his own union (or political persuasion) even though he belongs to a different department of the plant. Management usually desires that communication lines in grievances follow the scheme of the plant organization.

The shop steward in action. Grievance handling is the main task of the shop stewards, but they share the field with other agencies. Among them is the "Conseil des Prud'hommes," a special labor court which attempts to mediate or, if necessary, decides individual labor disputes. The court consists of an equal number of employer and worker members. If this court is evenly divided on a dispute, a justice of the peace sits with the court and casts the deciding vote. He also acts instead of the "Conseil des Prud'hommes" where no such court exists.[11] Appeals against decisions of the labor courts or the justices of the peace go to the ordinary courts. "The Union may help a worker prepare his case for the prud'hommes. In theory (often ignored in practice) a union official may appear in his behalf only if he works at the same trade: a throwback to the corporate origins of the institution."[12]

Another road for the handling of certain grievances is an appeal to the inspectors of the ministry of labor. Since they are entitled to inspect plants to establish whether the labor laws have been observed, disputes regarding such issues may be referred to them. In addition, the inspectors engage in informal mediation procedures of labor disputes. Finally, they have the power of decision in regard to dismissals, especially dismissals of shop stewards and members of plant committees.

In some of the nationalized industries, special disciplinary committees exist, composed in equal numbers of management and employee representatives—the latter usually being appointed by the union. Collective agreements have led to similar committees being set up in the banks and the streetcar companies; these committees have, however, only advisory functions.

There is thus a good deal of choice before the individual worker in his grievance handling. The most frequent procedure is still for him to appear before his superior or "patron" to plead his case. Among the other procedures, that which involves the shop stewards has shown a decided tendency to be less and less frequently used.

In a large number of cases, beginning in 1948, plant committees have undertaken or attempted to handle grievances. This has added to the confusion surrounding the systems of grievance procedure and to their general lack of effectiveness. At the same time this phenomenon was a symptom of a process which helped undermine the work of the plant committees.

This evolution reflects to a large extent the weakening of French unions since their high tide at the end of the war. Being elected on lists proposed by the unions, the shop stewards appear to the employers, the employees, and the public at large primarily as union representatives. They share, therefore, in changes of the status and of the power of the unions.

Technically, moreover, the fact that grievance handling through the shop steward normally provides for no final arbitration of grievances has made this procedure relatively less attractive than others. Most contracts have only rudimentary clauses on grievance handling, the elaborate machinery of the American grievance procedure is unknown, and in particular there is no counterpart to the "impartial umpire," except perhaps for the labor inspector. He plays that part at least in some circumstances, though in others the final decision may be up to the courts.

The decline of the shop steward expresses itself also in the difficulties which the unions and the employees in general have in finding candidates. As early as 1950, a report indicates, the labor inspector told the then-minister of labor, that in some four fifths of all enterprises, it was difficult to find candidates for the shop steward elections.[18] No less significant is the fact that the number of abstentions in the elections rose to some 40 per cent. The lack of popularity of the office reflects the declining appeal of the unions as much as their failure to protect the shop stewards effectively against dismissals and discrimination.

In a number of plants with forward-looking management, however, the shop stewards have been accepted as a desirable link between the plant, the union, management, and the workers. As time progresses, this number may increase, just as the real and sincere acceptance of collective bargaining may advance in French industry. Perhaps the main question is whether the institutions, upon which industrial relations at the plant level are based, will be given a sufficient lapse of time to evolve in relative peace. However, that will depend primarily upon events outside the plants.

The Plant Committees

The legal basis of the plant committees is the decree of February 22, 1945, and the law of May 16, 1946. The legislation provided that collective agreements could modify the legal prescriptions, and the law of February 11, 1950, about collective agreements requires that reference be made in the agreement to the plant committees and that mention be made in particular to the methods by which the social institutions which the committees administer are to be financed. The law thus leaves a good deal of freedom to the interested parties. If, however, no use is made of this freedom (by a failure to conclude a collective agreement), then the legal prescriptions are effective.

They can be summarized rather briefly. Committees are to be instituted in industrial and commercial enterprises with at least fifty employees. This holds true even though the enterprise consists of several distinct but connected plants, none of which has fifty employees. The shop stewards are a plant institution; the plant committee relates to an enterprise; the English title is, therefore, not quite correct, but it has become the usage. If, on the other hand, the enterprise consists of widely separated individual plants—such as the branches of a bank in different cities—only those that have fifty employees set up committees. In that case there is also a central enterprise committee consisting of delegates (elected by majority vote) of each plant committee. The committee consists of the representatives of the employees and the employer or his representative. It is thus a joint labor-management committee. It is to meet once a month or more often, upon the call of the employer who also provides the meeting room, the material and, if necessary, the personnel at the disposal of the committee. Since the committee has only advisory functions except in the administration of the plant's social institutions, voting power is of little significance. The only occasion where voting power may matter relates to the committee's authority to transmit a report of its proceedings to the labor inspector. If the proceedings contain the accusation that management has violated a part of the labor legislation, this may cause an investigation by the labor inspector.

The committee is basically an organization devoted to cooperation between employees and management. It is thus not entitled to conclude collective agreements. In economic and financial matters of the enterprise, the committee is to be consulted. Thus it is to be consulted on questions of organization, administration, and the business situation. It is to be informed of the profit-and-loss situation and may make suggestions on the distribution of profits. Similarly, it may express its opinion on product and price changes. In the case of corporations, suggestions and opinions of the committee are to be transmitted to the general meetings of the shareholders. Moreover, two members of the committee, one representing the higher employees, the other the workers and the lower white-collar employees, take part in the meetings of the board of directors (Conseil d'Administration) of the enterprise. In technical matters, the committees may make proposals for the increase of output and profit; they study proposals of management and of workers, suggest how they can be carried out, and propose premiums for workers who made successful suggestions. Where no plant committee exists, its technical functions may be carried out by shop stewards.[14]

In social matters, the committee has equally limited powers. Since it has the task of cooperating with management in the improvement of the working conditions and of the life of the personnel, the committee is to be consulted on such matters as the establishment of the plant regulations and the schedule of vacations. The committee also intervenes when a shop steward is to be dismissed. Such a dismissal is legal only with the consent of the plant committee. In the absence of its approval — or if the plant has no committee — the labor inspector must approve.[15] The plant committee has, however, no power over dismissals of other employees, although it is to be consulted on mass layoffs or dismissals. There are some exceptions to this general statement: plant regulations adopted after consultation with the plant committee and the shop stewards may establish seniority rules for group dismissals; such rules are usually also contained in collective agreements (for example, those of the banks). The *statut* of the miners — a law regulating their wages and working conditions — contains detailed clauses about hiring and firing involving consultation with various representative organs of the employees. Even where the plant committee has authority, its decisions are subject to court review: from a decision of the plant committee or of the labor inspector, the employer may appeal to the labor court and then to a regular civil court. He may, however, under certain circumstances, go directly to the labor court or the civil court to ask for the annulment of the contract of employment, under a court decision of 1952.[16] As a result, plant committees and labor inspectors have been bypassed more and more frequently by employers who prefer court decisions to those of the plant committees and of the government officials. Plant committee members enjoy the same protection as shop stewards. The remedy for illegal dismissal is either damages or continued wages (wages for the remainder of the period of office of the shop steward or committee member). Since the term of office is one year for the stewards and two years for the plant committees, wages are paid only for up to one or two years, according to the case. In combination with the shift in jurisdiction mentioned above, this means that the protection given to shop stewards or members of the plant committee is rather weak.[17]

The widest authority is enjoyed by the committees in the areas of the medical and social services of the plant. Legally, all institutions of this kind are under the authority of the employer. However, for all practical purposes the cooperation of the plant committees is so indispensable in this area that the latter exert a good deal of real authority. There is also a feeling that employers have diverted the attention of the committees to social welfare matters in order to avoid having to deal with them on financial and economic problems. Thus the metalworkers' union of the Christian Trade Union Federation claimed in 1950 that "we have been 'had' by the employers. In giving us the social welfare projects, they have loaded us down with work. They have also turned our attention and efforts from the real work of the plant committee."[18]

The plant doctor is usually appointed or dismissed with the approval of the plant committee. The committee also examines the financial and the medical reports of the plant doctor and transmits them, with its own comments, to the labor inspector. Similar close cooperation usually exists between the committee and the social welfare worker (*conseillère du travail*) of the plant. She takes part—without vote—in those meetings of the committee in which questions of concern to her are on the agenda. Moreover, she reports to the committee on her activities.[19]

The main field of action of the plant committees, however, is the administration of the welfare activities of the enterprise. Where no plant committee exists, the welfare activities are to be administered by the shop stewards together with management (law of May 16, 1946). This does not seem to be applied in fact. Management alone seems usually to be in charge in the absence of a plant committee. The institutions concerned are of many different kinds, both in their objectives and in their legal status. They range in their nature from friendly societies (*sociétés mutualistes*)—mutual insurance groups against accidents, death, unemployment, and so on—to the factory canteen, and in their organization from self-governing legally independent bodies to mere branches of the plant. The difficulties of regulating such diversity by law are obvious. For the legally independent institutions (independent from the enterprise but associated with it), simple representation of the plant committee on the executive board has been provided for. For those which are part of the enterprise itself, legislation provides full administration by the plant committee under the authority of the employer. This latter group comprises a great variety of institutions: vacation homes, kindergartens, hospitals, canteens, social clubs, sports organizations, credit and relief funds, and so forth. For reasons which (to say the least) are subject to dispute, workers' housing is not under the committee's administration. The committee has only a right of supervision of the administration by the management (decree of November 9, 1945). The reasoning given is that workers' housing is provided by the firm to ensure a stable labor force. Economic, rather than welfare considerations, therefore, are said to be predominant. This, however, could be said with equal validity about most or all welfare activities of the firm. Another argument—hardly more convincing—is that a committee elected for one year is ill-suited for the administration of a long-term investment such as housing construction. Other welfare activities, such as the establishment of a vacation home, would seem subject to the same qualification. It is true, however, that the committees themselves do not seem to have been eager to get administrative authority in housing matters. In view of the notorious French housing shortage, the committees prefer to avoid involvement in as delicate and controversial a matter. The Communist-dominated trade union federation CGT has denounced attempts of some firms to transfer the housing administration to the plant committees as "maneuvers of the employers."[20]

Financing is provided by rather complicated systems. The plant committee may extract contributions from the employees, but this is rarely done and produces only insignificant amounts where it is. The committee may receive gifts and contributions from unions or local committees. By far the most important sources of revenue, however, are contributions of the enterprise.

The principle adopted by the legislation of 1945 is that the firm must continue to subsidize those activities which it did subsidize in 1945. New activities, therefore, must be the subject of new agreements with the enterprise, but since the plant committee is not entitled to conclude such agreements it is the task of the unions to do so. The problem of how to determine the amount of the firm's contribution has been greatly affected by inflation. The solution provided for in the legislation has been as follows: first the largest yearly contribution made by the firm in the three years preceding the taking over of the social welfare activities by the plant committee is determined; then the proportion of the payroll of that same year is computed which this amount represents; this proportion is then applied to the current year's payroll. The larger of these two amounts is the minimum contribution.[21]

The plant committees in action. There is a widespread conviction that of all the institutions created in the field of industrial relations at the end of World War II, none has been more disappointing in its practical results than the plant committees. Such an over-all judgment, though not without justification, is not too helpful. It may be better to discuss various aspects and varying degrees of this failure. For, even though the prevailing impression is that of a tremendous gap between the expectations with which the committees were welcomed and their actual achievements, there are considerable differences in performance among the committees.

In the firms where there were several plants, a central enterprise committee and individual plant committees were established. In these cases the plant committees have, on the whole, performed better than the enterprise committees. The jurisdiction of the first is limited to social and technical questions; that of the latter relates to economic and financial problems.[22]

Smaller firms have shown less receptiveness toward the committees than larger establishments. To some extent this distinction coincides with that between firms with individual owners and those run by professional managers. In France where privately held share companies (particularly family-owned) and companies with limited liability are quite frequent, the distinction made above is not identical with that between individually owned firms and partnerships on one hand and corporations on the other. Of course in the United States, too, the two classifications, though closer to each other than in France, would not precisely coincide. In the smaller firms where contact between employer and employees is traditionally close and often of a paternalistic nature, the committee is not only sometimes regarded as superfluous, but it also introduces a formalistic element into labor-management relations which the employers resent. The fact that an effective committee inevitably detracts from the employer's authority is far more obvious in the small firm. It is also claimed that the employees of the latter, perhaps because of their small number, produce good committeemen less frequently than is the case in larger establishments.[23]

In the light of this experience, voices have been raised advocating a return to the decree of February 22, 1945, which limited the committees to plants with more than 100 employees (while the law of May 16, 1946, reduced this number to 50).

Where the administrative center of an enterprise is at a considerable distance from the plant, the committee often finds its work paralyzed by the director's inability to make decisions without authorization by the Paris management: "In every question relating to the general administration of the enterprise, the director takes refuge behind the management in Paris while often emphasizing his efforts to obtain from the management concessions to the workers. This referral is a serious obstacle for the functioning of the plant committee." There are, however, other cases in which the very same situation leads to the opposite result — namely, that of giving the executive on the spot greater freedom of action and thus the committee unusual vitality.

Regional differences in the effectiveness of the committees have been claimed to exist.[24] Thus the eastern and the northern regions are said to have the most constructive committees, the southern committees to be submerged in procedural disputes, and so forth. What is expressed in these variations may be differences in industry-mix from region to region, with corresponding adaptations in the general character of industrial relations.

A realistic assessment of the committees' performance should distinguish between the various functions entrusted to them by the law: welfare, economic and financial, and technical.

Welfare activities. As was pointed out earlier, this is the area in which the committees have done their relatively best work. The range of activities that come under this heading is fairly wide: housing — with the restrictions on the committees' authority mentioned above — canteens, nurseries, kindergartens, infirmaries, gardens for the workers, cooperatives, mutual aid and solidarity activities, holiday camps, Christmas trees, children's parties; in the area of cultural activities most committees have concentrated on libraries, sports, and the use of leisure time.

In addition, the committees have an important part in the appointment of social workers in the plant, of plant doctors, psychologists, and so on.

There are considerable differences, even in this field, among committees, based to a large extent upon the size of the welfare funds made available to them by the enterprise. Referring to one such committee, a report said that "since it has no budget, it is entirely devoted to demands: premium pay, better working conditions, special allowances for families, children, old people, etc. . . . It does not administer any welfare work, does not even have a part in the administration of any welfare agency, but is merely being informed of their activities, criticizes their administration and makes suggestions. The plant director, through his welfare assistant, the labor adviser (*conseillère du travail,* a social worker with special training in labor problems) and the department heads, has the entire family service organization and its agencies in his hands." [25]

This, however, seems to be an extreme situation. More frequent are reports on cooperation between employer and committee in the social welfare field. Most committees are competent to administer social welfare; it is of direct concern to the workers, and — as was mentioned above — management often encourages the committees to assume responsibilities in this field. The CGT, for curious reasons which will be taken up later, also tends to push the committees in the direction of welfare work. Even among the welfare agencies, however, there seem to be some which the committees prefer to administer and administer well (home economics courses, sports activities), others where they are less successful (a consumers' cooperative, a plant library are examples given), and others which many committees prefer to avoid (vacation homes). Some of these differences are accidental; no generalizations seem possible.

Even in plants where management is cooperative, the budget of the welfare activities is often a matter of dispute. Special agreements departing from the legal prescriptions occur: indeed they are necessary for the financing of new welfare activities since the law merely refers to those that existed prior to the issuance of the decree of 1945. This puts a premium on past refusals to meet employees' demands. Moreover, the differentials in labor costs thus created have some bearing on competitive relationships so that more progressive employers are being punished. This may explain why an employers' group such as the "Association des Cadres Direigeants de l'Industrie" (Acadi) during a study session of the plant committees (February 24–25, 1951) asked for remedial action.[26] Another problem is that of the distribution of the funds among several plant committees in an enterprise consisting of several individual plants. This is a problem somewhat similar to that of allocating joint overhead costs, and no clear principle of solution has yet presented itself.

Paternalism is perhaps the most difficult problem facing the committees. It has two aspects: the paternalism of the "patron" bestowing blessings upon the employees; this may be avoided by transferring full responsibility for the welfare activities to the plant committee. There is, however, also the danger of the committee itself taking on the role of the benevolent father. This has become a very real problem in some German plants and has not been altogether avoided in France either. The greater danger seems to be that of employers' paternalism, the more so as employers have lately tended to withdraw welfare activities from the committees' administration, giving the plant committee instead merely the right to check upon the administration by the employer.

Welfare activities are only a part of the committees' sphere of action in the social field. They are also to cooperate with management in improving working conditions; to express their views on the work rules of the plant (*règlement intérieur*). In these respects the committees — where they exist — have performed well, but without exerting a very profound influence upon the "climate" of the plant. They have occasionally made suggestions in favor of the introduction of profit-sharing systems, sometimes with success. Incentive-pay systems related to productivity indexes have found little favor with the committees since the unions dominating the committees have commonly regarded such systems as simple devices for heightening exploitation. Some committees have made studies of the wage-structure of the plant, of production bonuses, and time-and-motion studies. Some of these have had practical results. In general, however, when the committees moved too close to the area of wages, employers have categorically refused to consult them. *Droit Social* reports a case in which the committee discussed the security measures to be taken during a threatened strike. This refers apparently to a steel plant connected with a coal mine, and the security measures were needed to prevent the drowning of the mine. This discussion is described as a "probably pretty rare occurrence." [27]

On the whole, however, the welfare and social activities of the plant committee were and continue to be relatively the most successful area of their functions. It is true that it has been affected by some difficulties still to be discussed, as well as by changing attitudes toward the whole complex of union-management relations. Yet with the reservations implied in these observations, the impression remains favorable.

Economic activities. There is consensus that in this area the committees have been least successful. "It is in this field," says Georges Lasserre, "that the committees have played the smallest part."[28] There, they also have met the sharpest resistance. There are a few cases — in some of the banks, for example — where plant committees have been effective in discussing and commenting on economic and financial problems of the firm, but these are exceptions.

The committees are given consultative status in economic affairs by the law; they are to serve as channels of information in both directions, to and from the management. In fact, they are usually not given information of any significance. Company reports are infrequent, and they are usually presented in such a fashion that the uninitiated will learn little from them.[29] There are few counterparts in the French corporate literature to the attempts of American companies to make their reports attractive and intelligible, although an evolution in this sense is underway.

This is the result of several factors. French business has, if possible, an even wider concept of "business secret" than its German counterpart.[30] Complaints about the disclosure of business secrets by staff members or shop stewards are not infrequent, and they serve to justify the refusal to answer questions asked by plant committees. The state of war carried on by large parts of French management with the unions, particularly the Communist-dominated CGT (although many employers refuse to make distinctions among the unions) provides additional support for the policy of secrecy.

Large numbers of French businesses are family-owned and family-run. This includes some corporations. Information about the business is thus regarded as tantamount to information about the personal finances of the owners.

Asking questions about business policies is widely considered as an attack upon the authority of the employer. Many are either sincerely indignant when the plant committee asks questions, or they pretend to be in refusing to answer. If they do answer, the information is delayed and incomplete.

Finally, the early postwar years brought on widespread practices of blackmarketeering and tax fraud. Employers are understandably reluctant to let the plant committees become aware of such facts. In one or two cases, committees have acted against the firm on the basis of such information, and reports of these incidents have lent decisive support to an instinct for secrecy which is already exceedingly strong. Two such cases, both in early postwar years and involving the CGT, are reported by Georges Lasserre:

> In the R. Oil Works at Marseilles, at a time when the firm was asking for a price increase, the enterprise committee discovered 54 million francs in concealed profits when only 12 million had been declared. They brought this to the notice of the Minister in order to prevent the price increase. Another curious example is that of a biscuit firm in Eastern France where the committee, at a time when things were scarce, exposed the existence of hidden stocks of flour. The flour was confiscated, and the business firm, which was then forced to get along with the small official allocations, had to lower production and dismiss some of the staff. This made the workers furious, and the committee was disowned by the trade union.

The law authorizes the plant committees to make suggestions for the use of profits. No case has come to the author's attention where such suggestions have been followed by the employer, and very few suggestions of this kind have been made in recent years.

The practices employed by management to avoid committee interference in economic or financial matters are varied. Consultation occurs after the fact, the excuse being that the decision had to be made in a hurry. In other cases, employers consult the committees so frequently that they are submerged by work—but the issues on which they are asked for advice are the insignificant ones only. (Lasserre reports that a firm consulted the committee on the color to be chosen for a tile floor.) Where there are both a plant and an enterprise committee (in an enterprise consisting of several plants, for example) the plant manager declares himself incompetent to answer questions on economic or financial problems. They are referred to the enterprise committee which meets only every six months. Of necessity, it deals only with a few questions at each meeting. A particular issue may, therefore, come up long after it has lost all its relevance.

The participation of plant committee members in the meetings of the boards of companies has been rendered meaningless by standard devices. Informal board meetings from which the committee delegates are excluded precede the official sessions. It is at the unofficial gatherings that problems are really discussed and settled. The official board meeting merely ratifies (as rapidly as possible) the decisions reached informally.

Reports also agree that the committees have shown the least activity and initiative in the economic and financial areas. This may be the result of the employers' efforts to render futile the committee's concern with economic matters, or it may be ascribed to the committee's lack of competence in this field and the average employees' preference for action on issues more directly related to their personal welfare.

Yet, while the over-all judgment of the committees' performance in the economic and financial areas is negative, there are some exceptions. Some committees have hired accountants who have done educational work among the committee members and, through them, among the workers themselves. In a number of other cases, committees have become channels of one-way information, from management to the employees. An investigation carried out in the area of Lyons indicates that of 31 committees, 12 felt—as the majority of their members stated—that there was a community of interest between business and the workers; and 19, that the committees did not show any concern for a community of interest.[31] Solidarity, however, also has negative aspects: committees with good trade union and political connections have been used by business establishments to obtain special favors for them from government. This happened primarily prior to 1947 when ministries decided on raw material supplies, price increases, and so forth. In other words, some committees have been active in the economic field, merely to become agents of a Syndicalist coalition of management and employees.

New functions have been entrusted to the plant committees and, in their absence, to the shop stewards by the decrees of the de Gaulle regime on "capital-labor association" (Association Capital-Travail).[32] Enterprises are encouraged to give premiums to their employees by having them participate in the results of the enterprise, as far as its capital, its financing, or the growth of its productivity are concerned. Plant agreements with the most representative unions are to be concluded on these subjects; where there are no unions, union-concluded contracts may be used as models. The unions must be represented by employees of the firm. Tax reductions are to be granted to encourage the conclusion of such contracts. The plant committee is to supervise the execution of the contract.

Little practical experience is available to enable an observer to judge what the new legislation may mean. The unions have expressed concern that owing to lack of information the employees are not able to take full advantage of the new decrees, while the enterprise obtains the full tax benefits provided for. They are also concerned that union influence in the new system will be quite weak for a number of reasons: unions must be represented by employees of the firm, no union representatives are members of the committees deciding on the tax benefits, the employers' duty to provide information essential to the functioning of the system has been left deliberately vague since otherwise no agreements would be concluded.[33]

The technical area. In this field, committees have performed useful functions, primarily right after the end of World War II, but their usefulness seems to have declined in more recent years.

Right after the liberation of the country, the CGT adopted a policy which favored the primacy of production over the satisfaction of the workers' immediate demands. The slogan then was: "First produce, then demand." [34] Since de Gaulle was anxious to keep the Communists out of such sensitive ministries as that of the interior, foreign affairs, national defense, and consequently shunted them off into the administration of economic affairs, the Communists were mainly responsible for economic policies. In this capacity, they were exceedingly "reasonable." Demands for higher wages were sharply opposed by them and the unions under their influence. The plant committees, in that period, were given instructions to assist, as far as possible, in the growth of production.

This was just a passing phase. Even before the Communists were forced out of the government by the rising protest of the workers against their low living standards, the plant committees changed their attitude toward the problems of production and productivity. Fear of unemployment, the impression that economic reconstruction was of greater benefit to the employers than to the employees, and that the emphasis on productivity merely served to conceal increased exploitation of the workers turned many plant committees from instruments for increased production into devices for increased economic demands on the part of the employees. When the Communist Party took up open warfare against the government, the CGT encouraged the committees to speed up and accentuate this change of attitude.

Beyond this, a certain sense of futility took hold of many committees. On major technical matters there was usually little they were able to contribute. Modern plants have specialized personnel which handles problems of organization and technique. The committees rarely had anything substantial to add to this work. Sometimes when they had important suggestions to make, employers refused to take them seriously, out of fear of losing their authority. The smaller and less significant suggestions, on the other hand, which some committees were able to make, did not usually give them a sufficient sense of accomplishment to encourage further initiative. It may be true, however, that the sum total of these suggestions sometimes — perhaps most outstandingly in the nationalized industries prior to 1947 — was of considerable significance.[35]

Reasons for failure. One fairly clear indication of the failure of the plant committees is the relatively small number of active committees. Exact figures are not available because the committees do not have to register. In 1954, however, the ministry of labor estimated that of 21,000 firms having more than 50 workers, 15,000 came under the law. Of those some 10,000 to 12,000 had plant committees. Fifty to 60 per cent of them were functioning more or less well. "The figures have probably gone down since then," reports Georges Lasserre, "but may have become stationary in the more recent past. Moreover, complaints about the difficulty of finding candidates for shop steward or committee posts have become increasingly frequent, and at the same time the number of abstentions in the elections has increased to some 40 per cent of the electorate." [36]

The main responsibility for this must be placed upon the shoulders of many French employers, a great many of whom have not yet accepted collective bargaining and unionism. The plant committees appear to them as a form of "socialization without socialism." [37] Union rights in the plant are a "domain where one may hold that the direct intervention of the law-maker has already gone beyond the bounds of the reasonable. It is an illusion to expect employers conscious of their responsibilities to freely admit rules which would prevent them from carrying on the normal functions of management in the enterprises for which they are responsible." [38]

It is generally conceded that the attitude of the largest French trade union federation, the CGT, must also be regarded as responsible for the failure. As was mentioned before, the CGT—by far the strongest trade union federation in the country—changed its strategy profoundly in the 1947–48 period. This change vitally affected the plant committees. From instruments of cooperation between workers and management, they were now turned into devices to carry on the class struggle more effectively in the plants. This not only sharpened employers' resistance but also diverted the committees from their assigned purpose. This development has been further emphasized by the numerous cases in which the same person was a member of the plant committee and a shop steward at the same time—often a result of the difficulty of finding suitable candidates for both jobs.[39] In this way the functions of consultation and grievance handling are combined in one person to the disadvantage of both tasks.

Observers agree, furthermore, that the lack of sufficient training and education among the workers has been a contributing cause of failure. It is significant in this context that the committees of white-collar employees have functioned relatively better than those composed of a majority of workers. There have been attempts on the part of the unions to prepare their members for these new assignments. But these efforts came late, in many cases so late that the workers' loss of interest in the new institutions had already set in. A small group of workers has undergone systematic training, but the large mass has hardly been touched.

The fruits of these efforts may still materialize. The educational efforts of the trade union centers have, on the whole, tended to grow. The universities of Paris, Lille, Strasbourg, and Lyons have set up industrial relations centers. Recent political developments in France may provide further impetus to the plant committees since de Gaulle seems interested in the development of collaborative institutions in industry. A law has been proposed which would give workers upon their demand the right to an unpaid leave of twelve working days per year. This leave would have to be used for attendance of courses at either the trade union federation or the universities.[40] In the words of Val Lorwin: "It is not possible to say that the committees have 'worked.' It is too soon to say that they 'cannot work.'" As to the shop stewards, their future is inextricably bound up with that of French unionism and the industrial relations system of the country in general.

The Union in the Plant

French collective bargaining distinguishes in law and in fact between "most representative unions" and others. While the Popular Front government originally seems to have considered giving the majority union exclusive bargaining rights — American style — political pressure quickly imposed a change toward a doctrine of union pluralism. After World War II, the strongest union confederation, the CGT (Confédération Générale du Travail), largely dominated by the Communists, attempted to obtain exclusive bargaining rights. Soon, however, the Christian Trade Union Federation (CFTC), supported by one of the most influential government parties, the MRP (Mouvement Republicain Populaire, a progressive Catholic party), obtained recognition from the government as a "most representative union." When later the non-Communist FO (Force Ouvrière) broke away from the CGT it also joined the list of recognized unions as did the CGC (Confédération Générale des Cadres, a federation of technical and supervisory employees) over the resistance of all other unions. The CGT, CFTC and FO represent all employees; the CGC, the *cadres;* and other unions have limited representation (an occupational group, a locality, an area).[41] A decree of January 7, 1959, has designated the federation of independent unions (Confédération Générale des Syndicats Indépendants) as "most representative." An appeal against this decision is pending before the state court (Conseil d'État). The federation is weak in numbers, exists only in a few enterprises, has no departmental organizations, and no congress has met for several years. It is questionable whether the federation is eligible to be declared representative under the terms of the law (Art. 31f of Part I of the Labor Code[42]).

The criteria by which such recognition is accorded are manifold; they range from size of membership to independence from employers and "patriotic attitude during the occupation." To a large extent, these are matters of judgment and are, therefore, often influenced by political pressures.

To be admitted to the charmed circle of most representative unions carries considerable benefits for the union concerned. Not only does the union acquire rights relating to collective bargaining and the so-called "extension" of such agreements by the government (that is, the process by which the agreement is given the force of law and extended to cover plants and employees in the particular industry or occupation not represented at the bargaining table), but the recognized union is also the only one which may propose candidates in the first round of the shop elections of stewards and plant committees. The union has the right to propose the recall of those representatives whom it nominated. It may, furthermore, appoint a representative to the plant committee with consultative status. As for the shop stewards, they may be assisted upon their own request by union delegates including those from nonrepresentative unions.

The struggle waged around the question of multi-union recognition had its counterpart in a debate on the election system for plant committees. The method originally introduced provided for the election of that list of candidates which obtained a relative majority. At the time (immediately after World War II), only two major trade union federations existed, the CGT and the CFTC. In the climate of patriotic enthusiasm then prevailing, an agreement was concluded between them providing for joint slates. Even then, this agreement was not carried out universally.

At the same time the CGT was pressing for complete trade union unity as did Socialist-led (or Communist-led) unions in many other countries of the continent where unions traditionally had been divided according to religions or political philosophies.[43] While these efforts succeeded in Germany and Austria, they failed in France as a result of CFTC resistance. When the CGT metal workers' union announced that the joint slates were only a prelude to "total trade union unity in the factory," the CFTC mobilized its political allies and obtained a shift to proportional representation in plant committee elections.[44]

Collective bargaining at the plant level may proceed under French legislation in either of two ways. It may be a plant agreement which adapts an existing national, regional, or local agreement to the individual plant, or it may be a special plant agreement not connected with any collective agreement of wider scope. In the first case, the purpose of the plant agreement is primarily to set down the methods of calculating piece rates and individual or collective output bonuses. In the second case, according to the law, the plant agreement can cover only the setting of wage rates and wage supplements.

However, the number of plant agreements of either type since the legislation of 1950 — though growing — has been rather small. In nearly seven years, 213 plant agreements and 309 riders to agreements have been signed. Some of these — the Renault agreements of 1950 and 1955 which took over some of the features of the UAW-General Motors agreements, for example — have had national significance. For a while it seemed as if some of the methods of American collective bargaining — the experimentation with pioneering plant agreements and the system of the key bargain — were to be adopted in France as well. Yet there has been no significant followup to the Renault bargain, and the fact that the French government extended by law some of the provisions of the Renault agreement to all French workers, indicated that American bargaining methods would find difficult going in France.[45]

One of the main hindrances to the development of plant agreements is the fact that many, if not most, French employers refuse to recognize the existence of plant trade unions or plant trade union "sections." The existing law does not prevent an employer from opposing the operation of a plant union by using the "disciplinary powers" inherent in his capacity as employer. According to a decision of the highest French Court, the Cour de Cassation, the right of French unions to conclude plant- or firm-wide collective agreements as provided in the legislation of 1950 does not give the union real status in the plant. Such agreements must in general be concluded within the framework of a collective contract which must be negotiated on at least a regional basis with an employers' association. The latter contract then sets minima with the plant agreement determining effective rates above the minimum. Attempts to give firm-wide agreements real meaning — the Renault agreement of 1955 set the pace for this — collapsed when the Renault contract in application failed to live up to the hopes it had created. Instead a new kind of plant agreement developed—for which the Dassault contract of March 1956 was the model—in which the personnel itself is a party to the agreement, completely disregarding the union.[46]

For a long time the French unions have demanded the right to appoint delegates in the plant who would represent the unions which signed the collective agreement in their dealings with management. These union delegates would be plant employees, but they would have the right to be assisted by union representatives from outside the plant. The union delegates would take part in plant committee meetings and those of the shop stewards. They would act as second-level grievance men for members of their own organization when the shop steward failed to reach a satisfactory settlement.[47] These unions would also enjoy such privileges as the right to put up posters without censorship on the part of the employer, distribution of union publications and collection of union dues in the plant, office space in the plant, days off for the union delegates to take part in union congresses, and so forth, without loss of their vacation rights.

When these demands were put forward in connection with the legislation of December 23, 1946, regarding collective bargaining, they were met by a stern refusal on the part of the employers. They supported their refusal by referring to the intimate relationship existing in France between some of the unions and political parties, the resulting danger of political conflicts being brought into the plant, the hostility between competitive unions, and so forth. Even though the validity of these points cannot be altogether denied, many observers felt that the real reason for the refusal was the traditional French employers' desire to be "master in their own house." In the currently valid law of February 11, 1950, no reference is made to these demands, but the law allows for the introduction into collective agreements of clauses relating to the free exercise of union rights—which is, in France, the conventional designation of the issues mentioned above.

As a result, a small number of collective agreements have been concluded, providing short leaves for union activity. Even without authorization in collective agreements, unions may appoint delegates in the plants, but there is no way of compelling the employer to deal with them. A good deal of confusion exists as to whether the plant has to provide space for union posters and announcements, and whether such announcements have to be submitted to management for approval prior to their being posted. Two legal texts permit the interpretation that the firm must provide such space, but this is merely an inference, not a clearly stated obligation, and management has generally been hostile to this interpretation. A few collective agreements contain clauses on these matters, and the Miners' Statute provides for union announcement boards in every mine.* The distribution of union publications and dues collection in the workplace are authorized by very few collective agreements, but the Miners' Statute contains such an authorization. Equally rare are agreements that would authorize the holding of union meetings or give unions office space in the plant. A clause in the Miners' Statute has been interpreted by the courts to exclude the participation of outside union representatives.

Other Workshop Representatives

In addition to plant committees, shop stewards, union delegates (in the few cases where the latter exist), there are labor representatives on the boards of nationalized enterprises, as well as other forms of worker representation in the plants.

In the mines and quarries, the workers elect safety delegates. They are protected against dismissal by being given super-seniority, American style, in their occupational group. For the underground workers in the mines, the safety delegates also fulfill the function of shop steward.

In establishments with more than 50 employees, safety and health committees are to be established.[48] Where a plant committee exists, the safety and health committee operates as its subcommittee. The area of activity of these committees is indicated by their title. In a number of enterprises, col-

* The *Statut du Mineur* is formally a law determining wages and working conditions in the coal mining industry. It was first enacted in June 1946, following the nationalization of coal mining. At that time the content of the law was agreed upon by the then-existing two major miners' unions — the CGT miners' union and the CFTC miners' affiliate — as well as by the National Assembly. In spite of its character as a law, the *statut* may thus be regarded as an agreement. However, the changes in Communist Party policy beginning in 1947 and the withdrawal of recognition from the CGT union for having prevented the continuance of essential maintenance operations during a strike have greatly affected the situation. Negotiations are now carried on between the administration of the nationalized coal mines, the "Charbonnages de France," their regional administrations, and the mining affiliates of the two non-Communist unions, CGT-FO and CFTC. The latter represent an estimated one third of the employees. With this rather important qualification, the *statut,* now sharply attacked by the CGT, may still be regarded as an agreement, and changes in it are still being made by agreement between the two non-Communist unions and the Charbonnages de France. After approval by the responsible ministries, they are then enacted by decree.

lective agreements provide for the establishment of disciplinary councils with advisory powers. The Miners' Statute establishes councils consisting of equal numbers of management and workers' representatives. They establish the disciplinary regulations — which must be approved by the mining engineer — and they act as appeal boards on lesser disciplinary sanctions, while sterner sanctions such as downgrading or dismissal require the previous approval of the council. The councils exist at the local, regional, and national levels, and appeals from a lower to a higher board are possible. The courts have greatly weakened the *statut* by deciding that violations of the procedure give rise to claims for compensation, but do not nullify the decision of management.

Safety committees. Little need be said about safety and health committees. They derive most of their authority from their cooperation with agents of the government. Thus the safety delegates of the miners cooperate with the mining engineers and inspectors who in the coal mines perform the functions otherwise entrusted to the inspectors of the labor ministry. The usual procedure consists of the safety delegates setting down their observations in a record book; management adds its comments. This book is regularly transmitted to the government inspectors. In the case of imminent danger the safety delegates communicate directly with the inspector. When the latter visits the mine for inspection, he may be accompanied by the safety delegates.

Similar contacts exist between the safety and health committees and the labor inspectors. The latter set down in a record book in the plant those violations of the safety and health code that the inspector has established. This book is open to the plant committee which, thereupon, may assure itself of management's compliance with the code. The committees in turn report serious accidents to the inspectors and must submit reports on their own activities to the inspectors at regular intervals. These reports deal with all accidents in the plant which have caused a stoppage of work and required compensation under the law.

Finally, the committees are in touch with the regional social security organization, which is entitled to ask the committees for information about safety and health in the plant. In exchange the committees may draw upon the technical assistance of the social security organization.

On the whole, these committees function well. It is perhaps significant, however, that their authority is derived from that of the agents of the government with whom the committees cooperate and that the ultimate sanction is the labor inspector's right to bring a plant management before a court. In other words, not even at this technical level is there real collaboration between the workers and management without the intervention of the government.

Workers' representation in nationalized enterprises. The basic scheme for the management of public industrial enterprises goes back to decisions of the French Trade Union Confederation (CGT) taken shortly after World War I. Although revolutionary syndicalism had disappeared as an effective organized force in 1914, the Syndicalist tradition was still alive among the unionized workers, and with it the fear of a powerful state and of "bureaucratization." This expressed itself in the proposal that nationalized industrial enterprises be administered by boards composed in equal parts of representatives of three groups: workers and other employees of the enterprise, consumers, and the collectivity. There were to be similar boards for the different branches of industry and a general board for all nationalized enterprises. These latter boards have not been created, only those for the individual enterprises or for industries run as a single enterprise. For the latter, this scheme was carried out by the legislation of 1945–47 organizing the many enterprises which were nationalized after World War II although the laws provide for a number of variations in detail of the basic scheme. Electricity, gas, the coal mines, a number of banks and insurance companies,[49] and the Renault automobile factory are outstanding examples of publicly owned industries and enterprises in which the unions are represented in the governing boards.

By no stretch of the imagination, however, can this representation be described as a representation of the workers themselves. In fact, in almost every case there is less connection between the workers in the French nationalized enterprises and the union representatives on the governing boards than there is between German workers in codetermination enterprises and the workers' delegates on their boards. In Germany normally the chairman and possibly vice-chairman of the workers' council are members of the board, and the workers have a good deal of contact with their council chairman. In France a similar situation exists in the Renault automobile plant and in the nationalized airplane factories. In these two cases the plant committee is the origin of the workers' delegation to the governing boards. In the other nationalized industries the "most representative" unions propose the names of the workers' delegates for the approval of the minister under whose authority the particular firm or industry comes. These are typically top union dignitaries far removed from the rank and file. Moreover, in actual fact the role of the governing boards has been quite insignificant.[50]

The Committees — A Summary Judgment

The various forms of workers' representation in the plant have had differing fates. As a general rule to which there are many exceptions, it may be said that those committees have been most successful which seemed most remote from an attempt to change the social system. The same principle applies to the committees that have different kinds of specific tasks; on the whole they have tended to perform with more impressive results the tasks which fitted most readily into the traditional functioning of the plant, while they have been conspicuously unsuccessful in those functions which most clearly would have tended to introduce new principles of management. Thus, as a sweeping generalization it may be said that the plant committees performed best in their administration of social welfare institutions, although even here exceptions exist, and they achieved the least success in the area of the financial and economic operations of the plant.

CHAPTER III

Germany

The German works council can trace its history back for more than a century. When the Constitutional Assembly met in Frankfurt during the revolutionary years of 1848–49, the formation of works councils (*Fabrikausschüssen*) was one of the institutions proposed. They were to be joint labor–management organizations, to deal with disputes and grievances, work out plant rules, set up welfare agencies, and so forth. Like the remainder of the objectives of this abortive revolution, the works council failed to materialize. Much later on (in 1905) councils with mainly consultative functions were set up in the mines of Prussia, and these were supplemented in 1909 by the institution of elected safetymen (*Sicherheitsmänner*) in the mines.

As shown earlier, the decisive step occurred during World War I, when, in order to maintain social peace, to obtain the continued cooperation of the labor organizations in the war effort, and to compensate for the sacrifices which the law imposed upon the works, the Auxiliary Service Law of December 5, 1916, instituted councils in the plants. Section 11 of the law provided for the establishment of workers' and employees' councils (*Arbeiter-und Angestelltenausschüsse*) in all industrial enterprises with more than 50 workers or (white-collar) employees. They acted as grievance committees and had the right to appeal to conciliation boards created by the same law and consisting of a government representative and three representatives each of employer and workers. In effect, this law gave legal status to the union representatives in the plant.

In the revolutionary movement of 1918, partly under the influence of the Russian revolution, workers' and soldiers' councils were formed whose status became one of the major issues in the struggle among the various currents within the German labor movement. The enactment of the works council law of February 4, 1920, which was based upon Article 165 of the Weimar Constitution was a compromise in which the left wing obtained the symbols of victory without its substance. The acceptance of the councils was forced upon the government by left-wing pressure, but the majority Socialists then succeeded in depriving the councils of their revolutionary functions.[1] The law provided for the establishment of works councils which were to perform two main functions — bargaining and managerial. Under the first heading came plant-wide negotiations leading to wage agreements within the framework of the collective agreement concluded by the union, the establishment of work rules, and the handling of grievances. The managerial tasks of the councils consisted primarily in their right to delegate two members on the supervisory boards of the companies.

Shortly after the advent of the Nazis the councils were superseded by appointed "work trustees" who were to cooperate with the employer (renamed "leader of the plant" by the new regime). Many reports on life in the Nazi-dominated plants point out, however, that unofficially the old works councillors continued to play important roles as advisors to the workers. The need of the workers for a workshop organization manifested itself when, right after the defeat of the Nazis, works councils sprang up spontaneously in many plants. Their existence was legalized by one of the early actions of the occupation authorities, the adoption on April 10, 1946, of Control Council Law No. 22.[2] This law, however, gave the councils only limited and advisory functions. Various West German states enacted their own legislation which came close to the model of the 1920 law. Some of the state works council laws granted the councils the right to participate in managerial decision-making on general economic matters. These clauses in the Hesse and Württemberg-Baden laws were suspended in 1948 by the United States military government; the official justification given was that decisions on the issue of workers' participation in management were to be kept in abeyance until the federal constitution decided whether the right to legislate in this area belonged to the federal or the state governments. After the establishment of the West German Republic, the fundamental works constitution law (*Betriebsverfassungsgesetz*) was enacted on October 11, 1952. This law applies to all enterprises of the private economy and those public enterprises which are organized in the legal form of share or limited-liability companies. It applies with modifications to *Tendenzbetriebe* (establishments primarily serving political, trade union, religious, charitable, educational, scientific or artistic purposes). All employees, except executives (not clearly defined) are subject to the law. Within the mining and steel- and iron-producing industries, the law on codetermination of May 21, 1951, also applies, supplemented by the legislation of August 7, 1956, referring to codetermination in the holding companies.[3]

To understand the works constitution law fully, it is necessary to become acquainted first with the codetermination law which not only preceded it but which also formed an essential part of its background.

Codetermination

When the victorious armies of the Western Powers occupied what was later to become the federal republic, they were greatly concerned with the decentralization of authority in German industry, particularly in heavy industry which is primarily concentrated in the Ruhr area. They knew that some of the outstanding employers in the Ruhr had been lending moral and financial support to Hitler, and they believed that the monopolistic structure of the coal and steel industries was contributing to the rise of antidemocratic and aggressive tendencies in Germany. There could be no question at the time of returning these industries to their former owners, some of whom were regarded as war criminals. By successive laws and ordinances, the administration of the coal mines and the steel works was entrusted to various agencies (trustees) appointed by the military government, until in 1949 new decentralized companies were set up to which property rights in the holdings of the former *Konzerns* were transferred. Parallel with these developments come a gradual relaxation of the earlier rules which restricted the output of steel in Germany. The resistance of the workers to these measures, which deprived them of their livelihood, played a part in the abandonment of the policy designed to limit the war-potential of German industry.

For a number of reasons — including the presence of a labor government in Britain which administered the zone of the Ruhr — the reborn German labor organizations were strongly represented in the temporary administration of the Ruhr industry. Indeed, in the climate of opinion of that time, no effective administration was conceivable without the participation of the workers who had been the most ardent anti-Nazi group and were making invaluable contributions to the reconstruction of the war-devastated country.

When legislative powers passed to the Germans themselves on the federal level, the unions were eager to have their new position confirmed by German authority. In this way they hoped to avoid the criticism that their influence was the result of the victors' benevolence, just as the Weimar Republic itself had been accused by Hitler of having been imposed upon the German people by the victors of World War I. To their surprise, the unions discovered that the Bonn regime was reluctant. It was only under the threat of a strike in the Ruhr, 96 per cent of the miners and metalworkers having voted for one, that the government hastened the parliamentary debates. The law on codetermination in coal and steel was finally enacted on May 21, 1951.[4]

With only 14 sections, the law is rather simple compared with the 92 sections of the works constitution law voted a year later.[5] It provides for labor participation in two of the three governing bodies of German share companies—namely, the board of supervision (*Aufsichtsrat*) and managing board (*Vorstand*)—but not in the general assembly of the shareholders. The first usually consists of eleven members, though in larger companies fifteen or twenty-one members may be elected. On the typical eleven-man board, labor is represented by five members, and the shareholders by another five. Of the latter, four are to be elected among the shareholders themselves, while the fifth representative, though elected by the shareholders, is a person without material interest in the company. On the labor side, one member each is proposed by the works council to represent the workers and the white-collar employees, after consultation with the unions and the trade union federation; two more members are designated by the union federation in agreement with the union or unions of the enterprise and its works council. A fifth member, designated by the union federation, is to be independent, that is, not an employee of the plant. The eleventh man is to be appointed jointly; in case of disagreement, there is a complicated procedure which culminates in his designation by a court. With the necessary adjustments this system applies also to boards of fifteen or twenty-one members, and with further modifications including a highly intricate system of indirect elections, to the boards of holding companies among whose operating companies those in the field of coal or steel represent more than half the total turnover.

Labor representation on the managing board (*Vorstand*) consists of a labor director who, like all members of the board, is appointed by the board of supervision but must have the approval of the majority of the labor members. He is to represent the viewpoints of labor within the management of the company, but at the same time he is a member of management—a somewhat delicate position, particularly in times of labor-management negotiations or conflicts. It is precisely this issue of conflicting loyalties which the British unions tried to avoid by their refusal to let members of the boards of nationalized industries continue to be union representatives. The German labor director requires for his appointment the approval of the majority of the labor members of the supervisory board. The members of the British board are appointed by the minister and are responsible to him alone. The German labor director continues to be a union member. Indeed, a special association, the "Verein für Soziale Betriebspraxis" (association for social plant management) has been established in Dusseldorf, essentially for the labor members of the boards of codetermination enterprises. Most labor directors belong to it; they pay an annual contribution of 1000 mks. (about $250); the labor members of the supervisory boards pay 300 mks. (about $75) per year. These high contributions are one of the unsatisfactory ways by which the high salaries and other forms of compensation of these labor dignitaries are put at the service of the labor movement. The labor members of the British boards must resign from their union offices and "surrender any responsibility to the Trade Union." They represent the "viewpoint" of the union, but not the union itself. Cases in which this conflict of loyalties and responsibility have come to the fore, at least from the point of view of the union member, have already occurred in Germany, though up to now they do not seem to have been frequent. One example occurred during the metalworkers' wage movement in the spring of 1958, when a number of labor directors were reported to have insisted upon their primary duty as members of the managing boards. Six directors are reported to have become members of the board of the employers' association of the steel industry. Altogether there are 36 labor directors in the iron and steel industry. There have been many predictions that serious cleavages in times of economic recession will be unavoidable.

From Codetermination to Works Constitution

The general functioning of the German codetermination system has been discussed at length in American literature. However, it is not the focus of our own interest at this stage. Some of the problems relating to this system will be presented below as well as later on in this study. Of concern to us at this point is the connection between codetermination and the general system of workers' representation in the plant. For the unions, the codetermination law of 1951 was merely a stage in an evolution which, in their view, was to spread codetermination from coal and steel to all of German industry. The decisive battle was still to come. Codetermination, though now embodied in German law, was in fact only the continuation of a system created by the occupation forces and limited to two industries. Whether and in what way this system was to be applied to German industry in general, what form workers' representation in the plant was to adopt, what the functions and rights of the workers' representatives in the plant were to be — all these and many other related issues were still to be settled.

As we have mentioned, several West German states, called *Länder* in Germany, passed works council legislation shortly after the end of the war; indeed all of them did with the exception of Rhineland-Westphalia, Lower Saxony, and Hamburg. These laws varied considerably from land to land, ranging from simple representation for grievance handling and bargaining purposes to the Hesse law of codetermination similar to that enacted later in 1951 for coal and steel. Under the circumstances it was not extravagant on the part of the unions to hope for the generalization of the principles embodied in the federal law of 1951 for all or most of the nonagricultural enterprises. But events quickly put an end to these hopes.

Out of the Nazi period, management had emerged with greatly impaired authority. Not only had some of the most outstanding industrial leaders been ardent partisans of the Hitler regime, but almost all economic activity had been at the service of the dictatorship or under its control. The downfall of the dictator dragged along with him all the management leaders. Public opinion, right or wrong, regarded them as associates of the dictatorial system. Many employers fled upon the approach of the Allied armies, a few (some of the most famous) were accused of war crimes. So great was the disorganization on the employers' side that it took until 1947 for the first employers' associations to reappear, first in the British, then in the American, and last in the French Zones.[6] The unions themselves, not being able because of their tradition to conceive of collective bargaining except through employers' associations, are reported to have asked the Allied military authorities for their establishment. The labor organizations, on the other hand, enjoyed a good deal of moral authority. They appeared as representatives of a class which had offered resistance to the Nazis and which had suffered persecution from the hands of the dictator. The occupation forces themselves — often against their wishes — found themselves compelled, in their search for possible non-Nazi candidates for public office, to draw upon labor representatives. The influence of some of the American labor organizations upon the United States military government was exerted in the same direction. In any case, the works councils, spontaneously springing up here or there, after the destruction of the Third Reich, were the few genuine centers of native authority.

This was reflected in the thinking of the political organization which soon proved to be the strongest in the country, the Christian Democratic Union (CDU), whose leader Konrad Adenauer was to become chancellor of West Germany. The CDU's Ahlener program, adopted in 1947, was strongly prolabor and anticapitalistic. Its condemnation of what it called "liberal capitalism" led it to demand workers' participation in plant management. The right of the workers to share in decision-making in the firm was described as a natural one, comparable to the rights which property conferred upon stockholders.

For the second largest party, the Social Democrats, codetermination presented something of a quandary. Although shaken in its fundamental beliefs by its defeat of 1933 and by subsequent events, the party still felt some attachment to the traditional demand for the nationalization of industry. Codetermination thus seemed to some of the party leaders an issue that would sidetrack the efforts of the movement from the basic demand for socialization. Yet, codetermination might prove to be a useful preliminary step toward nationalization, permitting the training of labor people for managerial responsibility. Moreover, the outstanding leader of the postwar union movement, Hans Böckler, was firmly committed to codetermination, and the Socialists were naturally eager to establish and maintain the closest possible understanding with the unions. In no case could the Socialists permit the CDU, their most dangerous competitors, to oust the Social Democrats from their position as the unions' natural and most reliable allies on the political scene. Thus the party inevitably became the most ardent advocate of union demands for a generalized system of codetermination, whatever the secret reservations of some of the party leaders may have been. The two main parties of West Germany were therefore to all appearances unanimous in their support of the codetermination principle.

Not the least important factor on the scene was the reconstituted German trade union movement. Out of the defeat of the divided union movement by the Nazi dictatorship in 1933, the common experience of oppression and persecution during the years from 1933 to 1945, and to some extent as a result of pressure from some of the military government officials in the various "zones" of post-1945 Germany, was born the desire to establish a united, nonpartisan labor movement. Traditionally, the German unions had been divided according to philosophical, political, or religious lines into a number of competitive movements, each with its own union federation. Under the Weimar Republic, by far the largest of these federations — that of the so-called "free" trade unions — was spiritually and personally allied with the Social Democratic Party. The Catholic Center Party maintained the second largest federation whose main support was among the white-collar groups, but also among the miners of the Ruhr. Pan-Germans and Communists each maintained trade unions, though those of the Communists came and went, following the tactical changes and maneuvers of the party. A small federation, named after its founders, Hirsch-Duncker, was associated with the Democratic State Party. All these organizations disappeared with the establishment of the Nazi dictatorship in 1933. The union leaders after 1945 resolved never to permit the emergence of another divided labor movement whose internal cleavages they held responsible for the failure to stem the rising tide of Nazism. Codetermination seemed an objective on which under the given circumstances both Socialists and Catholics could agree, thus providing the ideological basis for a unified trade union movement.

The gradual formation of unions, as prescribed by the military authorities, favored the unification plans of the union leaders. Progressing out of local associations to formations on a larger territorial scale, the unions established their West German federation at a congress in Munich in 1949. Rapidly growing, and led with great vigor by Hans Böckler, the organization soon reached a membership of more than six million.

The workers could rightfully claim to have made great sacrifices for the rebuilding of the war-devastated German economy. With their well-known application to work, their gift of organization and discipline, the German workers had made a decisive contribution to German economic reconstruction. The caution exercised for several years by the unions in their wage demands made for an unusually high rate of profit which, combined with a favorable tax legislation, led to an exceptionally high rate of investment.[7] In May 1952, at the height of the struggle for a favorable works constitution law, the German trade union federation (DGB, Deutscher Gewerkschäftsbund) issued a manifesto addressed to the workers which contained these statements:

> In 1945, the German economy was in ruins. While you were working at the reconstruction of the factories, offices and administrations, the men responsible for the breakdown of Germany disappeared from sight.
>
> You alone have accomplished what others have called the miracle of the economic reconstruction of Germany. Now attempts are made to prevent the achievement of a real codetermination of the employees in the plants and the administrations.

> This emerges from the draft of the works constitution law. It shows a clear design to prevent the realization of real codetermination of the wage-earners. It confirms the sacred privileges of the employers. It leaves the wage-earners in an economically subordinate position. Moreover, the bill deprives you of rights that were yours in 1933, which were guaranteed after 1945 in the constitution and laws of some of the *Länder* and which have demonstrated their worth in the difficult period of reconstruction.

A universal system of codetermination, it was claimed, could prevent a repetition of the pre-1933 situation in which big business support helped install the Nazi regime. Codetermination would fulfill, at least partially, the old dream of industrial democracy and extend democratic institutions beyond the political sphere into that of economic life. It would not only re-establish, but greatly enhance and improve, one of the most significant institutions of the Weimar Republic — the works council. Clearly, the expansion to other industries of the social system now firmly established in coal and steel seemed in the logic of things. Yet within a year after the law of 1951 was passed, the unions were compelled to acknowledge that their dream was not going to be realized.

The decisive element in the union defeat was the change in public opinion. The currency reform of 1948 set the stage for economic recovery. Every passing year of prosperity gave additional impetus to this change. An important symptom was the evolution of the philosophy of the Christian Democratic Party. Although it reconfirmed the Ahlener demand for codetermination during the campaign for the first Bundestag (parliamentary) elections in July 1949 and once again at the Catholic Congress in Bochum of September 1949, the party began a rapid shift toward the very same policy of laissez faire which it had so categorically rejected right after the war. When on September 20, 1949, Professor Erhard became minister of economic affairs, his program of neo-liberal capitalism soon became the official doctrine of the CDU. The long period of prosperity enhanced Erhard's reputation to the point that in 1958 he became the chancellor's deputy.

This was accompanied by what the opponents of the government called the "restoration" of the pre-Hitler regime, the re-establishment of the authority of the business leaders. Their resistance to codetermination on a wider scale was a crucial factor in the failure of the union demands.

Chancellor Adenauer took advantage of a strike threat of the DGB to shift the discussion from the substantive issues of codetermination to the problem of whether in a democratic society the unions should be allowed to put pressure upon the freely elected parliament. The unions proceeded nevertheless to call a general strike which took place on May 28, 1952, and in some industries — including the politically sensitive printing industry — continued until May 29. Nevertheless, two months later the Bundestag adopted (against the votes of the Social Democrats, the small Communist group, and a few members of the governing CDU) a law which fell far short of the unions' expectations.

The Works Councils

The legislation may be briefly summarized: works councils are to be elected in all eligible plants employing at least five employees. (If all employees refuse to elect a council, the election cannot be imposed upon them by employer, union, or government.) The size of the council depends on the number of employees. Where there are five to twenty regularly employed workers, the "council" becomes one person only. When twenty-one to fifty employees are eligible to vote, the council comprises three members. According to the number of employees, council membership may rise to thirty-five. Where the council consists of at least three members, workers and white-collar employees must be represented in proportion to their numerical strength. All employees above eighteen years of age may vote, all employees above twenty-one, who have been employed in the firm for one year and are entitled to vote in German federal elections, may be elected to the council. Elections are secret and held every two years. Where the council comprises at least three members, workers and white-collar employees vote separately, unless a secret ballot of each of the two groups has resulted in a decision for a common election. The system of proportional representation applies, unless only one list of candidates has been proposed. Lists of candidates may be proposed by at least one tenth of the employees eligible to vote. Members of the council are not entitled to any compensation except for expenses, but must be paid their full wages if they lose working time in the orderly performance of their duties. They enjoy protection against arbitrary dismissal and against discrimination. Upon proposal of one quarter of the council members, a representative of a union may be invited to participate — without vote — in council meetings.

Employer and council are to cooperate with union and employers' associations within the framework of the collective agreements. Council and employer are bound to keep peace. The right to take measures of industrial warfare is reserved to unions and employer associations. Strikes, therefore, cannot be called by the council. Conflicts between council and employer are subject to solution by special procedures.

The works council has a number of functions:

1) The council handles grievances.

2) It concludes agreements on piece rates, wage systems, and so forth, insofar as there is no collective agreement on these matters.

3) It may conclude agreements on wages or working conditions, supplementary to existing collective agreements insofar as the latter specifically authorizes the conclusion of such supplementary agreements.

4) In the case of dismissals the council is to be heard; it must be consulted if larger groups are to be dismissed or hired;[8] it has a veto power against new hirings in a few cases: (a) if the new appointment violates a law, a collective agreement, or a plant agreement (for example, hiring of female workers in plants which are not allowed to employ women); (b) if the new appointee is not qualified and has been selected for personal reasons only; (c) in the case of discrimination for reasons of race, religion, nationality, origin, political or union activity; or (d) if there are reasons to fear that the prospective employee would disturb the peace in the plant by antisocial or illegal behavior. In all these cases labor courts have ultimate decision if no agreement can be reached between the council and management.

5) It negotiates the work rules (beginning and ending of work periods, pauses, time and place of wage payments, timing of vacations, in-service training, order in the plant, safety, health).

6) It negotiates with the employer on changes in the plant (restrictions of activity, transfer of departments, merger, introduction of new work methods); a special mediation procedure is foreseen in the case of disagreements on these matters.

7) It supervises the enforcement of the applicable labor laws and of the collective agreement.

8) It administers the social welfare agencies of the plant.

In summary, the council is entitled to negotiate on wages and working conditions (supplementary agreements to the collective agreements or entire agreements when there is no collective agreement), on the plant rules, on hiring and firing of groups, on cases of discrimination, and on substantial changes in the plant. However, "regulation of rates of pay and other conditions of employment in work agreements is prohibited if these matters are usually governed by collective agreement in the industry concerned even if there is no such agreement actually in existence."[9] The council handles grievances. It administers plant welfare agencies. It supervises the application of existing labor laws and of collective agreements. For the rest, it may be heard or consulted, and it is entitled to information.

The chairman of the works council may call a plant assembly consisting of all employees — except executives — of the plant; union delegates of those labor organizations which are represented in the plant may take part in the assembly without the right to vote. Regular assemblies are to be held every quarter; they take place during working hours. The workers are compensated by the firm for loss of working time.

Three different systems for the settlement of disputes between council and management are provided for. Reference to the labor court may be made in disputes regarding hiring. Disputes regarding conditions of work (setting of shift hours, incentive rates, assignment of vacations, administration of employee welfare institution, and rules of employee conduct) are to be settled by an *ad hoc* arbitration board. Such a board consists of an equal number of council and management representatives together with an impartial chairman who, if necessary, may be appointed by the chairman of the labor court. Such a board operates in most cases only at the request of both sides to the dispute. Only in a few especially stated types of disputes may the board make a binding decision at the request of only one side. By special agreement the parties may substitute their own mediation procedure for the one provided for in the law. This has been done for the Ruhr mining area. In this case conflicts are brought before the mediation agency on the "level above the plant."

The third system applies to economic disputes, that is, to changes in the plant which may produce serious disadvantages for the employees such as curtailment of the activity of the plant or of substantial parts of it, transfer of the plant, merger, changes of the production process, and so forth. If disagreements on these matters arise between the council and management, either party may apply to the authorities for mediation or set up a mediation board which may make a nonbinding recommendation for settlement.

In addition to the workers' assembly and the council, the law also provides for the setting up of an economic committee in all establishments regularly employing more than 100 employees. This committee consists only of members of the establishment — one half selected by the council, the other half by the management. The members of the committee are subject to particularly severe rules of secrecy, even toward the members of the council. The economic committee advises management in all important economic matters. Management has to keep the committee informed on such matters insofar as such information would not endanger plant or business secrets of the establishments.

Finally, resuming a practice established by the legislation of 1922,[10] the works constitution law provides that the employees delegate their representatives to the supervisory boards of all share companies. Under the older legislation there were normally two employee representatives on the boards. The new law states that one third of the board membership must consist of employee representatives. They are to be elected by all employees in a secret ballot. The first two of these representatives must be employees. In other words, "outsiders" (in effect union representatives) can only be elected to a supervisory board if it consists of nine members or more. As a result, boards of this size are less and less frequent in order to keep out "outsiders." Management and the works council often agree that this is desirable. This regulation does not apply to the plants subject to the codetermination law which provides for a larger and differently determined employee representation on the supervisory boards of coal and steel plants. Whenever there are at least two workers' representatives on the board, one of them must be a worker, the other a white-collar employee. If more than half the employees are women, at least one woman must be delegated to the board.

Most frequently the council chairman and vice-chairman are delegated to the board, even though the law does not require this. In other cases, members of the council are elected. A trend toward the combination of various representative offices at the plant level is unmistakable.

The system in operation. So far we have been speaking mainly of the legal aspects of the councils. How does the works council operate in fact?

Elections are held every other year. Before the works constitution law was enacted, they were frequently held every year. However, by no means all enterprises entitled under the law to have a workers' council do in fact have one. No official figures are available, but a fairly reliable estimate by the *Neue Zürcher Zeitung* of January 5, 1963 puts the proportion of those without a council at some 20 per cent. These are mostly smaller enterprises with large welfare activities voluntarily provided by the management.

Nominations are usually put forward by the outgoing council jointly with the local unions. During the preliminary debates preceding the vote of the law, the Socialists proposed giving the unions the right to nominate candidates; this was rejected in favor of a scheme which gave this right to any group of employees. Actually, this means that the outgoing council members draw up the lists, often together with local union leadership or the union stewards in the plant, and then obtain the signatures necessary for a nomination (according to the law, one tenth of the voting members of the group, but no less than three, and no more than one hundred). The law leaves it to workers and white-collar employees to decide in a preliminary vote whether they wish to have joint or separate elections. Only when both groups — each by majority — so decide can there be a joint election. In that case the lists are usually so drawn up that the two groups are represented in proportion to their strength. (This was the practice in most elections prior to the enactment of the law in 1952.) When one group rejects joint elections, each group elects its own works council members separately. Such a decision is most frequent when the independent German Salaried Employees' Union (DAG) has strong support in a plant. The distinction between white-collar employees and manual workers in Germany, or between civil servants (*Beamte*) and all other employees, is well known as a main fact of German social life. It is consecrated by law, administrative practice, and the mores of the country.[11]

The lists of candidates should contain twice as many names as the numbers of seats to be filled, but often do not. However, when there is only one list, twice as many names must be proposed for the election to be valid. The number of seats to be assigned to each list is determined by proportional representation; from each list names are selected according to sequence. When there is only one list containing twice as many names as the number of seats to be filled, a majority decides who is elected from that list. Single lists are not evidence that there are no conflicts; the competing groups may have agreed on a common list and on the number of candidates each group will present for inclusion on that list.

Since there is now a united trade union movement (apart from the white-collar organization, DAG, and a small Christian splinter organization — other splinter groups being insignificant), it is supposed to be neutral in partisan politics. Yet political issues play an important part in council elections. For several years after the war, Communist influence among the works councillors was relatively strong. However, the unions themselves could officially do little to combat this influence, much as the anti-Communist union leadership would have wished to do so. In this situation, the party organizations in the plants maintained by the Social Democratic Party (SPD) and sometimes by the Christian Democratic Union (CDU) intervened in the election campaign. It was mainly the result of their efforts that Communist representation on the major works councils — apart from a few isolated and sometimes sensational cases — has been greatly curtailed.

Competition between SPD and CDU, however, continues and is frequently of far more than local significance. Reflecting the pattern of the political affiliation of the German workers, the great majority of the works councillors of known political affiliation belong to the SPD, the next largest group to the CDU; a small group is Communist.[12] Partisan competition extends also to representation on the council committees. Union influence on the councils represents another campaign issue.

Some campaigns are fought over the issue of separate white-collar representation and the relationship between white-collar employees and manual labor. In other cases conflicts exist over name lists; these are essentially personal rivalries. Sometimes, however, they do conceal conflicts over issues in the life of the enterprise.

However, many if not most elections are rather quiet and the only major issues, if any, are political or union affiliation or the personal popularity of various candidates. On the whole, there is little turnover among the council members. The term "professional works councillor" (*Berufsbetriebsrat*) well characterizes this situation.[13] In spite of the absence of ardent interest or of major social issues, participation in the elections is very high — 85 per cent being a reasonable estimate of average participation, and much higher percentages are not exceptional. Since many elections took place shortly after the new works constitution law was enacted and since elections have to be repeated every two years, a council election season has developed, the outcome of which is regarded as a measure of change in working-class opinion in Germany.

Those who are elected. Although no extensive statistical studies about the personnel of the councils, comparable to those made in Yugoslavia, are available, some impressions gathered by interviews or based upon the literature may be of some interest.

No one who observed the personnel and the activities of the German labor movement in the decade of the fifties can overlook the great gap that separated the old from the young in the organizations. The dividing line as far as birth date is concerned was somewhere around 1910. Men born prior to that date usually acquired their trade union training in the Weimar period and had some connection with the great era of the struggle for democracy. Those whose memory does not go back much before Hitler have a vastly different view of what the labor movement is and stands for. Moreover, the long break in the evolution of the movement — from 1933 to 1945 or 1946 — and the losses in manpower of the generation physically destroyed by the Nazis and the war or removed by emigration have all but eliminated the age group in between. The contrast between the older and the younger workers is, therefore, sharper than it would normally have been. Something vaguely akin to business unionism seems to appeal more to the younger men who have little ideological attachment to the movement; some of the older men are still hoping that somehow the world and Germany will resume where "normalcy" left off in 1933.

Generally speaking, the older generation still provides the great majority of the council members, not only because the older and more experienced men enjoy the confidence of the workers, but also because it is not always easy to find good candidates in sufficient number among the younger men.[14] Since the turnover of elected councillors is generally low, the inevitable result is that the average age of the members is high and rising. Works council members are usually re-elected term after term, and the chairman and vice-chairman in many instances have been on the council ever since the resumption of operations. The following is a description of the typical works council chairman:

> A man in his late fifties or early sixties, who has worked in the plant for twenty years or more, a solid family man, who is well known to a large segment of the personnel and well respected by both his colleagues and his superiors . . . they usually have a long record of trade union membership, which reaches back to the unions of the Weimar Republic, and in some cases even to imperial days. In their appearance, habits and views, they convey an impression of solidity, respectability, and responsibility. In many instances, especially of younger council chairmen, they also hold offices in the local organization of the union or in municipal or other politics.

The other council members are frequently similar in type to the chairman.

The predominance of the "father" type is not the result of accident. Paternalistic traits are inherent in the outlook of the people involved as well as in the actual operations of the system. The councillors treat the workers in a paternalistic way and are usually expected to do so.[15] The institution of works councils has undoubtedly helped to reduce the domineering attitude of management which was in any case difficult to maintain in the stormy days after World War II. But the change was not automatically one to a system of democratic partnership, but rather to joint paternalism. The significant fact is that in many cases the works council has joined in this system and has become a partner in a management team which administers the labor force of the enterprise with authority and benevolence. An observer writes:

Management and the works council often appear to the worker as complementary rather than competing institutions . . . [It] becomes a harmonizing agency, a sort of buffer between management and the worker, rather than an organ which takes an initiative of its own . . . Wherever codetermination privileges bring members of the works council still more closely together with management . . . a new stratum of industrial functionaries, to some extent sharing management prerogatives, makes its appearance. The sphere of management may thus tend to include a privileged upper stratum of the working class.[16]

The organization of the council. Having been elected, the council proceeds in turn to the election of a chairman and a vice-chairman; one of them must be a wage earner, the other a salaried employee (if the council has members from the two groups). In considerable detail the law sets out the ways in which the council is to operate. Thus, if the council has eleven members or more, it is to elect an executive committee consisting of three elected members of the council plus the chairman and the vice-chairman. Once again, if the council consists of representatives of more than one group, these groups must be represented in the executive committee. Management takes part in council meetings, either upon invitation of the council or because the council meeting has been called at the request of management. A representative of the employers' association may accompany the management representative. When one fourth of the council members request that the local union be represented at a council meeting, the union must be invited to send a delegate. Such invitations seem to occur only rarely. Representatives of all unions with members in the plant may take part in plant assemblies. A plant assembly is to be called every three months at the request of management or at the request of a quarter of the workers. Management is to be invited to the assemblies and may call in a representative of the employers' association.

When council work requires, members are to be freed from the regular duties of their job. This is normally the case for the chairman in smaller establishments and often for the vice-chairman as well. In larger plants all members of the executive committee of the council devote full time to their council duties. The employer bears all costs arising from the works council's activities.

If an enterprise consists of several plants, a general works council may be formed. It consists of two delegates each (representing different groups on the council) from each local works council, or of one delegate from each council if it consists of representatives of one group only.[17] The functions of such a general council are limited to matters of concern to the entire enterprise or several plants. It may not act on problems coming under the jurisdiction of individual plant councils.

Where more than five young workers — less than eighteen years of age — are employed, special representatives may be elected to the council. They have only consultative status and take part in council meetings only when special youth problems are being discussed.

Much of the council's work is done in committees. The most important of these groups, as we have mentioned, is the executive committee. Other committees are set up according to the requirements of the particular situation in the enterprise. Frequently-organized committees are those on personnel, wages, social benefits, accident prevention, housing, discipline, welfare, minors, disabled workers, and female employees.[18]

Most of their work refers either to issues which can simply be handled by direct confrontations by a council member with a company official, or to long-run problems. Often, the committees meet with their managerial counterparts. The social committee, for instance, may meet with the social worker of the plant, with the plant doctor and a representative of the labor director where there is such a member of the management team (in the codetermination plants, for example). They may discuss emergency financial assistance for individual employees. The youth committee may provide for the establishment of libraries, for sports installations and activities, financial assistance for theater visits and film groups, and so forth. The housing committee, meeting with the housing administrator of the enterprise, seeks to find housing for the workers, settles disputes arising out of housing problems, cooperates with the local housing authority, seeks to finance additional construction, and so forth.

Council and committee meetings are held in offices in the plant provided by the company. Normally at least one of the council members, usually a member of its executive committee, can be found there by employees with problems. Council meetings are held daily in the largest establishments, and weekly in many large and medium-sized firms.

Shop Stewards

Particularly in large plants the councillors are assisted by so-called "men of confidence" (*Vertrauensmänner*) or shop stewards. They have no legal status as have the works council members, but they do have experience and contact with all sections of the enterprise, which the council members do not have. In a number of cases, the shop stewards came from accident prevention committees whose members took on additional functions, particularly in connection with grievance handling. Normally these shop stewards are elected in secret ballot by the employees of a plant or a department. Elections usually take place shortly after the works councillors have been designated. The number varies considerably from plant to plant and from time to time; under the most favorable circumstances the stewards constitute about 1.5 per cent of the number of employees.[19] Sometimes the employees also elect substitute shop stewards.

Having no legal origin, the shop stewards do not enjoy the same protection against dismissal and transfer as the members of the works council. However, in at least one large plant, a special agreement between the enterprise and the works council has extended to them the same rights as the council members insofar as shop stewards act as agents of the council.

They meet in groups — during working hours — with council members. They receive information about plant problems and in turn transmit any grievances they cannot settle to the councillors. Often shop stewards are delegated along with council members to joint management-labor committees in the plant.

In grievance handling the shop steward is frequently the first man whom the aggrieved employee approaches, usually after an unsuccessful attempt to solve his problem in direct contact with the foreman. In some plants works councillors, when approached by employees before the grievance has come to the shop steward, refer the case to him. (There are, however, plants in which the council members in that situation refer the grievance to a department head.) The council intervenes only when the shop steward regards the problem as too difficult to be handled by him.

Although the works constitution law describes grievance handling as one of the functions of the works council, no details are given on the way grievances are to be processed. Contractual arrangements rarely deal with procedures. As a result, there is usually no regular sequence of steps in grievance handling as there is under most American agreements. In one plant agreement, however, employees are required to address themselves first to their department head and to approach the works council (or shop steward) only after this first attempt has failed. There is also a conspicuous scarcity of agreements specifying that no employee will be at a disadvantage for having presented a grievance to a shop steward or works councillor. Only one plant agreement containing such a provision has come to the author's attention. The sequence most frequently observed in German plants is about as follows: shop steward where there is one, works council, union secretary, labor director (in coal and steel plants under codetermination). On the management side the foreman is often bypassed in favor of the next higher managerial echelon; then follows the "master" or office chief, the department head, personnel chief, and director. It is of course a moot question whether the labor director should be listed on the managerial side where he properly belongs (but where some employees and some unions often refuse to place him).

Union Shop Committees

In many plants the union is represented by its own organs, also called *Vertrauensmann,* as is the shop steward. Frequently the shop stewards and union representatives are the same people.

Normally, the lowest administrative level of a German trade union is the local organization. There is a local membership meeting, comprising all members of a particular union residing in a given city or area, at which a local committee is elected; the local committee then elects a local chairman. As a rule, this organization includes workers from several plants, although it may happen if there is only one plant or major plant, all or most of the members in one local organization will have the same employer. In that case, the local organization will be the same as the plant organization. In the majority of cases, however, the local organization consists of workers from two or several enterprises. Then the union often attempts to establish a shop committee, but not always successfully.

The way the members of the shop committee are selected varies from union to union. They may be elected by the union members in the plant in direct and secret ballot, as the rules of the metalworkers' union so state, or appointed by those executive committee members of the local union organization who happen to work in a given plant. In practice there are great variations in carrying out the rules. In some plants there is one committeeman for every 30 workers, in others one for 70 to 80 workers. However selected, committee members are to perform some of the council functions. Thus, the instructions (*Richtlinien*) for the metalworkers' union list among the tasks of committee members the following:

> Giving advice to union members in the plant and information about the constitution of the metalworkers' union, collective agreements, wage and salary agreements, shop agreements and shop regulations. Participation in all measures to prevent accidents, to maintain safety in the plant and to protect the health of the employees.

Advising newly entering employees. Making them familiar with the situation in the plant. They are to be assisted in overcoming their initial difficulties and to be recruited for our union.

These activities, according to the statutes, are to be carried on in "close liaison with those members of the works council who are union members. The latter are ex officio members of the shop committee. Works council members and members of the shop committee have to take into account their special tasks and carry them out. Mutual recognition and support are necessary. The shop assembly must be prepared jointly. It is necessary that the will of the unions be expressed in the assembly."

The shop committee member is usually quite close to the rank and file. In a study of a group of enterprises belonging to the Mannesmann Company, one quarter of those interviewed named the members of the shop committee as "the best representatives of their interests," and one third named the works council.[20] In discussions accompanying the survey, the shop committeeman "appeared in general as the first and most immediate level of interest representation for the employees with regard to the different institutions of the enterprise."

In practice, the relationship between council and shop committeemen is not always harmonious. Works councils are known to have felt—just as does management in many cases—that the shop committee member as representative of the union is an outsider who interferes with the settlement of industrial relations problems "within the family." The infrequency of union participation in council meetings expresses this feeling. Friction arises also at the time of council elections when shop committeemen attempt to influence nominations and election results: the more the council feels and behaves as a junior partner of management, the more likely it is that friction will occur between the council and the shop committee members.[21] However, where the union organization is very powerful and active, "shop committee and members of the plant representation form a unity between which the separation of functions is no more than a legal fiction."[22]

Law and Practice

The spirit which the works constitution law was to embody is set out in Article 49 of the law:

1) Within the framework of the applicable collective agreements, employer and works council collaborate in good faith, working together with the trade union and employers' associations represented in the enterprise, for the good of

the enterprise and of its employees and under consideration of the common welfare.

2) Employer and works council must not do anything which might endanger the work and the peace of the enterprise. In particular, employer and works council must not carry out any measures of labor struggle against each other. This does not affect the labor struggle of parties entitled to conclude collective agreements.

3) Employer and works council are to meet once a month for joint conference. They must negotiate about questions in dispute with the serious will to reach agreement and must make proposals to each other in order to settle disagreements.

4) Mediators and authorities may be called in only after failure to reach agreement within the enterprise.[23]

As is common to institutional arrangements in the field of industrial relations, however, considerable differences exist between legislation and practice.

As was just pointed out, the works council — though it continues to "represent" the employees in some of the meanings of the term — has tended in many cases to become an associate of management. The relationship between council and employer is rarely one of conflict, even though the council has important bargaining functions (except when Communists control it). At first glance, this is rather astonishing. The council represents an interest group which, by tradition as well as by current experience, is often at odds with management. Indeed, the council of the Weimar period was frequently, at least until the latter part of the twenties, a leader in the disputes between "labor and capital." It is true that the law imposes on both sides the duty to abstain from "measures of labor struggles" against each other. When the shop committee of the union becomes involved in a strike, the works council members of the committee regularly withdraw from the committee for the duration of the conflict. But a similar clause existed in the works council legislation of the twenties and did not appreciably affect the council's involvement. The reason for the absence of clashes between council and management (indeed often the partial absorption of the councils into management) lies much deeper than the letter of the law.

One of the fundamental facts of industrial relations in Germany is the great concern of the worker for steady employment. Even though a state of full employment (and even extreme labor shortage) has prevailed for the last decade, there is still the memory of the terrible years of the great depression and the first postwar years. Anything that would seem to threaten the stability of employment, often anything that can be made to appear as such a threat, is regarded as a mortal danger by the West German worker. Industrial warfare has been branded as as much of a danger as the demand for "excessively" high wages. Therefore, cooperation between the works council and management meets overwhelming approval among the workers. Only in exceptional circumstances — particularly over issues seemingly related to social or legal status as in the Schleswig-Holstein metalworkers' strike over the waiting period in sickness insurance — has the German worker until recently shown combative spirit. Large strike benefits also played a substantial role in some of the strikes. (The particular issue in the metalworkers' strike was that of reducing the waiting period of the workers to that of the white-collar employees.) It is only in the last few years that aggressive wage policies have found support.

Stability of employment, moreover, means for most German workers not only absence or low level of unemployment, but also the permanency of their particular jobs. The lack of mobility of the West German worker, his attachment to a particular enterprise, his involvement in its life are conspicuous traits that have been pointed out by many observers. Having tied his own fate to that of the company, he expects from his council representatives equal attachment to it. The latter's cooperation with "the enterprise" is, therefore, but a reflection of the worker's own attitude.

The long term of office which is so frequent among works councillors adds to their quasi-managerial status. They acquire more and more understanding for the viewpoint of the enterprise; their special status and the very length of their term of office sets them apart from their colleagues. On the whole, this is accepted by the workers. Yet, there are occasional outbursts of dissatisfaction such as the election of a clear Communist majority in the council of the Westfalenhütte Dortmund in 1955. The welfare institutions of this company were widely regarded as excellent, and it is probable that the protest vote was directed more against the works council than against the firm. The almost permanent leaders of the council engaged in close cooperation with the managing board and the labor director, and in this particular case, it led to resentment. The Communist majority was overthrown in the subsequent elections of 1957. No fully satisfactory explanation has ever been offered for either of these events.

Of the tasks of the works councils, two would appear from the American point of view to come under the heading of union functions: the council's role in collective bargaining and in grievance handling. Some aspects of these functions and of the consequent relationship between councils and unions will be discussed in a later chapter. But some of the main points must be presented at this stage.

The Council and Collective Bargaining

Collective bargaining proceeds in Germany at two levels. The individual unions conclude master (*Mantel*) agreements with employers' associations. These agreements are most frequently regional in scope, sometimes national, rarely local. The terms set in these agreements are usually not the actual terms of employment, particularly not in the area of wages. They are minima, corresponding to the rates set in the Fair Labor Standards Act in the United States. Actual rates — and often other terms of employment — are normally above the contract rates. The contract sets a floor upon which the effective wage structure is erected. The distance between the contract rate and the effective rate — particularly when premiums and bonuses are taken into account — is often considerable. Changes in contract rates have, therefore, often little or no immediate bearing upon the effective compensation of many employees. Only indirectly and sometimes with considerable lag do changes of the contract affect the actual living standards of the majority of the workers covered by the contract.[24]

How are the effective rates determined? In addition to the master agreements between union and employers' association, there are two main types of labor contracts: shop regulations and shop agreements negotiated by the works council and a single company or even a plant of a company, and individual agreements concluded by a worker and management, with or without the assistance of the council. Of these, the shop regulations and shop agreements are supplementary to the master agreement; they adapt the master agreement to the local conditions or add items not contained in this agreement. The shop regulations deal primarily with work conditions; the shop agreement with rates. These documents may substitute a higher wage structure for the minimum terms of the union-sponsored agreement, add supplements and bonuses and, generally, improve upon the master agreement if the latter allows this. In addition, the individual agreement between worker and management may set his particular wage rate considerably above the level of the master contract, and somewhat less substantially above the rate provided for in the shop contract. Effective rates thus differ as a rule from those of the collective agreement, and frequently from the rates set in the shop agreement. Estimates of the distance separating effective and contract rates have been made among others by the metalworkers' union in the spring of 1955. The results indicated that the average difference for the male workers on hourly pay was 17 per cent, for female workers 13.5 per cent; the combined average difference was 16.4 per cent. There were, however, great variations among the different industries in which the union is represented. Thus while the average difference for male workers on hourly pay in the shipbuilding industry was 6.2 per cent, it rose to an average of 27.7 per cent in iron production. The unions, particularly the metalworkers' union, are greatly concerned about this fact since it, in effect, transfers the task of effective wage bargaining wholly or partly to the works councils. Fritz Salm, executive board member of the German Metalworkers' Union, says: "Work conditions and contractual wages in a regional agreement are as a rule oriented toward the economically weaker establishments. The distance between contractual conditions and the facts in the plants is, therefore, often rather big. The existing contracts do not offer sufficient security for the earnings and are often an unsatisfactory way to determine wages in the plant." Mr. Salm then advocates what he calls *betriebsnahe* agreements, that is, collective agreements coming close to the conditions existing in the plants.[25]

Sometimes negotiated wage increases have been partly or totally offset by a curtailment of the wage increments provided for in shop agreements or of voluntary fringe benefits. In order to prevent this "devaluation" of collective bargaining and to make union action meaningful for the rank and file, the unions have been demanding the adoption of so-called "effectiveness clauses." These clauses provide that any wage increases agreed upon in the contract would apply not only to contract but also to the effective rates. This is part of a union drive to "bring collective bargaining closer to the plant." [26]

Piece rates are bargained by the individual worker and the management. The collective agreement and the works regulations provide, however, some guiding principles. For instance, a guaranteed minimum established in the collective agreement must be retained; the average wage provided for in the agreement must be attainable for the average worker; only the types of rates and methods of measurement provided for in the agreement can be used.

Often the collective agreement also sets down the methods by which the rate negotiations are to be carried on, and the procedure to be employed in the case of disagreement on the rate to be set.

In some cases, it is the council which works out the contracts for the rates and conditions that really and immediately affect the worker, and in many other cases, the council intervenes with management in the negotiations of the individual worker on his particular rate.

In these matters the council actually bargains in place of the union. A bargaining function supplementary to that of the unions is entrusted to the council in a number of matters that are usually settled by shop agreement — unless law or collective agreement has taken pre-emptive decisions on these issues. They concern the beginning and end of the working day, "coffee breaks," time and place for the payment of wages, vacation schedules, vocational training, administration of social services limited to the enterprise, discipline, job and piece rates, setting up of principles of remuneration, and the introduction of new remuneration systems.

On all these matters agreement must be reached between the council and management. In the absence of agreement, a conciliation committee is empowered to make a binding decision.

Few conflicts have become publicly known. The council's reasonableness has been stressed. Management is just as interested in friendly relations with the council. By strengthening the council's position, management often hopes to weaken the union, and this not always without justification. Cases in which councils have been used against the union are well known, and others in which councils have kept the unions from obtaining information about individual enterprises are not infrequent. "During the Bavarian metal strike in the summer of 1954, there were several instances in which the works councils appealed to the workers to stay on the job or concluded plant-wide wage agreements, generally accepting the employers' unilateral offer of wage increases which were lower than those demanded by the unions — in clear defiance of the strike command."[27] No less important, perhaps, is the fact that wage increases granted by way of individual arrangement with a worker or by plant agreement with the works council are not of the same legal nature as wage agreements obtained by a union. The terms of a collective agreement concluded by a union are automatically part of each individual labor contract of union members and cannot be revised downwards or abandoned by individual agreement; wage increases, beyond the contract, granted by way of a shop agreement concluded with the council, do not have this protection. The company is free to withdraw such increases when conditions make this advisable. This gives labor costs an elasticity which management usually finds greatly to its advantage. It is, therefore, preferable from the business point of view to grant intended wage concessions to the council rather than to the union. (It should be remembered that the council cannot legally call strikes and does not in fact do so.) Finally, reasonableness toward the council makes for greater emphasis on settlements within the enterprise and consequently for greater loyalty toward it.

Again and again in interviews with German unionists and management people, it was said: "There are no conflicts between the councils and management." This is probably an exaggeration, but it does indicate, at least, a widespread impression. An extreme example of council-management collaboration against the union was the Bizerba case of 1956. The council chairman and the plant management collaborated in bodily removing the union representatives from a plant assembly. What added some spice to the incident was that the council chairman was a union member. Thus the fact that in the metal industry some 82 per cent of all council members elected in 1961 belong to the metalworkers' union is not yet a guarantee of intimate understanding between union and councillors. This membership incidentally is rather unevenly distributed between the members of the councils in the workers' groups (91.1 per cent) and white-collar employees (47 per cent). Of the council chairmen, 93.5 per cent were union members.[28] Moreover, the generally confirmed non-use of the conciliation procedures between council and management, provided for in the law, lends considerable support to the thesis of no conflicts.

Grievance Handling

The German worker has several choices in the handling of his complaints. He may talk them over with his superiors; he may approach the "man of confidence" or works councillor; or he may address himself to the union, perhaps by way of its shop committee or through the local union administration; or he may turn to the labor court. In one plant, the "Hüttenwerk Oberhausen A.G." (HOAG), a kind of plant court for disciplinary matters, has been established. The labor director — an old trade unionist, Karl Strohmenger — acts as chairman. There are three representatives each of the management and of the works council. A member of the personnel management department acts as public prosecutor and the chairman of the works council as attorney for the defendant. HOAG claims remarkable success with this system in reducing the number of accidents, absenteeism, and so forth.

The law states that it is one of "the general duties of the works council" to see "that effect is given to Acts, ordinances, collective agreements and shop agreements in favor of the employees"; and further to hear "any employee's grievances and, if these seem well-founded, to seek to remedy them by negotiations with the employer.[29] Moreover, as we have seen, the council has a right of codecision on a large number of matters out of which grievances may arise, such as discipline, the fixing of job and piece rates, hiring, regrading, transfers, and dismissals. In other words, the handling of grievances, arising out of different interpretations of agreements — even those concluded by the union — the protection of employees against dismissals, and the regrading of jobs are functions of the council. Indeed, a large part of council activities consists of grievance handling, sometimes with the assistance of the shop stewards, who then are acting as agents of the council members.

Recognizing the importance of grievance handling, some German unions have tried to shift the procedure and channel the complaints through themselves. In many cases this — if successful — merely means that the union shop committeeman passes the grievance on to a works council member who is a union member. The latter then handles the grievance as if it had come directly to him, but the union may expect to get the credit for whatever results are obtained. However, there are cases in which only the union can act in behalf of an employee with a grievance. If, for instance, the council has given its approval to a management measure which an employee believes affects him unfairly, the council itself cannot act for the employee, but the union can. Moreover, the union may intervene as a second step if the works council has failed to settle the grievance to the satisfaction of the worker. The union agency involved is usually the *Geschäftsstelle,* an intermediary union organization between the local organization and the top echelons of the union. (For white-collar workers the corresponding union office is the *Bezirk.*) This appeal may be made by the worker directly or through the union shop committee. The matter may then be handled by the director of the *Geschäftsstelle,* an appointed union official, or by someone on his staff — a legal specialist, an expert on collective agreements, or an expert on council matters. In a matter of great significance, the *Geschäftsstelle* may draw upon experts from the national office of the union.

In a number of cases — particularly alleged violation of labor laws, but also of collective agreements, work regulations, or individual work contracts — a further remedy may consist in an appeal to a special court existing under German legislation, the labor court.[30] In this court the union is represented by lay judges just as are the employers' associations. The labor court may be appealed to by the works council under certain circumstances on issues relating to the hiring of employees. In the case of a new employee, this may be done if the council has refused to give approval to a new appointee and management has gone ahead and made the appointment. However, in order to be able to appeal to the labor court, the council must base its objection on reasons specifically mentioned in the law: that the engagement would violate a law or contract, that favoritism was the reason for the appointment, that there is discrimination for racial or religious reasons or union activities, or that the applicant "would cause trouble in the undertaking by anti-social or unlawful conduct." [31]

However, the record would seem to indicate that referrals to the labor court by the works councils are rare indeed.

It is difficult, if not impossible, to ascertain which of the various channels for grievance handling is used most frequently by the employees, primarily because the situation varies from plant to plant (and within the same plant) but also because grievance handling in practice is often mixed up with the "social matters" under the administration of the works council.[32]

Welfare Institutions

The administration of welfare institutions established by the plant is indeed one of the main tasks of the works council and at the same time one of the mainstays of its and the plant's paternalistic power over the employees. Contrary to the practice that has arisen in the United States under the Wagner Act, the German employer may make unilateral concessions to the employees or some of them without going through the union. Indeed, he is expected to do so, and the volume and quality of the welfare activities of the plant increase its attractiveness as a workplace.

The range of such institutions is considerable. Emergency funds to assist employees by loans or grants, vacation homes, housing, health centers, and canteens are common.[33] Legally these are institutions of the enterprise and under its control. However, the council, particularly its executive committee and the chairman and vice-chairman, has a good deal of influence on the administration of welfare institutions. This ties it to management, gives it power to build a machine, and contributes to the atmosphere of paternalism in so many German plants. Moreover, contact between the council and the workers is greatly intensified by the welfare activities. So, too, is the cooperation between council and management, with important consequences in the relationship between works council and unions.

Managerial Functions

Managerial functions in the narrow sense of the word occur in three forms: by way of the economic committee, the representation on the supervisory board, and the labor director. It can of course be claimed that many of the council's activities are managerial; the council's right to participate in the discussion of matters of discipline or the scheduling of working hours may be regarded as giving it managerial status. However, we shall use this term in a restrictive meaning; it will refer only to participation in decision-making on the economic, financial, and technical aspects of the firm.

The activity of the economic committee comes under this heading. This is a new venture, one of the ways in which the legislation after World War II departed from the works council legislation of the Weimar Republic. The organization of the committee has been discussed. In practice it has been disappointing. Most employees, it is claimed, are not even aware of the existence of the economic committee, and references in the literature to its function are exceedingly rare. Plant journals do contain reports on its activities, but it is doubtful whether these reports are read by many employees. In conversations, at least, the economic committee is rarely mentioned. One expert whom we interviewed went so far as to claim that the committee is often regarded as a nuisance by its own members and by the directors of the company. Since it has no powers of decision, its meetings are often regarded as wasted time. Normally its members do not learn much that is new to them, and the directors seem to carry on the meetings in a perfunctory fashion.

Workers' representation on the supervisory board differs according to whether the enterprise comes under the special codetermination law or not. The limited representation provided for by the works constitution law — one third of the membership — was bitterly opposed by the unions who wanted to extend to all plants the greater representation granted labor in coal and steel. In a considerable number of enterprises, the law is being disregarded by management without union reaction.[34]

There is no need here to add to the voluminous literature on the functioning of the codetermination law.[35] In general, it may perhaps be said that the presence of labor members on the supervisory boards so far has had neither the catastrophic consequences that many observers expected, nor the profoundly beneficial effects that others hoped for. It is perhaps not unfair to say that the real test of the system may come only with a severe depression.

In any case, there has been an improvement in the flow of information reaching the workers' representatives. This has probably strengthened their hand in dealings with management but also tied them more closely to the plant and thus sharpened the problem of their relationship to the union.

The same set of circumstances has also brought to the fore the problem of secrecy.[36] Like most businessmen on the European continent, those in Germany keep secret business information far beyond what American businessmen would find necessary to withhold. The law on the works constitution makes the disclosure of business secrets a severely punishable offence. As a result of the law and of the general attitude of business and perhaps of the public, the council members on the supervisory boards do not pass their knowledge acquired at the board meetings on to their colleagues on the council and even less to their union.[37] This tends sometimes to make council leaders appear as junior partners in management and adds to the difficulties in the works councils' relations to the unions.

Representation and Labor Force Structure

So far we have been speaking of the relationship between the works council and the workers as if the latter were a homogeneous group. Only when referring to the white-collar employees did a distinction emerge between different work groups. To limit oneself to this differentiation, however, would be a crass oversimplification. For, in fact, the German labor force seems to be highly differentiated in many ways, including its attitude toward the plant, the union, and the works councils. Some brief remarks about this subject are thus necessary at this stage; further developments will be presented in a later chapter.

The author is relying primarily on personal observations and on a major investigation of some West German steel plants.[38] Some of the significant distinctions that have to be made are obviously specifically German or at least limited to countries that shared Germany's political and social development to a considerable extent and for some time. Other differentiations may be of more general validity.[39]

One of the most obvious distinctions is that between the workers who acquired trade union training prior to 1933 and those who joined the movement only after 1945. The pre-Hitler unionists are the predominant group in the works councils; they also regard the council ordinarily as their spokesman and are its main support in the plant.

Cleavages within the labor force arise also in the relationship between the very substantial refugee group in the plants and the others. In some cases this distinction may coincide with the one just mentioned, but this is not always the case. Many refugee workers come from the industrial areas of East Germany and have not only union, but also council, experiences similar to those of their West German colleagues. The refugees from outside the area of the Weimar Republic, primarily many of the so-called *Volksdeutsche* — members of the German-speaking minority groups in Eastern Europe — have a significantly different background. Differentiation and sometimes friction among these groups are to be expected.

Technological changes have introduced further elements of internal differentiation. The hierarchy of status in the work force and often the wage structure — frequently still inherited from semi-artisan days — no longer corresponds to the present operational structure of the labor force in German industry. The tension resulting from this is rendered particularly intense by the absence of a gradual modernization process in some parts of German industry which might have facilitated step-by-step adjustments. The reconstruction of German industry after its wartime devastation often took place at the level of the most advanced technology. As a result the separation between the uniformity of work requirements and the demand for authority by older men with high skills that are no longer needed led to considerable friction.

This is also reflected in changes in the way some of the workers themselves judge the criteria used in job evaluation. These problems would of course have occurred in any case, partly because rising standards of popular education reduced the scarcity of some skill characteristics. But the Nazi dictatorship delayed the necessary adjustments. The facility with which new technological processes could be introduced in the rebuilding of German industry added to the difficulties. Moreover, as many observers point out, the younger generation among the German workers has a different attitude toward work than its older colleagues — with less emphasis on loyalty toward the firm and on the virtues of tradition. Identification with the plant is far less among the younger members of the work force, and the "boss" plays less and less the role of a father or grandfather. Work is primarily a means to an end and is of "less comprehensive significance" than it was for the older generation.[40]

As a result the works council is confronted at times with the almost impossible task of representing a far from homogeneous work force. This, of course, is not unique. It is a problem that every major industrial union faces to some extent. For the council, however, it is complicated by the relative intimacy of common life in the plant which excludes certain forms of compromise. In any case, it is important to realize that the relations between the council and those whom it is supposed to represent are not free of pitfalls and that some of these difficulties are reflected in turn in the relations among the council, the unions, and other workers' organizations.

CHAPTER IV

Yugoslavia

The experiment of making workers' councils managerial organs in Yugoslavia is very recent. The practical experience may be said to have started after 1950 as part of the adoption of a system of economic decentralization. This followed upon a period of centralized administrative planning which had prevailed during the first postwar years up to 1950. The process of decentralization went through different stages and ups and downs. Between 1951 and 1954 some forms of decentralization were attempted which did not aim at giving workers' councils a real voice in plant management. Beginning in 1954 the councils acquired increased significance as managerial tools. Some further changes introduced since then may, in spite of some retreats, be interpreted as a gradual advance along the lines of increased autonomy for the firms. The stature of the councils tended to grow with the self-government of the enterprise. An experimental approach and a readiness — astonishing in an atmosphere as charged ideologically as that of Yugoslavia — to learn from short-run experiences and to stress empirical evidence were characteristic of this stage. However, the year 1962 brought a sharp reversal, and it is too early to judge what the more lasting features of the experiment will be. For a better understanding of the evolution, it is necessary to review the political circumstances and to outline the economic, social, and historical framework within which this process took place.

The Circumstances

The dominant facts are the poverty and the diversity of the country. It is essentially divided into two parts: the potentially fertile Pannonian plain, and the mountain areas of the southwest which contain unexplored mineral resources. Industrial activity of any significance was limited until very recently to the northwest of the country, the areas around Zagreb and Ljubljana, in Croatia and Slovenia respectively. Compared with them, much of the remainder of the country was in 1945 underdeveloped and almost completely free of modern industry. More than 70 per cent of the population lived on agriculture with extremely small agricultural enterprises predominating. Three quarters of the farms were less than 10 hectares (24.7 acres) in size. Since large-landed property was of little significance, land reform could do little to relieve the land hunger of the peasants. The contrast between the industrially more advanced areas and the rest of the country was reflected in substantial differences in the standards of living. Per capita income — though low everywhere — was almost four times as high in Slovenia (Ljubljana) as in Montenegro, while the average for Croatia was slightly more than half that of Slovenia. At the other extreme, Bosnia-Herzegovina and Macedonia were close to Montenegro. These differences, reinforced by historic cleavages and religious divisions, separated the country — formed as recently as 1918 — into rival regions whose battles, sometimes carried on violently, made democratic government exceedingly difficult, if not impossible. There are differences of religion: the Croats are Roman Catholics; the Serbs, Greek Orthodox; part of the population of Bosnia is Mohammedan. History added other divisions. For a thousand years the boundary between the eastern and the western Roman Empire ran along the Drina and Save rivers which separated Croats and Serbs. In 1918 the country was pieced together: Croatia, Slovenia, and Bosnia-Herzegovina came from the Austro-Hungarian Empire; Montenegro had been an independent state, as had been Serbia, after their liberation from Ottoman rule. Serbia felt that it had played a decisive part in freeing the Croats and Slovenians from Hapsburg domination and that it was, therefore, the natural leader of the new country to which it gave its dynasty. Croatia and Slovenia, on the other hand, regarded themselves as culturally and economically far ahead of the rest of the country and entitled to leadership or at least equality of status. These rivalries led to the assassination of a Croat peasant leader in open Parliament. This was followed by the establishment of a royal dictatorship in 1929 which most of the country regarded as a victory of Serb reactionaries. Later the King was assassinated.

Industrial development in most of Yugoslavia was limited until 1945 predominantly to extractive industries, most of which were in foreign hands. Foreign capital owned nine tenths of the mines, almost four fifths of the metal industry, and so forth. Almost all the minerals were exported; far more than half the lead, bauxite, antimony, and copper produced left the country before being processed. Only in Slovenia and Croatia did a native industry exist.

The internal divisions continued throughout World War II. After the occupation of the country by German forces, two underground movements arose, one led by General Michailovic, the other by the Communists under their leader Tito. The two waged relentless war against each other which ended in the elimination of Michailovic and the establishment of a Communist regime recognized by the Allies. The fact that this regime succeeded in maintaining itself on native soil throughout most of the war and in liberating a large part of its territory by its own forces gave it a prestige quite distinctive from the other Eastern European Communist regimes whose leaders came to power in the van of the victorious Russian armies. This explains, to a large extent, the success of the Tito group in its struggle for independence from Moscow. No less significant was the fact that at the end of hostilities Tito's troops controlled the largest part of Yugoslav industry as many businessmen had fled in fear of being accused of collaboration with the enemy.

Nationalization. Under the circumstances, nationalization on a large scale and the introduction of the Russian economic methods on Yugoslav soil were perhaps inevitable. In any case, the economic system set up after the end of hostilities generally followed the Russian example. In agriculture, this meant a land reform during which the properties of the *Volksdeutsche* (Yugoslav citizens of German extraction and German language), of "collaborators" and supporters of Michailovic, and of large landowners of Austrian or Hungarian nationality, as well as all properties exceeding 35 hectares, were confiscated and distributed among small landholders. Shortly afterwards, *Kolkhozes*—agricultural cooperatives Soviet style—were established, and the peasants were put under heavy pressure to join them. Those who refused did not receive tractors or fertilizer, paid a punitively higher income tax (20 per cent compared with 3 per cent for members of the *Kolkhozes*), and were forbidden to use hired labor. Deliveries in kind at low prices were imposed upon all peasants, running at an average of 82 per cent of the harvest, while detailed planning measures determined the use of the land.[1] The results were disappointing; although the number of *Kolkhozes* grew rapidly, their rate of output fell behind that of small private peasant enterprises. The labor force of the *Kolkhozes* was excessive, the government provided insufficient investment funds, and arbitrariness in setting delivery quotas added to peasant resentment. At the same time, industrialization was to be driven forward by large-scale investments; no less than 27 per cent of the national income was to be devoted to investment purposes, with transportation, electricity, mining, the metal industry, and manufacturing obtaining the lion's share of capital funds. Agriculture was neglected. A five-year plan was adopted with the objective of increasing industrial production fivefold. Russian support was to consist of an exchange of Yugoslav agricultural goods and industrial raw materials for Soviet capital goods. When the plan began in 1947, 82 per cent of all industry was nationalized; so were all banking, wholesale trade, and the important transport services.

Administrative planning. The plan set up production goals in the greatest detail, not only for the economy as a whole or for entire branches of industry, but for each plant separately, almost entirely eliminating nongovernmental initiative. This period is called the era of administrative socialism, because it was carried out as if running the economy and establishing socialism were exclusively matters of administrative procedure. Some 217 federal and republican (provincial) ministers gave orders to directorates, and they in turn to factory managers. The principle of complete unity of state administration and business management was introduced, the latter being totally subservient to the former. The number of government officials was enormously increased in comparison with prewar times. Even in industry, the ratio of administrative staff to workers increased from a prewar 9 to a postwar 15, and in commercial enterprises from 12 to 48 per hundred workers.[2] New enterprises were set up by special decrees which determined their trade name, organization, the amount of working capital, and the manner of management.[3] Ministries set production goals for all nationalized enterprises individually, allocated raw materials and fuel, gave credits for working capital, and carried out the distribution of finished goods. "It is characteristic that within this period very large enterprises were established whose organization encompassed the whole of the country, as for instance the State Bus Transport Enterprise (DASP), the State Goods and Textiles Trading Enterprise, the State Trading Enterprise 'Narodni Magazin' and some others." A director, appointed by the state and responsible to it, was the top manager of each firm. All other agencies of the enterprise were either subordinated to him or had only consultative status. In mid-1947 a reorganization of the state economic administration transferred some economic functions to so-called general and principal boards or directorates, intermediate between ministries and enterprises. Yet in the atmosphere of detailed centralized planning and administration, this feeble attempt at decentralization did not produce any significant results. The absence of an effective market for capital goods, administrative distribution of the majority of consumer goods, the existence of a black market for agricultural goods, the status of enterprises as mere extensions of the general plan administration — all these were the characteristics of this first period in the postwar reconstruction of Yugoslavia along Communist lines.[4] The "director's fund," whose distribution was within the province of the director alone, was the main instrument of plant autonomy. Only a sector of peasant production, in which, however, compulsory delivery and taxation were planned elements, was left free.

In an attempt to justify this system as an indispensable stage in the economic development of the country,[5] Yugoslav sources often quote the evolution of the industrial production index between 1946 and 1950. With 1939 as a base, these indices are presented in Table 1.

TABLE 1. Industrial production index between 1946 and 1950 in Yugoslavia

Industrial branch	1939	1946	1947	1948	1949	1950
All industry	100	79	121	150	167	172
Means of production	100	121	241	352	462	510
Raw material production	100	76	113	138	154	160
Consumer goods production	100	84	130	165	171	165

Source: Information Service Yugoslavia, "The Development of Workers' Self-Government; Management of Enterprises before the Introduction of Workers' Self-Government" (mimeographed).

These figures, however, vastly overstate the degree of recovery and expansion: first, because the figures include incomplete and partially complete investment processes, some of which were destined never to be completed; second, because of the well-known tendency of industrial production indices in countries in the early stages of industrialization to overstate the weight of new developments and thus exaggerate the rate of industrial growth; third, because the bulk of the country's output originates with agricultural enterprises, and there the results were disappointing. For the average of the years 1948–57, total yields in the main farming crops were still below the prewar average of 1930–39. Thus, wheat average yields of 1948–57 were 2,190,000 tons compared to 2,430,000 for the prewar period indicated; for corn (*mais*) 3,520,000 tons compared to 4,300,000; for sugar beets it rose from 616,000 tons to 1,320,000 tons and for potatoes from 1,650,000 tons to 1,920,000 tons. But at least in the case of sugar beets, this increase was obtained at the cost of a drop in the yield per hectare.[6] Finally, in considering the growth of industrial production, one must take into account the large proportion of resources devoted to investment in industry. Indeed, there are few Yugoslav economists who will not admit, privately, but often also publicly, that the system of "administrative socialism" resulted in failure.[7] Yet, whether this alone would have produced a change of "the system" is uncertain. In any case, it was the break with the Soviet Union which set off an evolution that led to a radical overhaul.

In 1948, Yugoslavia was read out of the international Communist movement, and this was followed by an economic blockade: the Eastern markets, which until then had absorbed more than half the exports (53 per cent in 1947) and provided more than half the imports (56 per cent in 1947) of the country, disappeared; military expenditures grew rapidly to cope with the new threat from the East. From slightly more than 10 per cent of the national income, defense expenditures rose to about a quarter in 1952. Only American and other Western assistance helped Yugoslavia to weather the storm. By an unfortunate coincidence, three successive droughts (1947, 1950, and 1952) greatly added to the troubles besetting the country.

The changeover. There was no immediate change in the fundamentals of the economic policy pursued. Indeed, the first reaction of the regime to the conflict with Stalin was to tighten controls. Circumstances created considerable changes in the actual operations. The five-year plan established in 1947 continued in operation, but the discrepancies between plan objectives and achievements grew. Even after the plan was extended to cover another year (to the end of 1952), the original objectives were far from being fulfilled. Civilian investments, which were to rise year by year and to attain the yearly level of 70 billion *dinars* in 1951, actually dropped from 1949 on and amounted to 44 billion in 1951. As Marshal Tito himself stated, "current production — 1952 — uses only about 30 per cent of capacity and runs at about 70 per cent of the five-year plan figures."[8] There is little doubt that even had the break with the Soviet Union not occurred, economic growth would have been unsatisfactory, and the plan would not have been fulfilled. The plan objectives were clearly overambitious as Table 2 would indicate.

The pressure on private consumption, which had to be satisfied with the difference between national income and net investment and had to share it with the government and the military, was bound to be tremendous, and consumption standards must have dropped considerably. In addition, there were many errors in the execution of the plan, inevitably following the highly centralized administration of the industrial system. Forced collectivization — even though Russia described it as too slow — further delayed recovery.

TABLE 2. National income and investment between 1938 and 1948 in Yugoslavia (in millions of dollars)

Income and investment	1938	1947	1948
National income	1040	880	960
Net investment	52	132	144
Difference	988	748	816

Source: United Nations, *Economic Survey of Europe* (New York, 1949), p. 47.

Yet two years passed between the break with the Soviet Union and the working out of a new economic system — a delay which may perhaps be related to a refusal on the part of the Yugoslav Communists to regard the cleavage as permanent. Out of this emerged the workers' councils. They were destined to play a key role in the new doctrine of Yugoslav communism and beyond the boundaries of the country. The root of this institution — but not its new function — may be traced back to legislation enacted in 1945.

A law on workers' commissions then created workers' representatives who were to be in "permanent contact with state organizations, the management of the enterprise and the union branch." [9] Another law gave union branches in the plant the right "to recommend to the director measures relating to productivity, improvement of conditions of work, workers' living conditions and questions relating to the problem of personnel." These "rights" were quite insignificant and ill-defined. In their later effort to describe Stalinist communism as the result of a "bureaucratic degeneration" of the pure idea, the Yugoslav Communists looked for new administrative organizations that could form the basis of a different, although still Communistic, economic system. Following is a semi-official version of this search:

The conviction that the state ownership of the means of production and the management of national economy by the state constituted only the inferior initial phase of the development of Socialist relations, which was to last only as long as it was indispensable, forced its way in an ever greater measure. It was made clear that the state and its apparatus should not be considered the sole infallible builder and main force of the Socialist society, but rather that it could develop further only if supported by conscious activity and immediate participation of producers and citizens in efforts aiming to solve all kinds of economic and social problems. This necessitated that the role of the state in national economy be confined solely to the functions which were still indispensable at that particular phase of development and that the decisive role of the producer whose democratic rights to participate in the management would be guaranteed by law and who would be interested materially and directly in as successful operation of enterprises as possible, be brought to the foreground.

Referring to the workers' commissions which were languishing in various plants and completely lacking in most, the vice-president of the Yugoslav government and leading theoretician of the party, Edvard Kardelj, in a speech on May 28, 1949, said: "This undeveloped spontaneous form should be further developed and transformed into a permanent form of the direct cooperation of workers in the management of our enterprises." Such a development, he said, would be a step forward in the growth of Socialist democracy and in line with the teachings of Marx and Engels. A first tentative measure was taken by the end of 1949 when workers' councils as consultative bodies were set up in some of the largest enterprises. They were elected by all employees in secret ballot. The number of plants with councils in spite of their severely limited functions then grew consistently, until on June 26, 1950, the Federal Parliament enacted the "Fundamental Law on the Management of State Economic Enterprises and Higher Economic Associations, by Working Collectives." There have been many changes in the operations and details of this law since 1950, some of which will be presented below. For an understanding of the law, it is necessary, however, to discuss first the political organization of the country as it emerged out of the legislation of 1952 on peoples' committees and further legislation in 1953. For soon after the works council law went into operation, close relations between councils and the peoples' committees were established.

The federal system. Yugoslavia has a federal system. The federation consists of six republics — Serbia, Croatia, Slovenia, Bosnia-Herzegovina, Macedonia, Montenegro — and two autonomous regions, Voivodina and Kossovo. The federal government consists of a legislative and an executive. Legislative authority was, until 1953, in the hands of a federal council and a nationality council. A producers' council was then established, while the nationality council was absorbed into the federal council. In effect, this means that the federal council consists of 280 members, designated by relative majority and universal suffrage, in one-member constituencies, plus 70 members elected by the assemblies of the six republics (10 each) and the two autonomous regions — Voivodina, 6; Kossovo, 4. Normally, the two groups sit together as federal council; when questions affecting the equality of the nationalities or the relationship between federation and republics arise, the delegations of the republics and autonomous regions meet separately and must agree with the directly elected delegates before a law can be adopted. The second chamber of the legislative assembly is the producers' council, elected by the various economic organizations according to the contribution of each economic group to the national income. Since national income is measured according to Marxian definitions, services (in particular the professions) and government administration are not represented at all. Only the "producers" of material goods, members of economic organizations, participate in the election. Thus, industry, agriculture, artisans, and commerce are represented. A look at the national income figures indicates that this is a device by which industry (the organized workers, such as the Communist Party) is given controlling influence at the expense of other social groups. In 1956, for example, industry contributed more than 43 per cent of the national income, while the share of agriculture amounted to less than 30 per cent. If construction (4.5 per cent) and transport (6 per cent) are added to industry, the combination has a controlling majority regardless of the way agriculture, forestry, commerce, and arts and crafts vote. In terms of labor force engaged in the different branches of the economy, however, manufacturing, construction, and transport represent only slightly less than 900,000 persons out of a labor force of some eight million. One ninth of the labor force is thus represented by a majority of the membership of the producers' council. Needless to say, this arithmetic is actually of only subsidiary significance. What is decisive is that no political organization opposed to the Communist movement is tolerated.

In most questions, the two chambers have the same authority. However, in foreign affairs, army matters, and education, the federal council alone is competent, while the producers' council wields some authority of its own regarding the economic organizations.

The federal executive is, in effect, a committee of the assemblies. However, the executive committee is separated from the administration; the organs of the latter are called secretariats. There are five of them: foreign affairs, national defense, interior, economy, and treasury. Three of these are headed by civil servants but foreign affairs and defense are under the direction of political leaders who are members of the executive. Each administration is under the general supervision of committees of the executive committee; the latter consists of 30 to 40 members. The purpose of this system is to separate the political from the administrative side of government and to prevent thereby the "bureaucratization" of the government.

President Tito is chief of state and chairman of the executive committee where he has veto power; but whenever he uses the veto, the ultimate decision is in the hands of the assemblies.

The various republics are similarly organized, except that they do not have a president (excluding Croatia and Slovenia) or secretariats for foreign affairs or defense. Education and public health are, instead, within the exclusive competency of the republics. In general, however, the division of powers and functions between the federal authorities and those of the various republics is not very clear.

The local committees are one of the main new features of the present constitution. They are of two kinds: municipal authorities in the case of urban settlements, and district councils which combine several rural communities; the latter preserve some autonomous rights in relation to the districts. The basic structure of the assemblies in both municipal and district councils is the same as in the case of the federal assembly: two assemblies, one general, the other representing the "producers." In the event of disagreement between the two, the dispute goes to the next higher authority—district or republic. Administration and municipal executive (the municipal people's committee) are also separated in the same way as in the federal government. Among the functions of the local commune is supervising the economic activities carried on in its territory. Its income consists of a share in the federal taxes levied upon the local business enterprises as well as of a direct tax it imposes upon these enterprises. The very important functions of the commune with regard to local business will emerge more clearly in our discussion of the workings of enterprises in the new Yugoslav system.

In addition, the commune is the main agent of state power in the local area—except for defense, police, statistics, and social security, which are reserved to higher authority. In the other fields the local commune is independent, but the higher authorities may suspend its actions on the ground that they contradict federal or republic laws.

Business in Yugoslavia

The operations of Yugoslav enterprises must be understood against this administrative background since there are several points at which public administration and business management enter into contact.

The bulk of Yugoslav business is state-owned. Only in small handicraft and some forms of domestic trade does private business survive. The official term for state-owned enterprises is "general social property." Employment in privately owned handicrafts is limited to five persons in addition to the owner's family. In farming, private owners are restricted to land not exceeding ten hectares of cultivated land; for larger families more may be allotted. Management of the state-owned enterprises on behalf of the community is in the hands of the "working collectivity" (the employees of the firm). Managerial activity is carried on by way of a workers' council, a managing board, and a director. Where there are fewer than 30 employees, the entire "working collectivity" performs the functions of the council, and only a managing board is elected.[10]

The council is the highest authority of the firm. It consists of 15 to 120 members according to its size, elected for a one-year term. By decree, the term of office was extended to two years in 1955 and 1958. The reason given is that a one-year term is too short to acquire the necessary experience. The election proceeds by universal equal suffrage and secret ballot, usually in the first four months of the year. Active and passive suffrage is held by all employees of the firm who have the right to vote in the general political elections. Elections are supervised by an electoral commission selected by the workers' council holding office when the elections are prepared. Lists of candidates are proposed by the trade union branch in the plant, or by at least one tenth of the workers and white-collar employees. In larger enterprises with several plants a joint council may be elected, with each plant choosing an election unit which then selects the members of the council. A proper representation of production workers as against the other workers and office employees must be established. The legality of the election procedure is supervised by the municipal people's committee and the district court.

The council — acting as a body, not as individuals — makes the fundamental decisions for the firm. It adopts the regulations and the plan of the enterprise, its wage and salary schedule, the budget, balance sheets, and profit and loss statements. It makes decisions on sale and purchase of assets, on credits for investment or working capital, on the distribution of that part of the earnings which the enterprise may dispose of, on expansion or the establishment of new plants, and so forth. Moreover, the council elects the managing board and supervises its activities.

The managing board consists of three to eleven members, depending upon the size of the firm, including the director who is a member ex officio. The board, too, acts only as a body, while the director has authority as a person. In general, the board translates the council's policy decisions into more concrete actions; it may also take decisions on current matters not within the province of the council. In particular, the board decides on managerial appointments in the firm and on individual complaints in the area of industrial relations against the director.

At least three quarters of the members of the board must be production workers; not more than one third of the board's members may be re-elected from among the members of the outgoing board; no one may be a member for more than two consecutive years. No such restriction on re-election exists for council members; the reason given for this difference is that the danger of bureaucratization is regarded as larger for the members of the managing board. To protect the members of the board against arbitrariness, they may not be given notice terminating their employment or transferred to another job without their consent during their tenure of office.

The director is the actual manager of the firm. He hires and fires, except for executives whose appointment and dismissal are in the hands of the managing board. He secures discipline within limits still to be discussed. He makes job assignments, and the like. In the area of industrial relations, however, his decisions can be appealed to the managing board.

He is at the same time part of the plant self-government and a representative of the community at large. He is, therefore, entitled to veto decisions of the workers' council or of the managing board which, in his view, contradict state regulations. In the case of continued disagreement, the people's committee of the municipality decides.

Ideally, therefore, all fundamental decisions are to be taken by the council and, in more detail, by the managing board. Day-to-day operations are entrusted to the director. Obviously, the borderline separating these classes of decisions is fluid. The precise location of the boundary will often depend on political circumstances external to the firm; in many other cases on the personalities involved, their competence in general, professional skill in particular, and last, but surely not least, their standing in the all-powerful party.

Theoretical problems of the council system. The theoretical model of a council-administered economy would provide for the councils to act as entrepreneurs within a framework to be set by central authority. This "model" gives rise to a number of fundamental issues:

1) How to enforce observance of this framework by the enterprise;

2) How to provide a yardstick for rational decision-making by the enterprise;

3) How to provide incentives for the enterprise as a whole to serve economic progress;

4) How to provide incentives for the employees to act efficiently.

In attempting to solve these problems, the Yugoslav policymakers were of course not free to choose among the technically available solutions. For political objectives, first the need to ensure the maintenance in power of the

Communist Party under Tito's leadership imposed severe restrictions. Second, the regime aimed at high growth rates in the economy, especially in industry. Third, the distance in economic development and living standards between the relatively advanced and the backward regions of the country was to be reduced in order to unify the nation. The evolution of the economic policies of the country since 1950—reflected in changes in the status and functions of the councils — is the story of the regime's attempts to find under changing circumstances appropriate solutions for the fundamental issues within the area of politically tolerable choice.

Planning, in the new system, took on an entirely different meaning from the one in the earlier phase. While formerly the plan authority was concentrated in Belgrade, and all other agencies including the individual firms were merely subordinate administrative parts of this supreme decision-making authority, planning now is limited by decentralized decision-making. The new plan is characterized by its lack of detail,[11] while in the past it provided for every item of output in each plant. Relying on the market, the new system tends to avoid as far as possible the use of direct controls. Price controls were abolished for many, though not all, consumer goods, but were retained for capital goods and raw materials. There is also a check on price increases. Physical controls are rare and apply mainly to foreign trade. Arbitrary and particular rules addressed to a specific enterprise which prevailed under the earlier system were frowned upon. General laws were to be the instruments of economic policy. For every plan goal, there were to be "adequate economic instruments,"[12] (incentives to attain it). Since rules are mostly general rather than specific or detailed, enterprises were free to act on their own, within the general framework. The plan, under the circumstances, became a statement of objectives regarded likely to be attained by the effects of incentives, operating through the market, rather than a list of specific instructions.

This compromise between direct controls and the operation of a market underwent several changes as the regime was feeling its way toward a new system. Up to the end of 1961, in spite of ups and downs, the trend seemed to be toward increased reliance upon the market. Changes announced in early 1962 indicated a sharp reversal and a return to tighter direct (particularly price) controls.[13] Whether this represents a more lasting departure from the liberalizing trend than previous changes remains to be seen, although a number of signs point in the direction of a general tightening of the regime. One of the most significant symptoms of this trend was the Djilas trial. However, for the time being the essentials seem still unchanged.

These fundamentals, as far as they are relevant for an understanding of the council operations, may be briefly summarized as follows:

1) The planning commission prepares various alternative plans and selects one of them for further elaboration. This alternative is worked out in more detail, but compared with the earlier system the plan now represents only outlines, primarily the fundamental "proportions." Leontieff's Input-Output Analysis is being used as a tool of Yugoslav planning. The plan is supplemented by a system of "economic instruments," that is, steering devices designed to make the economy move in the desired directions. Since administrative fiat is to be excluded from the arsenal of modern Yugoslav economic policies, the "economic instruments" are essentially economic incentives. On this federal plan are based various "lower" plans, those of the republics and districts. All these are called "social plans" as distinguished from the plans of the firms. The same principles apply to investment plans which are in the main forecasts with an indication of the instruments that are expected to call forth the intended volume and forms of investment. There are, however, some types of investment which the federal government undertakes by itself, primarily key investments—in steel, power, transportation. For the rest, investment is undertaken on the basis of expected rates of profit and return and of the rates of interest which the banks charge.[14] As to consumption, the federal plan gives "indication . . . of the rate of increase of personal incomes that the economy can afford."[15]

Apart from the key investments of the federal government, the actual operations of the economy are determined by the decisions of the individual enterprises. They are free to make their own plans, within the framework set by tax laws, the guaranteed minimum wages, and some rules on the distribution of net earnings (the word profit being strictly banished from the Yugoslav vocabulary). It would be an obvious misrepresentation to claim that Yugoslav enterprises are as free as American businesses. A list of the restrictions on the freedom of the Yugoslav enterprise appears quite formidable. The main restraints are the following:

(a) The state intervenes in the election of the works council and managing board and may, in certain cases, dissolve them.

(b) The director is elected by a state organ and can be removed only by it.

(c) The state may liquidate an enterprise.

(d) The economic plans of the federation of the republic may provide for specific restrictions and establish obligations for all enterprises or those of certain industries.

(e) Some parts of the plan of the enterprise need, to be effective, the approval of the state and may be amended by it.

(f) Special rules govern the disposition of net earnings by the enterprise.

(g) The pay scale of the enterprise must be approved by the trade union and the local community.

(h) Enterprises are restricted in disposing of their basic assets.

(i) Most of their financial transactions must be carried out on a non-currency basis by way of state banks.

(j) In some industries, state regulations prescribe the details of cost accounting.[16]

Compared with the system of 1945–50, however, the freedom is considerable. It is, of course, hoped that the plans of the various enterprises will conform to the pattern and the objectives of the over-all plan in that their actions will respond to the incentives provided by the "economic instruments." But this is a hope, and its attainment is not to be furthered by administrative action except when the "base proportions" (most fundamental relationships not clearly defined by the Yugoslav literature) are seriously endangered. In that case, legislative action will be justified.

2) Rational decision-making is partly based on the operations of the market. Relationship between costs and revenue and shifts in relative prices of cost and product items permit rational decisions on relative quantities of inputs and the product-mix. For a decade or so, it seemed that evolution moved in the direction of freer operation of the market. This trend was reversed as a result of unsatisfactory results in output and foreign trade during 1961. Output increased, but less than scheduled, and exports (scheduled to rise by some 13 per cent) fell by nearly 2 per cent. The regime reacted sharply in 1962, curtailing consumption and counteracting a fairly general price rise by forcing a return to the price level of December 1961.[17] The fear of inflation has been ever-present and seems now to have overcome, for the time being at least, the liberalizing forces in the country. To the extent to which price controls are to be used as permanent devices, administrative decision — either explicit or implied — will take the place of adjustments to changing market conditions. This, however, is a far less efficient guide for rational decision-making. Also a direct attack on the inflationary forces would seem more promising than mere repression of their symptoms.

3) The question of how to determine the success of an enterprise has been hotly disputed and continues to be the subject of debate. Without entering into details, the main issues are expressed in changes in the method of determining the basis for the various incentives. Thus the first method used, that of "exceeding the plan" in terms of physical units of output, resulted in a neglect of maintenance, of safety measures on the job, of quality, and so forth or in understating the capacity of the plant so that plans were set at low levels. Plan fulfillment in terms of value led to a shift in the product-mix: by concentrating production upon higher-priced items to the neglect of simpler products a higher value output can be obtained, and the system puts a premium on such shifts, even though from the point of view of economic rationality the choice of a different product-mix might be preferable.[18] A further disadvantage of using the value of output as the yardstick of success was that this system induced disregard of costs. It naturally became necessary to take costs into account as well.[19] Norms for the consumption of raw materials, and so on, were established. In effect, what would be called "profits" in a capitalistic enterprise became the key for income distribution in Yugoslav enterprises.

The system of incentives for the enterprise as a whole is then closely related to the market. Economic enterprises are, in principle, autonomous economic units. The incomes of the enterprises depend, therefore, on costs and sales returns on one hand, taxes to the various governmental agencies, federal, state and local, on the other. Interest on fixed and working capital figures among the costs of the enterprise. It produces some 13 per cent of public income. Of the taxes the most important are the turnover tax which yields some 19 per cent of public revenue, the tax on gross revenue of the enterprise, and a payroll tax. These taxes provide almost 60 per cent of public revenue.[20] In addition to the taxes, the enterprise must set aside resources for various "funds"—for depreciation, for general reserve, for expansion, for housing, and other social purposes. Until 1961 the trend was toward increased freedom for the enterprise to dispose of its earnings.[21]

4) While over-all net income of the enterprise sets the limits for the personal incomes of its employees, further restrictions must be taken into account. A wage schedule is set for the enterprise by the workers' council in agreement with the trade union. As far as possible piece rates are employed. Aggregate incomes based upon this schedule form the "fund of scheduled earnings." If the net income of the enterprise (after taxes) is insufficient to provide this fund, personal incomes may be reduced to the level of legally set minima. If necessary, the reserve funds of the enterprise

may be drawn upon, and the municipality may advance funds. As a last resort, the enterprise may be deprived of its self-government and reorganized.

When net income exceeds the "fund for scheduled earnings," a surplus exists whose disposal has been one of the major problems of the system. Low personal incomes tend to induce the enterprise (the council) to distribute as large a share of the surplus as possible in the form of supplementary income to the employees. This would defeat the industrialization drive of the regime. Severe restrictions on the disposal of the surplus were thus enacted compelling the enterprise to place most of the surplus in various funds, for a general reserve, for investment, social purposes, and so forth. This tended to curtail the amount available for distribution to the point where the incentive effects were defeated. A steeply progressive tax on distributed funds formed another stage in the evolution of the experiment until in 1961 the councils were given full freedom to decide.[22] This misfired from the point of view of rapid industrialization; the regime accused the councils of distributing too large a portion of the surplus to the employees. The return to stricter controls has been justified by this experience.

The distribution of these supplementary incomes is to be made as far as possible in a way designed to provide maximum incentives. Personal incentives are set at two levels — that of the work group and that of the individual. In deciding upon the distribution of the net income of the enterprise after taxes and the allocation of resources to the various funds, the workers' council proceeds through two stages: the distribution of personal incomes among the "economic units" — the subgroups within an enterprise — and, within each unit, to the individual employees. In both stages, incentive effects are to be aimed at. The council sets up criteria — quantity and quality of output, cost reduction, and so forth — which form the yardstick by which performance is to be judged.

The system in operation. To translate these principles into operation has been no mean task. The problems confronting this system in the Yugoslav economy are indeed difficult: unjustified (in terms of human effort) income differences among workers of neighboring enterprises, monopoly profits (and the gamut of problems that Henry Simons[23] labeled "syndicalism"), short-sightedness on the part of the workers' councils in allocating funds for distribution in personal income rather than for productive investment, and so forth. Yugoslav economic policy has been searching for ways to solve these problems, and different solutions have been tried out at different times. The tendency to change has at times been hectic. All solutions, moreover, have been rendered extremely difficult by the poverty of the country and the exceedingly low income levels, not only of the workers, but also of medium and higher officials in the various enterprises. The entire mechanism has been working under extreme pressure for higher living standards. To some extent, the system has tended to prevent this pressure from destroying it by using the demand for higher incomes as an incentive for bigger and better output. But, as we shall attempt to show, rewards and incentives seem relatively too modest to perform their functions effectively and the dictatorship, though mild by some standards, is oppressive enough to vitiate the fundamental philosophy of the system which is the encouragement of personal initiative.

In principle the market mechanism is to be of controlling influence. Physical controls having been eliminated, consumer freedom prevails with the attendant consequence of rationing by the pocketbook. Since price controls are predominantly applied to producers' goods, the consumer goods market is in the main free of outside interference.[24] This, however, means that the danger of monopoly profits and monopolistic prices is very great. In a country with a low development of manufacturing, poor transportation, and a tendency toward excess of effective demand over supply, various forms of monopoly are the most frequent type of market situation. The absence of advertising of brand names and of consumer attachment to particular products means little compared with the conspicuous lack of competition in most consumption goods.[25]

It is true that foreign trade offers opportunities for the government to reduce the power of monopolistic positions. By permitting the import of foreign consumers' goods or varying the import quantities or the so-called "coefficients" of exchange rates, that is, the particular exchange rate assigned to a given commodity under the now abolished system of multiple exchange rates, the government could reduce exaggerated prices and profits. The mere threat of such action might be used to keep monopolistic excesses in check. But this power is more theoretical than real, given the perpetual pressure upon the balance of payments on one hand, and the insatiable demand for consumer goods on the other. Foreign aid has at times enabled Yugoslavia to provide for substantial imports of foreign consumer goods, but this was barely sufficient to relieve acute domestic shortages and to prevent more rapid inflationary developments. Indeed the shortage of foreign exchange is such that it has become one of the main bulwarks of monopolistic power on the domestic market, even more effective as such than mere protective tariffs.

The profit margin of the enterprise may thus depend as much upon its monopolistic situation as upon its physical productivity. The main check that is presently available upon the exploitation of monopolistic power is tax policy. This, however, has to serve many other purposes, particularly that of counteracting inflationary tendencies and making resources available for investment. As a result of these divergent objectives, tax policy has undergone many changes over the years. A detailed study lies outside the scope of this investigation. Briefly, in the first stages of the new policy, the enterprise was assigned a minimum utilization rate of its capacity,[26] and its tax was set as a proportion of its wage bill which again was specified in the plan. Profits then remaining could be distributed by the enterprise. This was soon found to be a poorly devised system; enterprises paid out "an overwhelming share"[27] of their surplus as wage supplements and the setting of individual tax rates for individual enterprises violated the spirit of the new system and led to discrimination against the more efficient enterprises without necessarily eliminating monopoly profits. An additional progressive tax on "excessive distribution of profits" was introduced in 1953, but this was so high that it seriously affected the incentive for efficiency, except perhaps that it stimulated the elimination of surplus labor.

Very substantial changes in the fiscal system were made from year to year. Thus, while the minimum utilization rate of plant capacity was abandoned, annual depreciation rates in terms of the value of the fixed capital of the enterprise and a flat tax on this capital were introduced; enterprises had to borrow additional funds needed from the banks at competitive rates. The tax of the enterprise was related to its profits instead of the wages bill.

The determination of the wage bill and its distribution among the work force are central problems of this system.[28] Contradictory forces have been operating on Yugoslav policy with respect to the first of these questions. Governmental policy has been caught in a dilemma between the desire to make incomes dependent on the economic success of the enterprise—the incentive effect—and the need to compress consumption—the investment effect.[29]

The trend after 1952 has been in the direction of giving the enterprise increased freedom in determining how to use its net income after taxes. This freedom proved costly—by way of increased consumption—when economic growth slackened in 1961.[30] As a result, taxes were increased by new regulations in 1962 and enterprises were required to set aside a larger proportion of their earnings for depreciation reserves, general reserves, and other funds. A smaller part of earnings is thus available for distribution.[31]

How is this total then distributed among the employees? How are wages determined?

The Wage System

The basic principles of the wage system are as follows:

1) Primary responsibility in setting wages and supplements belongs to the works council.

2) The federal government sets minimum rates.

3) A kind of collective agreement providing minimum and maximum rates for typical jobs is drawn up by the union and the trade association of the particular branch. This serves as a model agreement.

4) The employee is entitled to a wage and a supplement, with the latter depending upon his performance, that of the enterprise, and of the work group to which he belongs.

5) The local community and the trade union are to approve the wage schedule as set up by the council.

6) As far as possible piece rather than time rates are to be used.

The works council is given basic responsibility for establishing the wage scales that are to apply within the plant. The common practice is for the managing board at the beginning of the year to draw up a tentative wage scale; this will include time and piece rates, bonuses, vacation pay, production norms, and so forth. This is posted in the plant, and all employees are invited to make comments and offer suggestions. The managing board then prepares a definitive proposal to the workers' council, the local people's committee, and the trade union. These three bodies meet; if they agree, the wage scale is adopted; if any one of the three bodies disagrees, a special arbitration body decides. It is appointed by the government of the republic in which the enterprise is located. It consists of equal numbers of representatives from the trade union and the trade association of the firm concerned; another member, the chairman, is appointed by the government of the republic.[32]

The conjunction of four elements — the workers' council, the trade union, the chamber (trade association of the enterprise), and the people's committee — is supposed to achieve a fair balance in setting wage levels.

> [The council] will have an interest in setting tariff rates as high as possible, thus reducing their liability to tax; the trade union will be interested in keeping rates of pay for the same or similar jobs more or less equal from one enterprise to another, and the chamber in keeping rates from one enterprise to another in

the same branch of activity more or less in line, while the commune — with an eye to its guarantee obligations [in case the enterprise faces financial difficulties, the commune is obligated to come to its assistance] — will be interested in holding down tariff-wages.[33]

The wage system has undergone many changes, just as has the system of determining the allocation of the net income of the enterprise. Gradually, the councils were given increased freedom in distributing wage increments. They were instructed to provide premiums for all jobs in which it was possible to measure objectively the worker's contribution to improved quality or increased volume of output and reduced costs. Enterprises are to give:

premiums to the workers performing the jobs on which the general success of the organization depends, or for the success achieved in implementation of specific tasks aimed at realization of a better organization of work, economy in materials and other costs, achievement of greater productivity of work and better quality of products, or decrease of expenses of the economic organization. The title to the premium and its level are prescribed on the basis of the tasks specified in advance and the criterions for determination of the success achieved.[34]

In addition, for all workplaces and jobs the work effect of which can be measured, the economic organization must prescribe the obligatory effect to be achieved within a determined time unit (norm). All premiums must be paid out of the earnings of the enterprise.

The reference to premiums for "workers performing the jobs on which the general success of the organization depends" is particularly significant. The general trend of council-made wage schedules has been egalitarian. Director's salaries frequently amounted to no more than twice the base wage (or three times the wage of unskilled workers) in the plant. Egalitarian trends also prevailed in the distribution of premiums. Pressure from above was exerted to provide a greater spread in the wage structure.

This is just one aspect of the general problem of striking a proper balance between the need of providing incentives, the requirements of the development of the enterprise, and the egalitarian tendencies of the workers' self-government. All this must be seen against the background of powerful inflationary pressures originating partly with the industrialization policies of the regime, partly with the low incomes of the population and the consequent eagerness to distribute the largest possible part of the income of the enterprise. While greater incentives may appear, at first glance, to add fuel to the inflationary fire, neglect of incentives may have even greater inflationary effects by curtailing output and reducing productivity. It is this observer's judgment that so far the proper balance has frequently not been attained, with the error mostly in the direction of insufficient incentives as distinguished from general distribution. The evidence for this lies, we believe, partly in successive revisions of the wage structure aiming at establishing higher incentives, but also in the great amount of "black" work (moonlighting in American labor parlance) performed after hours either on the worker's own account or as an employee of an artisan. This practice implies that the worker "goes slow" on his main job in order to preserve his strength for the second job, where, paid by results or working under close supervision, he must put in a good day's work. The prime importance of the "main" job for the worker is that it provides him with social security benefits of great value.

The incentives are weakened, moreover, by the tremendous importance of social security in the worker's real income. The counterpart of this is a large contribution to social security. Aggregate deductions from the worker's gross income are estimated at, on the average, more than half or even close to 60 per cent of his gross income. Among these deductions are social security (approximately 35 per cent), contributions to the housing fund (approximately 10 per cent), and personal income tax (approximately 11 per cent). Effective increases in direct payments to the workers are thus exceedingly costly to the enterprise. With steeply progressive taxes on the wage bill of the enterprise and high deductions from the workers' gross income, a small increment in the net payments to the workers requires very heavy expenditures. This meets the objective of keeping consumption levels as low as possible, but it threatens to make for ineffective incentives.

This is, perhaps, a symptom of the quandary in which a Communist system finds itself whenever it uses economic incentives. They inevitably clash with the egalitarian philosophy of the regime. Unlike the Soviet Union, which has wholeheartedly chosen inequality, Communist Yugoslavia seems undecided which way to go, but the logic of the system would seem to push it toward increasing inequality. Complaints about excessive increases in income for the benefit of managerial employees ranked high among the motivations for the reforms of 1962. These alone, however, can hardly have been more than a small fraction in the increase of total personal incomes during 1961 by about 21 per cent. Productivity rose by merely 2 per cent and production by 7 per cent. This discrepancy obviously resulted from the general relaxation of the rules on income distribution.

The Councillors

The first general works council elections took place in 1950, following the enactment of the law about the self-government of the enterprises. Official Yugoslav statistics report that 84 per cent of those eligible to vote took part in the election. Together with the councillors elected prior to the enactment of the law (those with consultative status who continued in their functions until elections took place in their plants), there were altogether 155,166 members of works councils. In enterprises with more than 30 employees, 114,313 members were elected.

Detailed statistics are available for later years. An official study for 1956[35] tells us that the great majority of workers' councils was elected in manufacturing, mining and quarrying, trade, and catering and handicrafts, even though some 7 per cent of all councils functioned in agricultural enterprises. One quarter of the council members represented white-collar employees. Of the others, slightly more than half were skilled workers; highly skilled workers formed less than one fifth of the council membership on the workers' side. The typical council member was male (84.8 per cent) between twenty-six and thirty-five years of age (45.3 per cent), while the council presidents were slightly older (46.9 per cent between twenty-six and thirty-five and 30.6 per cent between thirty-six and forty-five with only 4.4 per cent up to twenty-five years of age as compared with 12.9 per cent of the council members). In professional skill, the presidents ranked far higher than the ordinary members; 85.7 per cent belonged to the two highest skill groups as contrasted with 70.5 per cent of the council members. Only about 10 per cent had secondary school or university education. Presidents of managing boards had about the same characteristics as their colleagues presiding over the councils.

Statistical information is also available on the types of questions dealt with in council meetings. About 40 per cent of all the issues before the councils can be described as economic, financial, or technical problems of the enterprise, ranging from its plan and statements of its accounts to production costs, quality, and realizations. Salary, norms, and distribution of profits — subjects that refer directly to the workers' income — represented only one sixth of the items on the agenda, a smaller fraction than labor relations, labor discipline, and "economic crime" taken together.

According to close observers, an interesting evolution has taken place in the nature of the council's work. Early meetings of the councils, it is said, were taken up overwhelmingly by personal issues, many of them the grievances of one or two individuals. During the next stage, the discussions focused primarily upon methods by which the short-run incomes of the workers in the enterprise in general could be increased. Only gradually did interest shift to long-term consideration of the economic, financial, or technical problems, which are the real assignments of the councils. This shift may reflect progressive education of the council members and of the workers in general, or it may correspond to the growth of the councils' responsibilities under the shifting legislative and administrative arrangements. Whatever the cause or mixture of causes, the evolution seems to indicate that workers' participation in management, as far as subject matter is concerned, has moved in the direction desired by the law-makers.

Of the three types of business issues — technical, financial, and economic — the first seems to be handled best by the councils, while financial issues seem least understood. Moreover, there are substantial regional differences in the level of competency with which the councils handle these issues. As can be expected, the councils in the industrially more developed areas (Slovenia and Croatia, for example) are more effective and deal with wider issues than councils in Macedonia or Montenegro where industry is in its earliest infancy. Interviews have confirmed also the obvious expectation that experienced industrial workers make better councillors than workers from rural areas who are just entering their industrial careers.

The educational effects of the system are closely related to the fact that council members are normally elected for no more than one year.[36] More than a third of all workers and white-collar employees have so far served as members of workers' councils. With the passage of time, more and more workers will have the experience of council membership. The shorter the period of office, the greater is the number of employees who, at one time or another, participate in council work. However, the educational value of the experiment is almost precisely the inverse of its merits as an effective device of management.

Members of the councils are subject to recall, but this seems to occur only in highly exceptional cases. Thus, during 1956 only 998 councils members were recalled, 0.8 per cent. Among the reasons given for the recall, laxity and "economic crime" are separately stated in the statistics; about one fifth of the recalls were ascribed to each of these two reasons, with the rest grouped together under "other reasons." Economic crime stands for theft, corruption, and the like. There is a general impression that "economic crimes" have become an important factor in the economic life of the nation. Marshal Tito was reported to have complained that "the provisions of the nation's criminal code dealing with such crimes were mild—the maximum penalty being fifteen years imprisonment."[37] He said that some people had embezzled millions of *dinars* and had paid with only short prison terms, making the crime worthwhile. Recalls were carried out at the instigation of various authorities: organs of self-government (of the local commune) and the "collective" (the workers in the plant) were responsible in 60 per cent of the cases; state authority, the director, and the political organization in the remainder of the cases (less than 10 per cent).

Somewhat more frequent is the recall of members of the managing boards. This occurred in 476 cases and affected 1.2 per cent of 40,232 board members. Organs of self-government were most frequently responsible for the recall; the political organization was responsible in about 8 per cent of the cases. It is of course possible that political motives were operative in the recall of the council or board members by other bodies.

The above figures refer to enterprises with more than 30 employees. Among them are a few large enterprises—say with more than 1000 employees—or fair-sized enterprises with several shops. Some attempts at adapting the council system to these situations have been made, but it would seem that no full solution has yet been found for the problem of how to make self-government effective under such circumstances. Shop councils, the development of smaller election units in the plant, and so forth, have been proposed.[38] A large percentage of Yugoslav enterprises, on the other hand, has fewer than thirty, but more than six, employees. In these firms, all employees are members of the council; the only elected body is the managing board. Even this seems in many cases excessive organization. It has been suggested that either the workers' council represented by the "working collective" or the managing board be suppressed.[39] (Enterprises with six employees or less do not elect either council or managing board. Their functions are performed by all employees.)

Elections are free and secret, according to the law, and all workers are entitled to vote provided they have the right to vote in political elections. Official statistics for 1956 tell us that of 1,363,788 employees, 1,329,890 were entitled to vote, that is, all but 34,000, or almost 98 per cent. We are further informed that 1,169,058 did vote (all but 160,000, or 88 per cent). Of a total of 6854 lists of candidates, 6599 were proposed by the trade union branch. Only 255 were "unofficial" lists. Of 124,204 workers' councillors, 121,648 were elected from trade union lists. In other words, only 2556 councillors proposed on nonunion lists were elected, that is, about 2 per cent.

Such "unofficial" lists can be proposed by one tenth of the employees of the enterprise in question, but the statistics indicate that this method is not frequently used. In some cases mild pressure has been sufficient to persuade opposition groups to abandon attempts at establishing unofficial lists. In other cases the police or the party intervened. The fact that a few such lists succeeded in getting some unofficial candidates elected is of course no evidence for real freedom in the election procedure.[40]

The supervision of the legality of the elections is in the hands of the local commune and of the district court. Complaints can be formulated by all candidates, proponents of lists of candidates, the union branch of the enterprise, the local commune, and the district authority. If irregularities are established which may have influenced the outcome of the elections, new elections are ordered.[41] This kind of supervision of the regularity of the election will not necessarily inspire confidence among potential oppositionists.

The function of the members of the workers' councils and of the managing boards is honorary; they are not paid for their work in the organs of workers' management. They receive only compensation for wages lost while they are taking part in the meetings of these bodies. Throughout their entire stay in office, they continue to work on their jobs in the enterprise.[42] Decisions of the council are valid provided more than half the council members attend the meeting.

The Managing Board

The board consists of three to ten members, including the director of the enterprise who is a member ex officio. In 1956 there were some 40,000 members of managing boards, most serving on boards with three to eight members.

The boards act as the executive organ of the councils. They implement the council's policy decisions by giving instructions to the director, and they submit policy proposals. But they also act on their own: they decide appointments at higher levels, except for the director who is appointed by the local government; theirs is also the decision on grievances against the director on industrial relations issues.

At least three quarters of the board members must be production workers or otherwise engaged in the fundamental economic activity of the enterprise. Not more than one third of the outgoing members can be reelected, and no one can be a board member for more than two consecutive years. These clauses naturally act unfavorably on the board's effectiveness, given the small number of workers qualified to serve on it; such restrictions tend to emphasize the educational functions of board membership at the expense of their managerial tasks.

Protection for board members is provided by clauses in the law which prohibit their dismissal during terms of office as well as their transfer to other jobs during that time without their agreement.

The Director

The director is the executive organ of both the workers' council and the managing board and thus the principal representative of the enterprise. At the same time, as appointee of the local people's committee administering the commune, he is a representative of the state and sees to it that the activity of the enterprise corresponds to the laws and administrative regulations. He may, therefore, suspend the execution of any instructions of the council or board which in his view violate law or regulations. In the case of a conflict, the organs of the local community decide.

Among the functions of the director are hiring and firing (except for managerial jobs), job assignments, and discipline (except for severe cases which go before a disciplinary court appointed by the workers' council). Grievances against decisions of the director may be formulated by any worker; as was pointed out above, they come before the managing board for decision.

Almost all directors are male; only 49 out of 6030 (less than 1 per cent) are female. Almost half were in the age group of thirty-six to forty-five which makes them older than members or even presidents of workers' councils. Their educational qualifications do not seem high: less than 10 per cent had university education; less than a quarter, secondary school education. Two thirds had only primary or junior high school education (which ends at the age of 14). Their skill qualification, however, is high: almost 90 per cent belong in the two upper reaches of the four existing skill groups. Only in agriculture are there many unskilled directors — one third of the total.

Nine and three tenths per cent of the directors were relieved of their office during 1956 — a total of 563; 61 of them were removed at their own request. Laxity and "economic crime" were the reasons in a quarter of the cases. The supervisory authority was responsible for more than half the dismissals — a sign perhaps of insufficient authority exercised by the councils or managing boards or of excessive outside supervision.

The procedure for the appointment of the director as well as for his dismissal provides for the ultimate decision to be taken by the people's committee of the local commune. For the appointment there is a public competition whose outcome is decided upon by a special committee of the people's committee. This is not a competitive examination, but rather an announcement of the opening in the press. Candidates then submit documents about their education and experience and are interviewed by the selection committee. One third of the members of the special committee consists of persons designated by the workers' council of the enterprise concerned.

From the scheme to the practice. In the scheme of things there is a clear division of functions among the three organs of self-government in the enterprise: between them and the workers themselves, between the enterprise and the outside authorities of the state, between the union and the party. In actual operation, as may be expected, these relationships do not usually correspond to the scheme.

The councils are to set policies on fundamental questions; the boards are to translate these into daily operations; the director is to carry them out. Thus, the council may decide on an enlargement of operations. The managing board, upon study, may come to the conclusion that this would require the purchase of additional space, building materials, and hiring of additional workers; it may furthermore appropriate the necessary funds, authorize borrowing, and so forth. The director then would try to obtain foreign exchange for the purchase of machinery, engage in the actual negotiations to get the necessary credits, and hire the workers for the enterprise. But just as in an American enterprise where the lines separating different levels of management and those separating management from administration can only rarely be drawn with precision and permanency, the actual distribution of authority in Yugoslavia differs from plant to plant and from that planned in the system. Thus, councils have sometimes themselves decided technical and operational problems which should have been left to the board or the directors. More often, the latter have in fact decided policy questions while the council just endorsed these decisions. Autocratic directors and autocratic managing boards are frequent. In the backward regions of the country they will almost inevitably be autocratic until a better educated industrial working class can be developed. Perhaps more serious is the situation where a combination of political "pull" and indifferent council gives a director or a small group on the board full authority. Vice versa, a director, though incompetent and lacking in interest in the enterprise, may prove irremovable because of political protection. In that case, the managing board or some managerial employees may in fact perform his functions.

Some of these deviations from the intended system are inevitable, and no change of legal texts would help.[43] They are the outgrowth of poverty and ignorance "in a country in which at the outset 20 per cent of the population was illiterate."[44] Other shortcomings are the equally unavoidable consequence of the political autocracy which interferes with the efficient operation of any democratic agency that is supposed to develop under it.

It it not easy, however, to distinguish between the restrictions on workers' self-government which the dictatorship inevitably involves, purely technical shortcomings of the system, problems created by poverty and lack of industrial tradition, and, finally, the congenital difficulties of any system of workers' management. Just like most other countries in rapid industrialization, Yugoslavia is suffering from constant inflationary pressure. Good harvests and foreign aid may help reduce it; at other times it vitiates the entire system and leads to a return to repressive control measures which are basically in contradiction with the entire system.

One of the by-products of such controls is their differential effect upon the earnings of enterprises and of the workers concerned. The lack of consistency and of clearly understandable criteria for the establishment of differential controls has aroused the resentment of the workers. In the strikes in the Slovenian coal mines in January 1958, this element entered to a considerable extent. During January 1958, the coal miners of Trbovlje and other coal areas of Slovenia struck under the leadership of their own works councils. A number of them were reported to have stayed underground for two days in a protest against low wages. The strike led to the intervention of Miha Marinko, President of the Slovenian Republic. It ended in price increases of coal which enabled the mines to pay higher wages. In effect, this was a strike against the federal price control authorities. Although this was the first officially reported strike in Yugoslavia in a decade, reliable reports spoke of twenty strikes during the winter of 1957–58, most of which were protests against excessively low wages, combined with rapid price increases. Other strikes in the Sarajevo area arose out of conflicts among the employees over the distribution of profits.[45]

In the wage area, however, controls alone do not create problems; it is primarily the exceedingly low wage levels. "Moon-lighting" and petty pilfering on a large scale are the inevitable results. Seeing that most workers live in fact and of necessity on income(s) exceeding those provided in the salary schedules, it might be wiser to grant salary increases. Moreover, the system employed in determining relative wages puts political pressure behind the demands of unskilled or low-skilled workers and thus greatly reduces the skill premium. Given the scarcity of higher skilled workers and the need for them, this may interfere with efficiency:

> The views of the mass of unskilled workers — that, because everyone has the same needs, everyone has to get the same pay (with which we may sympathize but which, for the time being, are economically disastrous) — have in a certain number of enterprises led to a leveling of wages and salaries. Indeed, this view was even impressed on the community as a whole when in 1952 the trade unions fixed the salaries of the directors on the basis of the wages of unskilled workers multiplied by three in small enterprises and by five in the largest enterprises; this procedure set a limit for the highest salaries in the range of $65 to $110 per month! The consequences were lack of responsibility, lack of initiative, lack of incentives, and, only after all this had become obvious, the radical correction of wage differentials in 1957.[46]

The use of incentive pay systems is still far less frequent than the law recommends.[47] And since the funds available for premiums and the surplus available for distribution are often insufficient, the incentive aspects of the system tend to be weak. Low productivity, political pressure in the plant, and heavy taxes thus combine to counteract the freedom given the enterprise to dispose of its surplus and to reduce inefficiency.

A further hindrance to the effectiveness of the system is a multiplicity of controls. The government machinery includes the following inspections: financial, foreign exchange, market, building, sanitary, veterinary, and labor. In addition, there is tax inspection and supervision by the bank in connection with loan transactions and by the social security institute. "It is not rare to find at the same time in one enterprise representatives of different financial inspectorates sent by various institutions. It even happens that the other inspection services — from the municipality to the federation — each in its own domain, simultaneously carry out their control in an enterprise."[48] Controls seem to exist for their own sake, and the workers' council and even the managing boards learn only rarely what the results of the various inspections have been.

The System from the Worker's Angle

How does Stepan Babic, the man on the work bench, experience the new system? There is little doubt that there has been a real improvement in his standard of living compared with the situation up to about 1952. Real wages have risen from their intolerably low level, although they are still among the lowest in Europe. It is difficult to find reliable measures of this change, particularly since the figures of the earlier period — based upon the prices of unobtainable rations — are highly fictitious. But no observer of Yugoslav events would question the fact that real wages have risen. The increase of the domestically produced national income is, however, no reliable guide to this change, not only because of the high and fluctuating level of net investment and national defense spending, but also because of the very profound influence that changes in outside economic relations have played and continue to play in the evolution of the Yugoslav economic system.

Equally important is a distinct improvement in the quality of the products offered the consumer. This is a fact which most Yugoslavs point out, but which finds no expression in the statistics, even though it greatly contributes to the improvement of the standard of living and to bringing some joy into the daily life of the worker. To some extent, it is the result of the element of competition introduced into the Yugoslav economy by the system of decentralized decision-making; another, perhaps immediately more significant, cause was a temporary reduction of inflationary pressure by a combination of circumstances; for as long as inflation was rampant, any merchandise, however shoddy, could easily be sold.

There are some indications, too, that the return to material incentives produced a greater pride in workmanship and increasing recognition of the importance of competency. It is assuredly too much to say that competency has become more important than party membership; a dictatorship could hardly afford to abandon reliance on party loyalty as a primary criterion in the selection for appointments and promotion. But the recognition has been growing that party membership alone is not a sufficient qualification for managerial authority. The selection of directors, though still not free from political considerations, takes competency more and more into account.

Stepan is thus better off than before 1952 — provided he has employment. One of the first effects of the introduction of economic accountancy into the system was the release of unnecessary workers from many enterprises in order to increase the volume of profits and decrease the number of those who would share in them. Many of those then rendered unemployed have since found their way back into jobs, but concealed unemployment is still one of the dominant issues of the Yugoslav economy. The system of hiring is, under the circumstances, of great importance to the unemployed.

The intention of the government was to have all hiring go through a public employment service. These offices were established by the local authorities and were supposed to cooperate within each republic to refer job-seekers to any appropriate opening within the republic. However, only a part of the actual hiring seems to pass through these offices. In all cases but one, when we raised the question of how additional workers would be obtained, the answer failed to refer to the public employment service. Instead the enterprises seem to rely on recommendations by current employees or on the job-seekers who present themselves at the factory gate. Stepan, if he were to look for a new job, would most probably make the rounds of the enterprises in the area where he lives. If he is a highly skilled worker, he would have few problems; indeed, if he were willing to go into one of the new industrial areas in Macedonia, Montenegro, or Bosnia, he might find himself the object of relatively enticing offers. But a low-skilled or unskilled worker might go without employment or have to accept inferior and occasional jobs for long periods.

What does Stepan do if he is fired? The dismissal is proposed by the director and ratified by the council or a special council committee for dismissals. Notice given up to the fifteenth of each month takes effect as of the fifteenth; notice given after the fifteenth takes effect on the first day of the following month. The law provides for an appeal to the board of management or, in special cases, to the council. A further protest is possible to an arbitration board set up by the local people's committee; it consists of the president of the people's committee as chairman, an arbitrator proposed by the people's committee of the particular industry, and another proposed by the local union. The ruling of this board is final except in cases of breach of law, when an appeal to a court is possible — for instance if a worker is given notice during illness, sick leave, convalescence, annual leave, during pregnancy or while she has a child up to the age of eight months, during military service, while he is a member of the workers' council or of the managing board, as specified in Article 330 of the act respecting employment relationship of December 12, 1957. If Stepan has served in the enterprise for a long time, a longer period of notice is required (for service of five to ten years, two months notice is required). If it is a case of mass dismissal as a result of a reduction in operations, the workers' council must first decide how many workers are to be laid off, with the director selecting those to be discharged.

The union appears only in a highly subsidiary fashion in this entire procedure, and this opens the general question of to whom Stepan will address himself when he feels unfairly treated in the plant.

There is an almost embarrassing wealth of grievance procedures available to him: the workers' council, the managing board, the director, the union, the Communist Party. Which of these, if any, Stepan selects depends on a great many circumstances. If he is a member in good standing in the party, he will most probably turn to it with his complaint. Where the director is a strong personality, he may be the court of appeal against decisions of the foremen and department heads. In the early stages of the council system, the workers' council was often enlisted in support of personal grievances. Sometimes — although the author has no personal knowledge of such a case — the employee may even follow the course suggested by the law and appeal to the managing board against decisions of the director.

One of the frequently used methods of presenting grievances, particularly those of a whole group, is not listed among the publicly acknowledged ways of grievance handling: The workers present themselves *en masse* at the director's office and demand redress. This is in effect a suspension of work, comparable perhaps to a sit-down strike, the typical weapon of poorly organized workers.

Equally noteworthy is the fact that the union is hardly ever mentioned by anyone in connection with grievance handling. This illustrates the peculiar status of the union in the system of workers' councils — a topic still to be treated at greater length.

CHAPTER V

Poland[1]

The Polish workers' council has attracted far less attention abroad than the Yugoslav experiment in workers' self-management. To some extent, this relative neglect may be justified by the greater success of the Yugoslav council system. Yet, the Polish workers' council cannot be written off as a complete failure, and the history of its rise and decline carries many lessons of fairly general validity.

Compared with its Yugoslav counterpart, the Polish council system was far more spontaneous. While the Tito regime introduced the councils by decree, the Polish councils had their beginnings in voluntary movements in various plants and were only later, as a result of an almost revolutionary change, endorsed by the Polish Communist Party and the regime. There is, nevertheless, a very important analogy between the developments in the two countries: in both, the councils were to be an alternative to a highly centralized economic and political system whose defects they were to remedy without, however, destroying ultimate political control by the Communist Party.

Economic and Social Background

Polish economic and social developments since the end of World War II[2] seem to fall into three main phases. The first extends to 1948, the second from 1948 to 1956, and the third covers the period from 1956 to the present. During the first phase, the Lublin Committee, set up by the Soviet Union during the war, gradually extended its control — both geographically, to cover the entire national territory, and politically, by eliminating in particular its Socialist competitors. Poland was officially designated as a popular democracy, different from a dictatorship of the proletariat, and this difference was to consist partly in the continued existence of private farming and some form of private enterprise in nonagricultural activities. The second phase was introduced by the defeat of the "nationalistic" Gomulka wing of the Communist Party in August 1948 and the consequent accession to power of the party wing led by Bierut, which insisted upon patterning the economic and social system of Poland upon the orthodox Stalinist model of the Soviet Union. The forced "merger" of the Socialist Party (PPS) with the (Communist) Workers' Party in December 1948 (or, more accurately, the absorption of the Socialists by the Communist Party) marked an eight years' suspension of effective resistance to Communist orthodoxy. The revival of the anti-Stalinist struggle in 1956 (the Poznan strike and street demonstrations and the return to power of Gomulka) marked the beginning of the third phase which includes the present time.

Economic policy during the first phase has some parallels with "war communism" in Soviet Russia. Land reform after the model of the Bolshevik measures of November 1917 was accompanied by the nationalization of large-scale, and portions of medium-sized, industry. The industrial enterprises were combined into larger undertakings and placed under the administration of fourteen central boards which in turn came under the supervision of various ministries. At first, it seemed as if a significant role was to be reserved for private enterprise and that no coercion was to be applied to bring small peasants into agricultural collectives. Industry was to be divided into a nationalized, a cooperative, and a private sector in what reminded some observers of the Russian NEP policy.[3] Others described this stage as the Socialist Party's conception of "a 'golden mean' between the model afforded by the Soviet Union and that of the leading capitalist countries of the world."[4] However, this balance was soon destroyed, and a Stalinist era began. In the fall of 1947, the offensive against private enterprise in industry and farming was carried forward. In March 1948, the Socialists abandoned their struggle to maintain their independence. Partly under the impact of the Yugoslav-Soviet dispute, the Polish Communists purged themselves of "rightist-nationalist" elements, represented in the person of Wladyslaw Gomulka, and proceeded to shape the economy of the country according to the Soviet pattern.

Pressure was exerted upon private enterprise which rapidly reduced its share in industrial output from 9 to 1 per cent. The cooperatives were subordinated to the economic ministry. (Oskar Lange's capitulation on this point marked the end of Socialist resistance to Communist domination.) The scope of the instructions which the State Commission of Economic Planning issued to the enterprises was widened to the point where the individual manager was left only room for two kinds of decisions: to reduce costs, and to exceed the plan objectives (provided available material enabled him to do so). Prices were kept artificially stable for long periods, and could consequently not perform their function as guides for rational decisions as to products and factors of production. Instead, direct orders specifying in detail and in physical terms the size of the output of the individual enterprise, the product-mix, the factors of production to be used, as well as the prices to be paid and to be charged, were issued to the managers. In the plants themselves, the authority of the manager became sovereign: committee administration, and the influence of the trade union committee, of the party cell, and of the workers' committees were eliminated. A highly centralized and authoritarian economic system was set up, corresponding to the equally centralized political dictatorship which was established after the forced merger of the Socialists and Communists.

Management became incredibly top-heavy. Under the State Commission for Economic Planning were some twenty economic ministries dividing various branches of economic activity among themselves. The next lower administrative layers were formed by nearly two hundred "central administrations" and several hundred "associations." Below the latter in authority were the enterprises, which were regarded as mere branches of the associations with correspondingly little authority.[5]

The rate of economic growth, once the first stage of postwar reconstruction was completed, was unsatisfactory. The actual figures, at first glance, would not seem to bear out this judgment. National income rose (in 1950 prices) from 80.3 billion *zlotys* in 1949 to 117.9 in 1953 and to 138.9 in 1955. This represented an annual growth rate of 10.1 per cent for the period from 1949 to 1953, and of 8.6 per cent from 1953 to 1955. These accomplishments fell far short of the ambitious plans, however. Thus national income was scheduled to reach the level of 133.9 billion *zlotys* in 1953, while achievement amounted to only 117.9; the plan figure for 1955 was 167.3 billion *zlotys,* but the result was only 138.9. While industrial growth, particularly that of heavy industry, was more rapid than the average growth of the entire economy as a result of "an extraordinary concentration . . . of all possible resources"[6] on industrial development, agricultural output lagged far behind, showing average annual growth rates of 1.4 per cent (1949–1953) and 4.6 per cent (1953–1955).[7] Moreover, a very high and increasing share of the national income (a staggering 40 per cent in 1953) was allotted to accumulation. This meant that the volume of production available for consumption rose far less than the gross national product. Since at the same time population increased rather rapidly (from 23.5 million in 1948 to 27 million in 1955) and agricultural production failed to meet plan expectations, consumption levels proved unsatisfactory. Hilary Minc, the main architect of Poland's economic policy at the time, admitted in a speech on October 9, 1951: "We recently had difficulties in supplying the population with several important items. These difficulties manifested themselves on the market of agricultural products where . . . a severe lack of meat and insufficiency of certain other products have been felt. On the other hand, because of insufficient supplies of several agricultural articles the prices of products sold by the peasants on the free market, such as milk products, vegetables and potatoes, have recently risen."[8] Also, the sacrifices imposed upon the population did not hold out the hope of rapidly rising consumption levels for the future. There was, for instance, a "phenomenal rise of investment in stocks, for which no precise explanation can be given."[9] The suspicion does not seem unwarranted that at least a part of this meant "accumulating stocks of unsalable goods resulting from an unsatisfactory pattern of output . . . and some of the waste in production processes may, through the accounting system, have inflated the estimate of stock building." The familiar upward bias of the official production index under conditions of early and rapid industrialization contributed to the overstatement of the growth of industrial output, as did the inevitable deterioration of the quality of goods in the race for "plan fulfillment." Military requirements also played a large part in the growth of investment.[10]

By the end of the six-year plan in which Poland was engaged (1955), many of the shortcomings were ascribed by public opinion to the high centralization of the economic system and the use of administrative orders in regulating it. The demand for decentralization was widespread; popular slogans were the "rehabilitation of the enterprise" and the observance of "objective economic laws."[11] The events of the Twentieth Party Congress in the Soviet Union (Khrushchev's revelations about Stalin) greatly contributed to unrest and discredited the regime.

The Council Movement

Two currents merged in the evolution toward the workers' councils: workers' resistance to low living standards, bureaucratic controls, and political oppression, and the technicians' rejection of inefficiency and waste which they related to political interference. These two currents were united in a double objective: one political, the other economic. The political objective was to find a road to socialism which would be different from that of the Soviet Union, particularly from its bureaucratic centralism; in the area of economics, the goal was to carry out a shift toward administrative decentralization and to introduce incentives which would improve efficiency and thereby raise the standard of living. Yet the unity of the two currents was not permanent, as events soon were to prove.

The first signs that workers' councils were widely regarded as a means for attaining these objectives appeared early in 1956, several weeks before the strike of Poznan on June 28, 1956, which paved the way for the great changes of October of that year when Gomulka came to power. Some of the shortcomings of the "administrative" system had become so obvious that as early as the fall of 1955 the central committee of the Communist party recommended to the workers of the nationalized industrial plants that they seek out the sources of the troubles and make proposals to be considered in the elaboration of the new plan to cover the years from 1956 to 1960. (The official title of the Polish Communist Party is United Polish Workers' Party; we shall use this term or the expression "Communist Party" as an equivalent.) One of the centers from which new ideas emerged was the famous automobile plant (FSO) of Zeran with about 6000 workers.[12] There, long deliberations in the party organization in the plant, the plant committee (the union group), and in full assemblies of the workers and white-collar employees led to proposals that were later labeled "workers' autonomy." L. Gozdzik, secretary of the party cell in the Zeran plant and one of the driving forces behind the idea of the workers' councils, reports:

When we learned the facts [revealed in the report by Khrushchev to the 20th Party Congress in the Soviet Union] we understood what had happened to the Communist Party in Poland, our Comrades and later in the Yugoslav affair. Our eyes opened regarding the "nationalist rightist deviation" [the ousting of Gomulka in 1948] and the reasons which led to it. We started looking for ways to repair the damage . . . This was on the eve of the Party Activists' Conference in Warsaw in April . . . There . . . we said everything that was on our minds. This meeting was tumultuous . . . But this was the first real discussion after the period of silence and of lies; things reached a stage where many people in the room were horrified and almost fainted. This conference was followed by prolonged discussions in our midst . . . We examined the ways which would permit the working class to have the feeling that it was really administering the enterprise. Many ideas were agreed upon. Many differences appeared. Cautiously we proposed setting up a technical council capable of coordinating our efforts in the economic field . . . Then we thought that it would not be bad if we had in the plant a workers' council to direct the enterprise, to determine its economic administration and its organization and at the same time to guide it and make recommendations to the directors for execution. We examined this proposal, first in the party committee, then in the other meetings which in those days occurred frequently. The discussion was often stormy.[13]

Actually, two kinds of ideas were developed which led to two different institutions: the "experimental enterprises," and the workers' councils.

Each was a device for dealing with the larger problem of giving some degree of autonomy to the enterprises and providing some material incentive for efficiency. The "experimental enterprises" were engaged in "trying out new management techniques for interesting the staff and workers in efficiency by allowing them to share both in profits and in the responsibility for results." In most of these experiments, efficiency was measured by money profits and no longer by physical plan fulfillment. In some experimental firms, profits were worked out according to a special set of prices and according to strict cost-accounting rules, which included charging interest on all working and fixed capital.[14] A suggestion for the establishment of such experimental enterprises came as early as June 1956 from the workers of the J. Krasicki plant, while pressure for greater plant autonomy in general came from the VFM motorcycle factory in Warsaw which became one of the experimental enterprises. The plants chosen to be "experimental" were larger firms whose managements were considered of sufficient caliber to warrant being given greater autonomy than the rest. The experiment was intended to be limited in time and is now terminated. Although the most successful managerial methods of the experimental plants were to be applied on a larger scale, so far little seems to have been done.

The Poznan Strike of June 1956 gave powerful impetus to the drive for the establishment of workers' councils. Among the demands put forward by the striking workers was a call for "industrial democracy." The question of the degree of influence exerted by the Yugoslav developments on those in Poland with regard to the workers' councils has been widely discussed in Poland and is not easy to answer. Many Polish authors trace the origin of the councils back to those set up in Polish plants in 1944–1945, after the end of the Nazi occupation, which put abandoned plants back in operation. W. Domino in *Gos Pracy* of February 1, 1957 says: "The idea of the workers' councils was not dug out of ideological archives by some theoretician of the new principles of our political regime, nor transplanted from sunny Yugoslavia. The idea was reborn where it had existed, namely, in the conscience of the working class."[15] Giving the enterprise more autonomy meant having someone perform entrepreneurial functions in the industrial enterprise. Who was that to be? A return to private entrepreneurs was excluded by the internal and external power situation of the country, as well as by the Socialist ideology of most people involved in the events — including even the sharpest critics of the existing administrative system. To give the director the authority of the entrepreneur and the necessary material incentive to use it effectively would have made him in effect a private capitalist. Another argument used against this proposal was that, if the incentive was large enough to be effective, the outlay required would be too big for the poor country.[16] To put the union shop committees into the position of responsible managers was difficult because of the disdain in which the unions were held by most of the workers at the time. In the eyes of most workers, the unions had become another governmental authority concerned with "fulfilling the plan" rather than defending the interests of the workers. A widely used expression in Poland at the time referred to the unions as simply "the second government." Attempts on the basis of the resolutions of the seventh Plenary Session of the Communist Party Central Committee to enhance the authority of the shop committees of the unions failed because "the unions were much too compromised among the workers." One writer characterized the union shop committees as follows: "Under the title Shop Committee we understand usually a group of union functionaries which distinguish themselves by these main virtues: Loyalty and obeisance toward management, activity for plan fulfillment, with more or less indifference for the interests of the wage earner; they have a special position in the plant; namely, that of functionaries separated from the personnel and tied more closely to management than to the workers."[17] Workers' councils seemed to offer the best answer to the problem. Many plants set them up spontaneously — the first apparently was the automobile plant in Zeran — in different forms and with differing jurisdiction. They often had political ambitions. Reorganization of the state, the party, and the unions to free them from "bureaucratic control" was a widespread slogan. In the economic field, many councils attempted to translate into fact the propaganda phrase of the regime according to which the workers were "managers" of the enterprises. Some of the councils aimed at reducing waste, improving quality, and increasing productivity in the industrial plants. Vague ideas about profit sharing were widely accepted, and the economic efforts of the councils were expected to lead to an improvement of wages far beyond the concessions which the government made in April 1956 to reduce the tension in the factories.

When in July 1956, the party (and, in August, the unions) moved to satisfy the rising pressure of the workers for "the extension of workers' democracy in the plants" (expression used by the seventh Plenary Session of the Communist Party Central Committee in July 1956), events had passed beyond their powers of decision. The unions were attempting to channel the workers' movement into their union shop committees and had prepared a draft law intended to strengthen the position of the committees in the plants. This attempt was unsuccessful. With the rise of Wladyslaw Gomulka, the movement for workers' councils received support from above, since it was regarded as one of the elements in the popular move to overcome the centralistic and bureaucratic tendencies of the Stalinist legacy in Poland.[18] The supporters of the council idea were a political force that could be marshaled against the Stalinists within the party. Moreover, some groups hoped that the councils themselves might turn into new administrative units of the state, introducing a vital element of self-government which might undermine the centralist system.

When Gomulka came to power in October he declared:

> We must approve and welcome the initiative of the working class regarding a better organization of industrial management and working-class participation in the management of the enterprise . . . The leading organs of our economy, of our political life and of the state must work intensively to assist the initiative of the workers and to make more general — where this is possible — the proposed forms of organization.[19]

The objectives of workers' self-government were to be: "produce better, less expensively and more, in order to raise the standard of living of the workers and of the entire nation," solve difficulties such as excess personnel and excess of "administration," and reduce production costs. With the approval of the new party leadership, the number of workers' councils increased rapidly.

Functions of the councils. A decree, dated November 10, 1956, provided for the "extension of the rights of nationalized industrial enterprises." A law of November 19, 1956 set up rules and regulations regarding the workers' councils, while another law of the same date laid the foundations for the so-called "fund of the enterprise" for the year 1957. The first established the basis for decentralization in economic decision-making by giving the enterprises a greater degree of autonomy. Yet even at the height of the drive toward decentralization, the Polish firm had only modest powers. It has been said that it obtained only two additional freedoms: it was free to save raw materials, and to engage in so-called "side-line" activities, that is, activities beyond the scope of those provided for in the plan for the enterprise, with the profits derived from such activities having a direct and full effect on the profits of the enterprise and consequently on staff earnings. The fact that "side-line" activities remained outside the control of plan authorities led to the growth of several subsidiaries, often quite unrelated to the main business. Thus the Cegielski plant producing locomotives and tools went into the fabrication of Gramophones. The reference to the two freedoms may be an exaggeration; yet only by contrast with the previous system is it meaningful to speak of the autonomy of the enterprise.

The workers' council law provided for the institution of councils in three groups of nationalized industries — manufacturing, construction, and agriculture — if the majority of the employed workers of the enterprise wished to establish them. The councils, in the words of the law, "administer the enterprise which is national property, in behalf of the personnel." The councils were to have the following functions: (1) They determine the organization of the enterprise and establish its work regulations. (2) They advise on improvements of production, combat waste, and the like. (3) Within the limits of the collective agreement (concluded between an industry association and the corresponding union) and of governmental instructions to the enterprises, and with the approval of the shop committee of the union, they determine production norms, wage schedules, regulations on premiums, the distribution of the "fund of the enterprise," and, in particular, that part which is to be devoted to the staff. (4) Finally, they express their opinions about the activity of the enterprise and approve its balance sheet.

The "fund of the enterprise" — introduced as early as February 1955[20] but greatly expanded in November 1956 — consists of three items: (1) An amount equivalent to 1.5 per cent of the wage bill for all enterprises which achieve their planned profit. (For those who fail to do so, the contribution to the fund is reduced to 0.2 per cent of the wage bill.) (2) Half the profits obtained beyond the return provided for in the plan. (3) All profits from activities accessory to the plan — "side-line" activities. The law sets down certain rules about the destination of the fund — the maximum to be used for cash payments and the share that has to go to workers' housing and other social purposes. The distribution of the fund within the limits of the law is within the province of the council.

Theoretical implications of the council system. The introduction of the council system had far-reaching implications. The "model" of a council-administered economy[21] would provide for the councils to act as entrepreneurs within a framework to be set by central authority. As was pointed out in the preceding chapter, this model gives rise to a number of fundamental issues:

1) How to enforce observance of this framework by the enterprise;
2) How to provide a yardstick for rational decision-making by the enterprise;
3) How to provide incentives for the enterprise as a whole to serve economic progress;
4) How to provide incentives for the employees to act efficiently.

1) The problem of how to enforce the observance of the general objectives of economic planning — the framework of the operations of the individual enterprise — had been solved in Poland during the first phase of the Communist regime by tight administrative controls. The enterprise had been treated as a mere executory agency of the ministry. The economic plans established centrally by the government for each year were "broken down into a large number of directives which were, at least in principle, legally binding on the enterprises . . . The directives were usually numerous and pettifogging in detail, leaving managers too little opportunity to develop their own initiative." The decree of November 1956 on the extension of the rights of nationalized industrial enterprises reduced the number of problems on which directives could be issued to eight — total value of the output which the enterprise was to sell, the quantity of the most important items in the product-mix of the enterprise, the total wage bill, profits (or losses), the share of the profits to be turned over to the central (government) budget (or the subsidy to be obtained from it), the value of that part of the enterprise's investments which was to be financed by the central budget, the limits of capital repairs in the enterprise in terms of value, and the size of the working capital. Within the framework of the directives on these items, the enterprise was to make its own decisions. The Yugoslav council system went further than the Polish council in reducing the significance of administrative rules. The observance of the general framework is to be obtained in Yugoslavia primarily by a set of economic "instruments," essentially based upon incentives of the same type that a capitalistic economy employs. The plan is simply a statement of desirable objectives whose achievement depends upon the effectiveness of the incentives.

2) Neither Yugoslavia nor Poland has dared to go far in permitting the price system to function freely. Even at the height of the movement for economic decentralization, the Polish Economic Council, set up in the wake

of the October movement to advise the government on economic policies, rejected a system of "spontaneous price-formation beyond the control or influence of the state."[22] Price controls, particularly for producer goods, have been retained. Even though reforms carried out in 1960 have produced certain adjustments in price relationships that have made the price system more flexible and more realistic, this seems only temporary relief. The new prices, set in 1960, are to remain unchanged for several years;[23] as a device for the guidance of rational decision-making, they are thus likely to be decreasingly useful as time passes, even if it is admitted that the price reform improved the situation.

The fear of free prices is closely associated with the inflationary dangers confronting any nation embarking upon what has been called "hot-house industrialization"; Poland has not been free of this danger. Indeed, the issue of inflation was one of those involved in the tension between the "old-line" or Natolin group, which was in control prior to October 1956, and the more "liberal" party wing which came to power under Gomulka.[24] Controlled prices have been regarded as a method of repressing the danger of inflation. Moreover, the techniques of planning employed so far require the use of stable prices for the purpose of computation. Even if actual prices could be permitted to fluctuate and to adjust to changes in costs, the prices used by the planners in the making of the most important economic decisions would have to be kept artificially stable and consequently be different from the market prices.[25]

3) Under these circumstances, economic rationality can operate only as far as the price system — and the instructions from above — permit. Within these limits, the system requires that incentives be provided for the enterprise as such and that its employees exert themselves to obtain results that are favorable to the economy as a whole. At first sight, the distinction between the incentives to the enterprise and those applying to the employees may be bewildering. However, as a counterpart in the capitalistic economy, there is a difference between the interests of a company and those of its managers, its staff, and so forth.[26]

Following is an outline of the economic incentives applied in the management of state-owned industrial enterprises in Poland in 1960.[27]

I. Incentives acting on the enterprise as a whole
  A. Principles of financing
    1. Financing of stocks in some percentage (10–20%) from credits
    2. Fund of development of an enterprise
    3. Financing of small investments from the enterprise's own funds

    4. Different forms of bank credits, at different rates of interest
  B. Other incentives
    1. Prizes
    2. Fines for undue [incorrect] deliveries, and so forth
II. Incentives acting on the employees of enterprises
  A. On white-collar employees
    1. Salary (fixed, basic salary depending on position of employee)
    2. Premium (quarterly or monthly payment dependent on the improvement of the year's results of the enterprise)
    3. Reward (quarterly payment calculated annually dependent on the improvement of the year's results)
    4. Special rewards for inventions
  B. On workers
    1. Wage (per hour, per piece, and so forth)
    2. Premium (dependent on economies of raw materials or similar achievements — obtained by only certain workers)
    3. Reward (quarterly payment, calculated yearly, dependent on improvement of the year's results of the enterprise)
    4. Special rewards for inventions

A set of rules introduced in March 1958 made the contributions to the fund of the enterprise and thus the source of the incentives for the employees dependent upon the increase of the profits from year to year. The proportion of the profits that may be transferred into the fund grows with an increase in the excess of current profits over those of the preceding year. Conversely, a reduction in the rate of profit compared with the rate of the preceding year leads to a cut in the rate of the contribution to the fund.

Numerous flaws can be pointed out in this system. It rewards enterprises whose performance at the start is particularly poor and encourages the concealment of reserves. The search for a better solution continues. A counterpart of a somewhat different nature, in a capitalistic society, may be seen in the endeavor to prevent monopolistic profits.

4) Individual incentives are of three kinds: bonuses for white-collar workers, incentive-pay systems for manual workers, and participation in the results of the enterprise for both groups. This last item is labeled "reward" and appears in the outline under IIA.3 and IIB.3. Of these, the most significant has been the participation in the results of the enterprise.

Legislation requires that cash payments from the fund do not exceed 8.5 per cent of the wage bill of the enterprise; 25 per cent is to be devoted to workers' housing and general social purposes (welfare, vacation homes, and the like). As global figures for 1958 indicate, 69 per cent of the enterprise funds in industry has been devoted to bonuses and individual payments, 26 per cent to housing, and only less than 5 per cent to "social investment" in general.[28]

The limitation of the cash payments means that, at most, one thirteenth of the annual wage bill (that is, an additional monthly wage) can be paid out. Illegal wage payments, however, may have added to this proportion. They are reported to have run to nearly half a billion *zlotys* in 1958 (in addition to a total wage bill of 123 billion *zlotys*).[29]

The distribution of the bonuses among the employees has given rise to sharp debates. In some plants, the workers favored an egalitarian distribution: the same amount was to be paid to every employee with variations only positively for seniority, or negatively for absenteeism. In other plants, the bonus was figured as a percentage of base pay. Votes in the plants seem to indicate that most workers favor the first system. Opposition to an egalitarian distribution has pointed out that such a concept is at variance with the idea of material incentives which the new policy is said to favor. The professional economists, whose voice is highly respected in Poland, have in their large majority supported the incentive arguments. A modest degree of compromise seems to be established by the frequent practice of excluding from the distribution those workers found guilty of prolonged absenteeism, alcoholism, and lack of discipline. This, however, is no real solution. Both the limitation of the total amount of the bonus and the trend toward an egalitarian distribution tend to weaken the system's incentive effect. The size of the actual cash payments as a proportion of the wage bill seems to vary a good deal from enterprise to enterprise. In light industry in 1958, it is reported to have varied between 1 and 22 per cent.[30] Such variations would tend to strengthen the incentives.

In principle, this egalitarian trend should be counteracted by the premium-pay system whose introduction and spread are greatly favored by the regime. But it has been often opposed, openly or indirectly by the workers. Moreover, piece-rate norms have been set very loosely, so that workers have been overfulfilling them by 50 to 60 per cent in most industries, and even by 100 per cent in metalworking. "Little or nothing was done to tighten up the norms when labor-saving equipment was introduced."[31] Recent reforms may have brought about some improvement.

Altogether, therefore, the idea of incentives seems to have been respected more in principle than in fact.

The councils in operation. Since the law is silent on a great many issues of organization, practice has varied a good deal from plant to plant on such matters as the number of councillors to be elected, the organization of the elections, the election committee, and so on. The law does specify, however, that there is to be a presidium of the council — which, in effect, does most of the council work — and that its members serve without compensation, except for time lost. Moreover, wherever possible, two thirds of the council members must be manual workers (rather than white-collar employees). This regulation has actually been rarely observed. On the average, it is estimated that only half the council members are production workers; the remainder are white-collar employees, engineers, and technicians.[32] The proportion of workers is rather low on the often all-important council presidium, and since the establishment of councils is voluntary, only one third of all enterprises (but three quarters of all industrial enterprises excluding artisan establishments) have councils.[33]

From their very beginning, the councils suffered from the fact that their relationship to management was not clearly defined. In many cases, this relationship reflected differences in their quality and their objectives. The councils themselves complained about the fact that "the legislation . . . is insufficient and often contradictory." The council president of the M-5 plant in Wroclaw states: "So far the results of the activity of the workers' councils depend many times upon the goodwill of the director of the enterprise. The council ought to have wider jurisdiction regarding the decisions of the directors."[34]

With regard to the choice of the director and his main assistants, the law states (Art. 13) that "they are appointed and recalled by the proper state authority, in agreement with the workers' council." This may appear to give the council veto power, but the next sentence indicates that "the workers' council has the right to make proposals regarding the appointment and the recall of the director and his assistants." Similarly, even though the council is to make major policy decisions, the director alone may decide in urgent matters and merely inform the council of the decision at the next meeting (Art. 16). Moreover, the director has veto power over all council decisions which he regards as contrary to the law or to the plan. Appeal may then be taken to the responsible minister.

According to the law, the workers' council is to manage the enterprise in the name of the staff while the enterprise is national property (Art. 2 of the law on the workers' councils). As spelled out in the legislation, the term "management" meant that the council could express its views on the plan of the enterprise during the process of its formulation by higher authority and then translate the definitive plan into detailed decisions.

Clearly, this definition of the councils' role falls considerably short of the authority of management as understood in the West. From the beginning of the council experiment this fundamental ambiguity was created by the reluctance of the authorities to give the enterprises full autonomy. The central direction for construction materials in Poznan is reported to have said: "We do not recognize the workers' councils. The direction of the enterprise must carry out only the recommendations of the central direction." Even the experimental enterprises complained about their narrow supervision by the central directions. The competency of the councils was narrowly circumscribed by the limitations of the authority of the enterprise itself. A contradiction thus existed between the idea of the council as a managerial device and the reality of close supervision of the enterprise by higher authority.

No less significant was the contradiction between the objectives of the councils as seen by the intelligentsia and those the workers themselves had set. For the intellectuals and technicians, the councils were to be the managers of the enterprises and, at the same time, cornerstones of a new democratic order. They were, therefore, to concern themselves primarily with the long-run interests of the enterprise. The workers, however, favored the councils mainly in the hope that they could produce real wage increases in the immediate future. For them the councils were to represent their interests—their only real representation, as the unions had long ceased to be concerned.[35] This combination of two essentially divergent, if not contradictory, assignments in one organization proved impossible. Differences between the two views of the nature of the councils were inevitable. Indeed, the very measures they took for a long-range increase in productivity, and thereby of wages, accentuated the conflicts. The elimination of waste, the reduction of surplus labor, the struggle against pilfering, and the reorganization of the plants hurt a great many workers in the short run and caused, insofar as these measures were effective, a decline in the earnings of working-class families. Attempts to eliminate surplus labor—estimated variously at between 10 and 40 per cent of employment at a national average—ran into workers' opposition which gave the discredited unions an opportunity to stage a come-back. They appeared as defenders of working-class interests against the councils. The development of side-line production often appeared as the best compromise obtainable under the circumstances.

Failure to reform the wage structure often forced the councils to administer a system which was hard to defend from the point of view of fairness as well as efficiency. In particular, time and piece rates had grown far apart. Base pay was very low; in contrast, standards for piece rates had been set at very low levels. Skill differentials were insufficient, and piece rates frequently had been set for operations which could not be measured. As a result, highly skilled work was sometimes paid at lower rates than unskilled labor.

The maintenance of discipline in the workplace, the reduction of rejects, the maintenance of quality standards, and the struggle against drunkenness and absenteeism were also part of the council assignments. One of the sources of great disappointment for the supporters of the October movement was the fact that in 1957 absenteeism was greater than the year before. A report on the FSO works in Zeran indicates that on one given day almost one quarter of the work force was absent. On most of the issues, the council and at least some members of the labor force found themselves on opposite sides.

To the reluctance of the regime to give the enterprises real autonomy and to the rapidly developing cleavage between the intelligentsia and the working-class groups backing the councils must be added a third factor which prevented them from obtaining significant short-run results: the key to the success of an enterprise was frequently outside that enterprise. Breakdowns in the raw material supply, failures of electricity and transport, and delays in ministerial decisions were usually far more important factors in determining results than anything the councils could do. In the words of Professor Edward Lipinski: "As long as there are no changes independent from the councils, in the supply of raw material, in indispensable deliveries and in equipment, as long as cooperation is not organized in a rational fashion, it is impossible for the enterprises to function well. And if they cannot function well because of objective difficulties, no council will be able to change this." [36]

Given these highly unfavorable circumstances, the councils acquitted themselves rather well. Incompetent directors have been dismissed, excess manpower has been laid off or used in the development of new products, and the wage structure has been successfully rearranged in some plants. In other cases, they were reported to have given freer play to staff men with technical qualifications, to have reduced the number of rejects, or to have increased production. In-plant training of personnel under council sponsorship has contributed to an increase and an improvement of the production in the precision-instrument establishment, Swierczerski, in Warsaw. Exports now go to Belgium, Brazil, India, and China. A good deal of council effort was directed toward the elimination of waste in order to reduce production costs and increase profits. Less impressive are the achievements in the struggle against pilfering (which actually seems to have acquired a great economic significance),[37] absenteeism, and alcoholism.

There are also, of course, many cases in which the councils performed rather badly. Excessive spending on wages, failure to observe the rules regarding the distribution of the enterprise fund by the allocation of too large a proportion of the fund to cash payments, and insufficient emphasis on the reduction of production costs are among the criticisms most frequently heard. As time went on, the situation seems to have become worse rather than better.[38] Lack of pride in work, low work discipline, and irregular work attendance have been pointed out by many observers.[39]

The decline of the councils. The period during which the councils functioned with some degree of effectiveness was very brief. The internal contradictions of the system soon caused the movement to lose its impetus. In early 1957, Gomulka himself turned against the protagonists of the idea of making the councils fundamental factors in the economic and the political life of the country.

The idea of forming regional associations of workers' councils, and making them the cornerstones of a new, less dictatorial political and administrative system,[40] was rejected as early as February 1957 by Gomulka. Three months later the Communist leaders described the functions of the councils as "comanagement" rather than "management." Clearly, the political leadership was no longer in favor of giving them effective power, assuming that it had ever wished to do so. Yet, when in April 1958 Gomulka made a speech advocating the setting up of the "conference of workers' self-government," thus undermining the council system, this came as a surprise to most observers, even in Poland itself.

Gomulka stated that the workers "through their representatives have the right to participate in the management of their plants, that is, to supervise and control the activities of management."[41] He described it as an error to believe that "the plants are to be administered by the workers." At the same time, he declared that the institution of the workers' councils "is good, it has passed its first trials."

Workers' self-government, according to Gomulka, is a concept far wider than the workers' councils. In addition to the councils, the working class possessed its organizations in the form of the party and the unions. "These organizations cannot be kept out of the workers' self-government. A workers' self-government limited to the workers' councils alone is bound to limp. It must carry on an anemic life."

First, said Gomulka, this conception which limited workers' representation to the councils has caused councils and union committees in the plant to take opposite positions — the first dealing with managerial problems, while the tasks of the union shop committee "would be reduced to the handling of the problem of the interests of the workers." Even more important for Gomulka, it would seem, was a second consequence, flowing from the then existing system: "Limiting the workers' self-government to the workers' councils makes it more difficult for the plant committees of the party to assign to the party a leading role in the plant."

The tasks of the workers' self-government, according to the Communist leader, are twofold: organizational-technical and social-educational; that is, it must analyze production problems and mobilize the workers for the solution of these problems. To divide these two and refer the first to the councils and the second to the union shop committee is "unrealistic," according to Gomulka. "A clear proof is the short strikes which have taken place in a number of establishments over the distribution of the fund of the enterprise or rather because of the demand to make payments out of a nonexisting fund — nonexisting because the workers had not produced it."

Gomulka, therefore, announced a new system: In all plants, those with councils and those without, a new institution was to be created, a conference of workers' autonomy, or workers' self-government. It was to consist of all members of the workers' council, of the union shop committee, and of the party (cell) committee in the plant. This conference was to be superimposed on the workers' council so that the latter would become the executory organ of the conference. The presidium of the workers' council was to be enlarged to include the managing director of the plant, the chairman of the union shop committee, and a representative of the party cell. The conference would discuss all questions coming under the competency of the council and make decisions binding on the councils. Gomulka then went into considerable detail on the preparation for conference meetings to insure that all its members would be kept fully informed of all developments in the plant.

In establishments where no council existed, none was to be formed. The conference would then consist only of the union shop committee and the party cell committee which would jointly elect a subcommittee. This subcommittee would then perform the functions of the council, namely, to carry out the decisions of the conference.

The design of the conference makes it perfectly plain that the party cell was to assume control over the activities of the workers' council. As if to underline this fact, Ignacy Loga-Sowinski, chairman of the central committee of the trade union federation, expressed his support for Gomulka's stand in the following terms: "The Conference of Workers' autonomy, organized — as seems to me proper — *under the chairmanship of the Secretary of the Party cell* — could coordinate the activity of the Party organs, the unions and the Workers' Councils in order to associate the staff with the achievement of these tasks." [42] This statement, read together with the decision to forego the setting up of workers' councils wherever they did not yet exist, was widely interpreted as heralding the end of the workers' council experiment. By being submerged in the conference on workers' self-government, the councils were subordinated to the party cell and the union shop committee. A further decisive step was made in December 1958, when a new law on workers' controls was passed which clearly changed the assignments of the conference from managerial to supervisory. Only those matters remain within the exclusive province of the workers' self-government conference which "directly concern the interests of all the workers and are of a nature demanding discussion and a decision with trade union representatives . . . These matters include resolutions on the enterprise's work regulations, on the division of the work fund, decisions on the provisions of living quarters for workers and on the social and cultural facilities offered by the enterprise." [43] The general economic functions of the conference are reduced to advice and expression of opinions. "Workers' controls extend over the enterprise's economic activities as a whole, but may not interfere in its management." In the area of social problems directly affecting the welfare of the employees, the conference retains its prerogatives. The councils themselves remain agencies for the execution of conference decisions. The simultaneous introduction of councils in the departments of larger establishments brings them closer to the everyday problems of the workers, but accentuates the change in their character from managerial organs to agents of grievance handling — under the supervision of the party and the union.

Conclusions

The main reasons for the councils' decline can be summarized as follows:

1) They were rapidly developing into a political threat to the party and the regime. Propaganda at council elections had become frankly anti-Com-

munist in many plants, and they formed the cornerstone of a possible anti-party organization.

2) They had alternative potentials, and neither was acceptable to the regime. They could become the effective management of the nationalized enterprise, but the Communists were unwilling to let the enterprises have the kind of autonomy to which the councils were aspiring (or to let the market make the decisions on resource allocation which the regime wished to reserve for itself). Alternatively, the councils could become representatives of working-class interests, thus filling the vacuum caused by the unions' subservience to the regime and the management of the enterprises. This, again, would have created unacceptable political risks for the party. Moreover, an effective defense of workers' interests might have raised wages, reduced investment funds, and thus prevented the achievement of the regime's principal objective — the rapid industrialization of the country.

3) From the first days on, Gomulka and a number of other leaders of the party seem to have had little confidence in the technical ability of the councils as managers. For a short time they gave in to the mass drive in order to derive political gains from it. Gradually and increasingly, the term "supervision" rather than "management" (or the more modest "comanagement") was being used to describe the main council function. The law of December 20, 1958 regarding "workers' self-government" completed this evolution by turning the councils into advisory bodies on all economic, financial, and technical issues. There is a striking parallel between the Polish evolution and that of the French plant committees which also turned into mere advisory bodies on financial, economic, and technical matters and retained real power only on issues relating directly to the welfare of the workers.

The "meat crisis" of the fall of 1959 set the stage for further changes. Cuts in employment, the dismissal of surplus labor in the plants, cuts in investment, a reduction of the excessively ambitious growth rate provided for in the plans, and a tightening of work norms were to bring relief and reduce the tensions in the social fabric. "Irresponsibility and indiscipline led to over-employment, unauthorized investment, over-expenditure of the wage fund, excessive overtime and unjustified absenteeism. Corruption, embezzlement and theft were also common; with a majority of the workers hostile to Communism, it was almost inevitable that they should be." Thus reports the *London Economist,* November 5, 1960.

The main achievement of this reform period seems to have been in the area of work norms, although the attempts to eliminate excessive employment and reduce investment do not appear to have been very successful. New piece rates have been set, commonly at lower (but often fairer) levels. Central control over the disbursements from the enterprise fund and plant investments has been strengthened. Some temporary and partial measure of rationality has been introduced into the price structure. While central controls have been strengthened — in the sense that the statutes have been made more effective — decentralization as an objective has not been abandoned. But it is even more clear than in the early days of the council experiment that the regime is not prepared to accept the full implications of decentralized decision-making.[44] It continues to pursue the illusion that it can combine incompatible elements in an effectively functioning system.

Significantly, all these important events have occurred without reference to the councils which by now are definitely removed from the center of the stage.

CHAPTER VI

The Councils and the Labor Movement: Structural Problems

In the course of history and in different countries, the term "labor movement" has had different meanings. In the United States it ordinarily refers to the trade unions. It is possible that in an extended meaning some institutions affiliated with the unions are included, such as a workers' education bureau or a health institute. But these are simply creations of the unions, or specialized union activities, or forms of union service to the members. In most of Europe and in many other areas "labor movement" has a much wider meaning. It refers to the unions, of course, but also and equally to other organizations: political parties, mutual insurance organizations (*mutualités*), cooperatives, and so forth. All these and many others are included in the meaning of the term.

The Concept of the Labor Movement

Among these branches of the movement the most important, in addition to the unions, are the political parties (such as the British Labour Party, the Scandinavian Social-Democratic parties, and others). In some countries the union-party relationship poses delicate problems. In France there is officially no organic connection between the unions and any political party. Indeed, the virtue of such separation is regarded as so self-evident that the accusation of having violated the tradition is one of the main weapons which the non-Communist unions have used against the CGT. Yet there are fairly intimate, though unofficial and nonformalized, relations between CGT-FO (Confédération Générale du Travail-Force Ouvrière) and the Socialist Party, as there have been between the CFTC (Confédération Française des Travailleurs Chrétiens) and the Catholic Party (MRP—Mouvement Républicain Populaire), though these ties seem to have loosened a good deal since the early fifties. The nature of the relations between the largest federation, the CGT, and the Communist Party is more difficult to establish in detail since it is kept confidential. Yet few observers would deny the fact that they work far more closely together than the other trade union centers and the political parties with which they are in sympathy. Indeed, in both the FO and CFTC there are prohibitions against the holding of political offices by at least some of the union officials. No such prohibition exists in the CGT.

In Germany the traditional division of the unions according to their political or religious philosophies has given way, since 1945, to a united, nonpartisan trade union movement. This has created some stresses and strains. The majority of the union membership and particularly of the "noncommissioned officers" in the union hierarchy belong to the Social Democratic Party (SPD) as do the presidents of all the industrial unions. The supporters of the Christian-Democratic Party (CDU) form the most substantial minority within the movement, while the Communists are a poor third in mass support. However, the CDU is the leading government party, while the SPD is a minority of the electorate. This divergence of the relationship of forces within the unions and the general electorate has required continual accommodation between the two parties in the union movement and particularly within the leadership of the trade union federation (DGB).

Social-Democrats hold the majority of the top positions in the DGB, and CDU supporters, the rest. None of the top positions in either the DGB or in any of its sixteen affiliated unions is in the hands of avowed Communists. Some Socialists accuse their leaders of having been too accommodating toward the former Christian trade unionists. If they have been generous, it paid off in June 1956, when a breakaway movement of some Catholic trade unionists met only hostile response among the non-Socialist labor leaders in the DGB. The splinter movement has remained completely ineffective with the sole exception of the overwhelmingly Catholic Saar district.

In Yugoslavia and Poland the authority of the Communist Party is of course supreme within the state as well as within the labor movement.

It is indeed so great that the relations between the party and the unions have all the characteristics of party control. This, as well as party control over all expressions of organized working-class opinion, is one of the fundamentals of the situation and presents insuperable difficulties for the creation of independent, genuine representation of the workers in the plant.

The relationship between unions and political parties is thus different from case to case among the four countries considered in this study. In every one of them, however, it is also different from the American situation in that political loyalties play a far greater role in Europe than they do in the United States. The antipolitical tradition of the French labor movement would appear in this respect to come closest to the American pattern, but the difference in fact and motivation is considerable. The greater intensity of political loyalty in Europe may be simply an expression of the far stronger feeling of class solidarity. It gives to unions and political parties (and often to many other institutions) a joint basis in commonly held beliefs and social values. This fact does not prevent rivalries among organizations and, of course, leaders; but the common belonging to a working class or, even more, to a "labor movement" in the wider meaning of the concept establishes and maintains ties among the competitive organizations and leaders with the result that contradictory relationships of competition and solidarity exist and are stable. Many symptoms indicate, however, that there has been a decline of class feeling and class loyalty since World War II and that consequently the discipline which the "labor movement" can impose upon its affiliates and members is decreasing in effectiveness.

We are thus confronted with at least three elements in the labor movement: councils, unions, and political parties of the workers. The different and changing relationships among them need further examination.[1] In this context the organizational system of the unions is of primary importance. We now turn to a rapid survey of union structures in the four countries.

Union Structure

French union structure is exceedingly complex and varied. Most general statements need ample qualification in order to be applicable to any given union or situation. With this reservation it is probably correct to say that the *syndicat* is the lowest organization provided for in most union constitutions. It is of a highly varied nature. Perhaps the most frequent type is that of an amalgamation of smaller groups for an industry, a craft, or combination of crafts, in a town, city, or small region. The *syndicats* are thus, in a very rough sense, similar to the German local organization. In the Christian miners' union the *syndicat* normally extends over a coal basin (except that in larger basins there may be two *syndicats* in each pit, but more frequently in a group of pits combined in a concession). In the metal-fabricating industry the *syndicat* is often what American parlance would describe as an amalgamated craft union with a coverage extending over several towns and many plants.

The clerical, supervisory, or technical workers belong either to a separate union federation, the "Confédération Générale des Cadres" (CGC), or to a separate national *syndicat* of this group within the industrial union of the industry to which they belong. FO permits a double affiliation; the group may belong at the same time for instance to the miners' union and to a national engineers' union.[2]

The next higher level is usually a regional organization which, however, in most cases performs no other function than to allow for regional representatives to be elected to higher union bodies. The supreme union body is a general congress which usually meets every year or every two years. The delegates to the congress are elected by the *syndicats*. In between congresses a national council functions; it is elected either by the *syndicats* or by regional groupings of *syndicats*. In addition to the national council there is a national bureau elected by the congress.

Thus, the basic and most important organization is the *syndicat*. Indeed, the national union may properly be described as a federation of *syndicats*. The *syndicat* administers itself through delegate bodies or general membership meetings. The latter are held mainly in times of crisis or for election purposes. It is the *syndicat*, not the national union, which is usually represented at the congress of the trade union federation. In the non-Communist unions, however, the *syndicat* is usually not in close contact with the individual members. This is left to a so-called "section" which, however, is rarely mentioned in the constitutions.

The section may, but need not, coincide with union membership in a plant or a separate craft. In many cases it consists of union members in several plants — that is, a craft group smaller than that of the *syndicat*, but still covering several plants. The section is the group which acts in the name of the *syndicat* in behalf of the individual member (that is, it engages in all the activities that the *syndicat* sponsors). In fact this makes the *syndicat* an intermediary organization among the members, the section, and the upper echelons of the union hierarchy. However, the section does not make policy but only carries out decisions of the *syndicat* or of the national union.

Some of the functions which the section performs in behalf of the *syndicat* within the plant were set out in earlier discussions.

The CGT prefers to have one *syndicat* in a plant. Some of the other unions may break it up into several in large plants. The CFTC, for instance, may have one *syndicat* for the clerical workers, another for engineers and technicians, and a third for production workers.[3] The CGT would combine all these into one *syndicat,* if all subordinate organizations were to carry out the wishes of the top leadership. However, this is not the case. At the same time, the CGT tends to give each plant a *syndicat* rather than a section. It thus comes closer to American organization systems in this respect than do other French unions.

German unions are based on local organizations (*Ortsverwaltung*) which assemble their members according to their place of residence, not their place of work. Thus the metalworkers' union has a local in an industrial town which may combine the metalworkers employed in a dozen different plants belonging to a dozen different firms. The local organization may be limited to workers of a particular plant if it so happens that this is the only metal-working plant in the area. In this case the local organization coincides in scope with a shop organization American style. This, however, is the result of accident rather than design. Moreover, the local organization is merely an administrative, not a policy-making, unit. Union policies are decided on much higher levels.

Union structure extends upwards from the local organization to the *Geschäftsstelle* whose director is usually appointed by the executive committee of the national union. This is normally the lowest level of full-time union officers. A *Geschäftsstelle* may take care of many local organizations. In the coal-miners' union, for instance, there are some 18 *Geschäftsstellen* in the Ruhr, the area between Cologne and Dortmund, with almost 1000 local organizations, and outside the Ruhr, 19 *Geschäftsstellen,* and about 700 local unions.[4] The *Geschäftsstelle* may have a professional staff — a legal expert, collective bargaining technicians, works council specialists, and so forth — and it may maintain branch offices in a number of important towns in its area.

The next higher level is the *Bezirk* (district) under a full-time director appointed by the national executive committee of the union. The director is often assisted by a fairly large staff whose services are available to *Geschäftsstellen* in the *Bezirk*. The 18 *Geschäftsstellen* of the miners' union in the Ruhr are grouped into 5 districts, and the 19 *Geschäftsstellen* outside the

Ruhr belong to 4 districts. The districts report in turn to the national executive committee. The district and *Geschäftsstellen* directors used to be elected by delegate meetings in their respective areas, but this system has changed — partly in a move toward greater centralization of union administration in Germany and partly to remove Communist union officers from the lower echelons.

Where union shop organization once existed, as it did in the pit-organization of the miners, it has been abandoned in favor of a residence-based organization. Instead — increasingly in the last few years — the German unions have tended to send out roots from their local organization downward into the shops. This has been done by the *Gewerkschaftsausschuss im Betrieb* (union shop committee). This committee consists of those members of the executive committee of a local who work in the plant in question plus, ex officio, the chairman and vice-chairman of the works council, provided they are union members. In the metal industry, however, the members of the shop committee are elected by all members of unions affiliated with the DGB (not merely the metalworkers' union). Candidates must have been union members for at least 52 weeks and have paid their dues accordingly. Those works councillors who are union members are also union shop representatives. On the average, there is a committee member for every 20 to 25 union members; in plants with less than 20 members, one shop representative is to be elected. If there are more than four shop stewards in a plant, a chairman or an executive committee is chosen. Every month there is a joint meeting of the executive committee with the leaders of the local organization, and the union shop representatives are instructed to cooperate closely with those works councillors who are union members.

Yugoslav and Polish trade unions have roughly the same structure and can, therefore, be discussed together. Predominantly, they are industrial unions, although a few craft associations exist as well; together they form a confederation of trade unions. In Yugoslavia, in 1954, there were 22 industrial federations and 11 other occupational associations. The basic unit of the union is the branch, which takes on a variety of forms. Most often there is a trade union branch in a given enterprise. In large enterprises separate branches may be formed in independent departments. Then a committee is formed for the entire enterprise which integrates and coordinates the work of the departmental branches. It is thus either a plant organization or a departmental organization of the union which is in most direct contact with the workers.[5] For small plants, artisan workshops, and the like of the same industry, a joint branch is usually formed. The employees of state, cultural, and educational institutions are organized in professional rather than industrial associations, and their branches are territorial in nature.

The next higher organizations in the union hierarchy are local and district committees which supervise the activities of the branches in their areas. In Yugoslavia the role of these intermediary organizations has been greatly enhanced by the emphasis which the new organization of public administration placed upon municipalities and districts. As a result the intermediary union bodies have been reorganized in three layers: a district trade union council supervising the work of the trade union committees of several municipalities, each of which has a municipal committee to supervise the activities of the local trade union councils in each of the localities or villages forming the municipality. However, the municipality which is the seat of the public district administration (the "capital" of the district) has at the same time a municipal committee and a district council. On the other hand, districts with little industrial development have only a district council which performs the functions of the municipal committees. The branches report to the municipal committees. The district councils are the lowest union body directly represented at the congresses of the trade union confederation held every four years.

Above the district councils there are committees of the different republics and the national executive committee of the individual union.

With the exception of Germany, where there is only a union shop committee but no union organization in the shop, the unions in the four countries are based upon union shop organizations which, to some extent, form the basis of the union structure. The weakness of the French union and the peculiar and highly restricted role of the Polish and Yugoslav unions in the industrial relations systems of their countries are important facts to be kept in mind in everything that follows.

Unions and Council Elections

What are the relations between councils and unions? One aspect of this problem relates to union functions in council elections. A summary of the council election systems in presented in Table 3.

Both shop stewards (*délégués du personnel*) and members of the plant committee in France are elected on lists established by the "most representative unions" in the plant. While the original legislation provided for elections by majority, a change made in 1947 introduced proportional

TABLE 3. Election systems of works councils in the four countries

Description	France	Germany	Poland	Yugoslavia
Type of representation	Joint: plant committee Separate: shop stewards	Joint: 1) Supervisory boards — codetermination 2) economic committees Separate: works council	Joint: works council (meets with director)	Joint: works council management board (with director)
Type of election	One college for blue-collar and lower white-collar; another for engineers, department heads, and foremen	Separate for blue- and white-collar unless both groups decide for joint election	Joint	Joint
Special group representation	In larger firms at least one seat for engineers and department heads; otherwise to be arranged by employer and trade union agreement	One white-collar representative required if council has three members	Two thirds to be blue-collar	Sponsors of lists of candidates are invited to preserve the ratio of production workers to others. At least three fourths of management board must consist of production workers
Term of office	Two years	Two years	Indefinite	One year, but extended to two years.
Nominations	First election round by unions; second round by groups of proponents and unions	Outgoing council and other groups particularly unions. Unions appoint workers' members of supervisory boards in codetermination	Groups of proponents	Trade unions and other groups of proponents
Right to vote	Age eighteen, and six months with firm	Age eighteen, and civic rights	All employees	All employees who have right to vote in political elections
Who can be elected	Age twenty-one, and one year in firm	Right to vote in political elections; one year in firm	Indefinite	All employees who have right to vote in political elections

representation with two rounds of elections. If in the first round fewer than half the eligible voters take part in the election, then a second election takes place; in the second round new candidates can be nominated, and nominations need not be made by unions alone. Since the highest court (Cour de Cassation) has decided that blank or invalid ballots are not to be counted in determining whether half the voters have taken part in the election, second rounds have become more frequent, and the influence of the unions on the elections has consequently diminished.

If a candidate nominated by a union has been elected, the union retains a certain measure of control over him during his two-year term of office, and the union has the right to propose his recall. To be effective, this proposal must be confirmed by the majority of the voters in the group (white-collar, manual workers, and so forth) in which the particular candidate was originally elected.

The safety delegates in the mines are also chosen by a system of proportional representation. The candidates are usually nominated by the unions. In some industries the health and safety committees are subcommittees of the plant committee and elected by the latter.

Union influence is somewhat enhanced by the right of each "most representative union" in the plant to name a delegate who is entitled to take part in the meetings of the committee. If several unions are represented in the plant, and they belong to one or several confederations, it is the latter that are entitled to send delegates. This information comes from a ministerial circular of July 31, 1946. A major issue developed with regard to union representation in central plant committees because the law was silent on this. After lower courts had decided against union representation, the highest court (Cour de Cassation), on October 9, 1958, reversed the lower-court decision.

German workers' councils are elected every other year on the basis of lists usually proposed by the outgoing council and often with the assistance of the union local concerned. The law permits any group which obtains a certain number of signatures to propose a list of candidates. Normally, however, this is done by the council and union jointly unless a major conflict has arisen within the plant. In many cases such a conflict has resulted in the introduction of a Communist-inspired list.

The preparation of the works council election is one of the main tasks of the union shop committee. Thus, among the "directives" of the metalworkers' industrial union (I.G. Metall) for the shop committee members is the "working out of the election slates . . . for the elections to the works council and to the board of supervision [of the company] according to the works constitution law under the direction of the local [union] . . . [*Ortsverwaltung*]."

The nonpartisan character of the new German trade unions has made it impossible in most cases for the union leadership to undertake an open campaign against Communist penetration of the works council. This has led to political parties being involved in the election campaign.

Since the enactment of the works constitution law, the question of whether wage earners and salaried employees should vote on a joint list or separately has assumed major importance. As we have mentioned, a first vote of the two groups separately has to decide whether or not joint elections are to be held. Only if both groups so decide can a joint election be held. The campaign over this issue usually hinges on the presence or degree of influence of the German Salaried Employees' Union (DAG).

When the German unions were reconstituted after World War II, the white-collar employees were to be organized in unions that were to be part of the DGB. As in the past, the gap between white-collar employees and manual workers often proved too great. White-collar employees usually feel vastly superior socially and intellectually to their blue-collar colleagues. In a common organization with manual workers, the white-collar employees fear that their special status and interest will be neglected or submerged as a result of the greater number of manual workers. German legislation contributes to this feeling of separateness by making substantial differences in layoff procedure, dismissal pay, and compensation in the case of sickness between white-collar employees and manual workers. (The German branch of the International Business Machines Corporation abolished these distinctions on its own in 1958 — a new departure in German industrial relations which many German employers seem to have resented.) The DAG, splitting off from the DGB, expressed these feelings of separateness. In many industries a majority of the organized white-collar workers remained in DGB unions: yet, there is a sharp rivalry between DGB unions and the DAG, which often expresses itself in competitive works council election lists.

Occasionally, two or three DGB unions are represented in a plant. This may lead to separate, if not competitive, lists in the strict sense of the word, but the unions frown upon such splitting of union votes and recommend that joint interunion lists be established instead.

Where union influence is very slight or absent, works council elections may not be held at all, even though the plant is entitled to them under the law. Thus the I.G. Metall reports that in 1957 only 7392 plants in the industry held such elections as compared with 7426 in 1955, even though the number of eligible plants had increased.[6]

Union influence upon the works councils may be approximately gauged by the proportion of works council members who are union members. This is not the same as the proportion elected upon union lists, because union members also appear on so-called name lists, that is, lists sponsored not by any union but by groups of employees. In 1957 the I.G. Metall reported that 81.1 per cent of the works council members belonged to the union as compared with 78.1 per cent two years before. Since union membership in the industry is estimated at only half those eligible to vote, union influence obviously extends considerably beyond dues-paying membership. Of the 18.9 per cent of the council members who were not members of the I.G. Metall, only 4.9 per cent — about one fourth — were organized in non-DGB unions.

The union prepares the elections by discussions in the union shop committee and membership meetings with the participation of officers of the local union organization. Wherever possible, union membership meetings are held in the plants after the slate has been prepared in order to present the candidates. Furthermore, general workers' meetings are held where the union-sponsored candidates are encouraged to participate in the discussions. In general, the unions devote a good deal of their energy to the preparation of the council elections.

In Poland the unions played no significant part in the council elections. This is understandable in view of the fact that the councils partly arose in opposition to the unions, which had ceased to have the workers' confidence. In fact, the councils here and there performed some of the duties which the unions failed to assume or carry out effectively. But this is (or was) a departure from the intended scheme of things and led to considerable rivalry. The solution to the problem of competition was to subordinate the councils to the party rather than to the unions. In principle, since the council was to perform managerial functions, the union would have had to negotiate with the council rather than cooperate with it. By combining councils, union branch, and party cell in one conference of workers' self-government, the system turns bargaining, if it survives at all, into an internal affair of the conference.

The Yugoslav unions, probably somewhat less discredited than their Polish counterparts, propose lists of candidates for the council elections. Such lists may also be sponsored by the employees of the plant or by groups of them. The number of sponsors must be at least one tenth of the number of employees in enterprises up to 500 employees, and at least equal to the number of council members due for election in enterprises having more than 500 employees. Incomplete lists may be proposed; the number of required sponsors is then reduced to half. The lists must contain the names of production workers in the same proportion as that represented by the labor force of the enterprise.[7]

The Council and the Parties

A discussion of the relationship between workers' representation in the plant and the political parties must start by emphasizing two essential propositions:

1) Workers' councils — in the generic sense in which we have been using the term — do not maintain the same kind of relations with all political parties. They, or various groups within the councils, make distinctions among the parties. These distinctions vitally affect council-party relations.

2) The role of political parties in public life, in the labor movements, and in the life of the plant differs from country to country. It varies among the four countries examined in this study and between them and the United States. In addition, it has undergone considerable changes over time.

Traditionally, European labor organizations and workers' institutions have been closely associated with some political parties, neutral toward very few, and sharply opposed to others. In some countries, unions have been organizationally integrated into political parties; in others, union leaders have at the same time been members and often leaders of political parties. The variety of relationships makes generalization difficult, but the fact is indisputable that the unions in the four countries considered in this volume maintain highly differentiated relations with different parties. The apparent exception to this is France where some currents of organized labor, following the Charter of Amiens,[8] have emphasized their independence from all political organizations and at the same time criticized the CGT because of its control by the Communist Party. But this exception is more one of form than of substance. True, the leadership of the CGT-FO is prohibited by tradition and constitutional rules from accepting political office, while the CGT is without doubt controlled by members of the Communist Party. Yet no informed observer would quarrel with the assertion that the CGT-FO is on friendly terms with the Socialist Party — or, at present, since they are divided, Socialist parties — while the CFTC is closer to the MRP (Mouvement Républicain Populaire, a Catholic party) than to any other political organization, though relations have cooled off considerably since the de Gaulle government came into office.

Within a given council, members of various unions or of various political parties may be represented. This, of course, is more likely to occur in France and Germany than in Poland, though some non-Communist parties of a highly peculiar nature are tolerated in that country, while multi-party representation is impossible at least overtly in the one-party system of Yugoslavia. Given the preponderant role played by the Communist Party in the working class of France, it is only reasonable to expect that Communists form the largest single group of councillors. Little direct evidence of this is however available.

Special mention must be made of the role of party groups in German council elections and activities.

It is true that political activity in the plant is prohibited by German law, even for works councillors. Yet, both major German parties which are represented in the leadership of the DGB — the Social Democrats (SPD) and the Christian Democratic Union (CDU) — maintain party groups within the unions. Those of the SPD are called "social working communities" (*Soziale Arbeitsgemeinschaften*); the CDU groups function under the label "social committees" (*Sozial-Ausschüsse*). In addition, other less official ideological groups of these parties function in some plants. Thus in 1952 a "Christian-social fellowship in the DGB" was formed for the promotion of the Christian point of view within the unions. (More church-inspired is the Catholic Labor Federation, KAB.) It published a bimonthly *Gesellschaftspolitische Kommentare* (Comments on Social Policy).[9] Undoubtedly the Communist Party and probably some other political groups have also established organizations in the plants. Since the Communist Party was declared "illegal" in 1956, the party cells in the plants have gone "underground." However, ample information on Communist activity in the plants is available. Thus the German Industry Institute reported in December 1959 that the union federation of the Eastern Zone (FDGB, Freier Deutscher Gewerkschaftsbund) had sent many "instructors" into West German, particularly the Ruhr area, to work with Communist works councillors in the plants. The number of Communist plant bulletins is said to have increased from 156 at the end of 1958 to 287 at the end of 1959, including 63 publications in the mines.

The SPD operates through full-fledged party groups in the plants but has had certain hesitations. The party, perhaps out of fear of being accused of splitting the unions, has not had any consistent policy on the activities of such organizations. (Siggi Neumann, chief organizer of the SPD plant groups, resigned from his party post in 1954 and joined the headquarters staff of the metalworkers' union. Herbert Wehner, vice-president of the SPD, is an ardent advocate of close relations between SPD and the unions.) Given, however, the considerable strength of the Social Democratic Party among the West German workers and particularly in the lower and middle echelons of the union hierarchy, informal SPD groups may be said to exist in any case in many, if not most, West German plants.

A special department for party work in the plants exists at SPD headquarters and publishes a brief monthly *Arbeit und Freiheit* (Work and Freedom). In addition there are some party publications for specific plants. For example, both SPD and CDU publish papers in the Opel factory at Rüsselsheim near Frankfurt.

While an open attempt made in 1955 to split the unions and re-establish a special Christian labor federation has been unsuccessful outside the Saar area (membership of the splinter group is estimated at 190,000), the unions have been rather unhappy about the formation of ideological groups within their midst. Yet they have not dared to move openly against the CDU groups out of fear of endangering their unified organizations. A symptom of this somewhat ambiguous attitude is a resolution adopted by the DGB Congress of 1959. It dealt in vague terms with the relationship between DGB and CDU trade unionists and requested that "special interests and special organizations be abandoned in favor of mutual interests." A proposal to declare membership in the Catholic KAB incompatible with union membership was turned down.

This ambiguity expresses the fact that party groups have played and continue to play important roles within the unions, particularly with regard to the councils. This was the case during the first decade following World War II. Since the unions had become officially nonpartisan, they found it difficult if not impossible to intervene in the council elections to keep Communists out. This task was therefore left to the political parties who dealt with it either by way of their groups in the plants or their local organizations. In many cases this simply meant that the union or council leaders in their struggle against Communist attempts to win seats on the councils designated themselves as members of their respective parties rather than as union or council leaders. Yet this necessity to use the protective coloration of the parties gave the latter considerable status in the representation of the workers in the plant. During the first postwar years, both the workers and the general public examined the outcome of workers' council elections to a considerable extent from the point of view of partisan politics. This is still the case in Austria.

Some caution was — and perhaps still is — required in interpreting the election results. As was mentioned above, the Communists were in fact often the only effective opposition to existing councils. When dissatisfaction with the council arose among the workers in a plant, Communists were likely to exploit the situation and to offer their services to those who wished to remove the incumbents. A vote for the Communist-sponsored or at least Communist-supported opposition list, therefore, did not by any means necessarily imply that the worker favored the Communist Party. In almost all cases no other equally practicable way existed to change the council or to stir up the council leaders. This explains to a large extent the sporadic, highly localized, and sudden election victories of the Communist-sponsored lists for the workers' councils which the newspapers reported in sensational fashion. The outstanding case occurred in the Westfalenhütte in Dortmund where the Communists obtained 16 out of 25 seats. These cases must be distinguished from some of the more consistent and steady successes which Communists scored in a few plants of the Ruhr where they had genuine support. On the whole, the decline of the West German Communist movement has tended to reduce the incidence of both the spectacular and the more regular Communist council successes. Most elections are now mainly a test of the degree of union rather than of political influence, and the unions report carefully the percentage of unionists among the elected councillors.

Nevertheless, political parties continue to exert influence upon the councils. This is less the result of a generally high political interest in the public at large, which all observers agree does not exist in Germany of recent years, but rather of the political involvement of the small group which participates actively in the work of the unions and of the councils. Among these "activists" political loyalties are relatively intense, and they tend to form the cohesive ties among the elite which dominates the social life of the plant. The weight of political loyalties has been reduced, even as far as these elites are concerned, by the loss of influence of the labor movement in general and of the SPD in particular in the West German Republic. No other ideology, however, has taken its place, at least in the older generation whose influence predominates in the councils. For the younger men and women private life has become paramount so that this generation plays a less than proportionate part in the councils, as well as in the unions and the party. For those who matter in council affairs, even if not for those whom they represent, political affiliation is still a key fact in the formation of formal or informal groups. Party influence on council policies is less significant. The leading councillors are practical men of considerable experience, and they are rarely in need of party advice on matters within their province. Party influence thus is exerted mainly in the choice of personnel and by way of the personal contact which party members maintain among themselves.

CHAPTER VII

Problems of the Bargaining Councils

The various organizational arrangements of union-council relations give some indication of the lack of ease that exists between them. The American system in which workers' representation in the plant is a union function has the advantage of simplicity. It reduces the problem essentially to one between different levels of the same organization. This simple solution has not been adopted very widely outside the United States. Why not?

In France and (throughout most of modern history) in Germany, unionism has been traditionally divided according to political or religious philosophies. This has created a need for a representative organ of all the workers in the plant which could rise above the level of union divisions. As a result, workers' plant representation must to some extent be independent of the unions.

In some form or other this kind of problem exists in every country where unionism is less than 100 per cent. Then the issue is one of who is entitled to speak in behalf of a work group which consists only partly of union members. In the United States the solution adopted by the Wagner Act and retained in subsequent labor legislation is the majority principle. An attempt at introducing it in France failed before it had really gotten under way in 1936. The principle of the "most representative union" applied to the French trade union situation would have given control, in most cases, to the CGT, then under Socialist majority leadership. This was impossible under the political conditions. Public opinion was ill-disposed toward an attempt to "impose the trade unionism of a particular politico-philosophic persuasion upon workers following a different philosophy." In 1936 the minority would have been represented by Catholic workers under the inspiration of the CFTC. After 1948 majority representation would have imposed control by the Communist-dominated CGT upon Catholics and the Socialists of FO.

Under the circumstances, the solution finally adopted was that of having shop stewards and later plant committees elected under a system of proportional representation. This device ensures some degree of cooperation between the different union (and nonunion) elements represented.

A similar scheme was adopted in Germany for like reasons. In the Weimar Republic the German trade union movement was divided into several competitive federations. The largest was the Socialist-inspired ADGB — called "free trade unions" — with affiliated craft and industrial unions; the second in size was the Catholic federation. Other unions of varying strength were pan-German, Communist, and "Hirsch-Duncker" — a democratic business unionism inspired by the example of British craft unions in the middle of the nineteenth century.[1] This division was overcome by the establishment of a united trade union federation in 1949. Yet the tradition of proportional representation has survived. (As will be remembered, the new Catholic splinter organization has not reached any significance outside the Saar district.) It is true that for some time Communist candidates played a not inconspicuous part in works council elections; it is conceivable that unions and government would have been united in eliminating Communist representation in the councils by a system of majority representation had this been their only concern.

The political cleavage is, however, not the only one which confronts councils in France and, to a rather insignificant extent, in Germany. The social distance separating white-collar employees and manual workers plus the further distinctions among the various white-collar groups — particularly the *Beamte,* the higher functionary of public administration — requires the creation of a special channel of expression for each group. This is provided by the possible arrangement of separate election colleges for the two main groups in combination with proportional representation. The latter creates the possibility that relatively small subgroups among the white-collar employees can be represented in the council.

The council thus becomes an integrating device where the unions themselves either are not able to provide such integration in their own midst or are not strong enough to prevent minority groups from having a voice in the chapter. In other words, councils appear to be means for giving effective voice to the work force of a plant where there is either a low degree of union organization or strong divisions among the unions and powerful opposition to the suppression of minority representation.

This is not a fully satisfactory explanation, for, in 1936 and in 1945, the French CGT undoubtedly surpassed the relative degree of union strength of the American unions at the time when they were granted the principle of majority representation. The same holds true for the German DGB after its reconstitution following World War II. Nevertheless, proportional representation continued in Germany and France in the election of workers' representatives in the plant.

The reasons probably lie deeper than mere numbers. They are related, first of all, to the traditional intensity of political, religious, and ideological feelings in Germany and France. Moreover, the currents representing these feelings are organized bodies, backed commonly by more or less powerful political parties. The unorganized workers whose representation was handed over by the Wagner Act to the unions wherever the latter had a majority suffered not only from lack of organized power, but, in addition, had no direct relationship to a political party which would speak in their behalf. Leon Blum could not deprive the CFTC of collective bargaining rights even though the CGT undoubtedly represented a vast majority of the organized and (in 1936) unorganized French workers in industry; the CFTC was organized and had influential political support in the Church-supported political parties. Nor could the Weimar coalition in which the Catholic Center Party played a key role permit the ADGB to force the Catholic unions of Germany out of the bargaining process during the interwar period.

The political climate of both countries added to this respect for minority groups — at the expense of union effectiveness. Where a multiplicity of parties and proportional representation existed in the political life of the nation, it was not easy to expel pluralism and proportional representation from the industrial relations systems. After 1948, pluralism became a defensive argument for all non-Communist unions in France against the overwhelming power of the Communist-controlled CGT. Once again political considerations prevailed over the requirements of union effectiveness.

In Germany the substitution of workers' councils for union shop organizations was facilitated by historical accident. As was pointed out earlier, the German unions were still engaged in major battles for their recognition when World War I broke out. In the overwhelming majority of the plants, union representation hardly existed or had to carry on clandestine activities. The protection which the Auxiliary Service Law of 1916 offered the union spokesmen in the plant was, therefore, gratefully received by the labor organizations. But in the long run the legalized council system meant that the unions were cut off from the plants and the rank and file. The grant of recognition by public authority — first the Auxiliary Service Law, then the works council legislation — proved in some ways a case of Greeks bearing gifts to the unions.

Union-Council Rivalry

The danger of union-council rivalry was realized as soon as the revolutionary movement of 1918–19 threatened to turn the councils into competitive organizations. Also, in sharp contradiction to the fear of revolutionary trends in the councils, the danger of their being motivated by "plant egoism" emerged. Karl Legien — then the outstanding spokesman of the German trade unions — speaking before the union representatives as early as February 1919 said, "The works councils are not an effective organization; they split the unity of the trade . . . All existing laws of solidarity cease to exist for them, everyone is invited to take what he can get."[2] Plant egoism has several meanings. It refers, for example, to the attempts of councillors to use their political influence to obtain orders for the plant to keep employees working. Primarily, however, plant egoism describes a heightened feeling of solidarity between council and management which the unions fear may ultimately lead to the formation of "yellow" or "company" unions (or in any case may weaken the cohesion and combativeness of the union). In the days of divided unionism in Germany this fear was strongest among the Socialists since the programs of the Christian and Hirsch-Duncker unions favored union-management cooperation in the spirit of the council legislation of the twenties. Today plant egoism is regarded as a threat by the now unified unions. A somewhat related problem is that of special council aggressiveness in enterprises run by Social-Democrats. Klenner refers to this problem in two variants: public enterprises run by labor representatives (Social-Democrats) and the so-called *Tendenzbetriebe* (enterprises of the party, the unions, and in a certain sense of social insurance). "The interests of the employed workers and white-collar employees are often opposed to those of the enterprise itself," says Klenner. Works councillors, in the interest of the people whom they represent, try to obtain particular favors from labor managers of the *Tendenzbetriebe*. Another form of plant egoism, finally, consists in the conclusion of plant contracts which go so far beyond the terms of the collective agreements that the union, by contrast, appears ineffective.

Management has, on the whole, shown a distinct preference for the existing industrial relations system, not only because it contributed to the lack of aggressiveness which the German unions demonstrated for some time during the post-World War II period, but also because it reduced the danger of competition based upon excessively low wage standards without imposing full wage uniformity. By far the most important reasons for the unions' "reasonable behavior" were, however, the fear of unemployment enhanced by the constant influx of millions of refugees, and — at the same time — fear of inflation, as well as the almost irreparable loss of self-confidence suffered as a result of the defeat of the movement by Hitler. The organizational problem discussed above may, however, prove significant in the long run while the other factors may lose their impact with the passing of time.

The most fateful consequence of the existence of the councils, from the point of view of the unions, is the distance between the labor organizations and the rank and file which the council often creates. Complaints about the lack of contact between councils and unions or even about cases of mutual hostility are also not infrequent. Fears to that effect were articulated during the interwar period while the council legislation was being drafted as well as shortly afterwards.[3] Even though the revolutionary element whose activities after World War I greatly accentuated these fears had been weakened (or in many cases eliminated), the problem of the interposition of the council between the union and the worker still remained. It is the inevitable result of the fact that the functions of the union of most immediate concern to the worker are in the hands of the councils rather than the union.[4]

True, the influence in favor of the workers which the council can exert within the plant largely depends in the last resort upon the power of the union, but this connection is not always obvious to the worker. For, in his daily needs, the councillor commonly provides the remedy without recourse to the union. The report of the metalworkers' union (I.G. Metall) for the year 1956–57, although obviously inclined not to dwell too extensively upon the shortcomings of the system, has this to say:

> Our report for 1954–55 referred to the differences in the attitude of the works councillors. The largest part of them operates in close contact with the unions, particularly the local officers. In the plants of these councillors disputes rarely arise which have to be carried forward to the last recourse.
>
> Another group of works councillors refers to the union only at a point when they cannot get along with the employer. But then the issue in dispute can usually no longer be clarified by negotiations, the points of view are crystallized, [and] reasons of prestige make acceptable solutions difficult to obtain. Such disputes are then commonly brought before the courts so that appeal must be made to the federal labor court.
>
> Other councillors, finally, in the case of conflicts with the employers, choose

from the beginning the line of least resistance and allow themselves to be frightened by the employers. These councillors push out into marginal areas of social policy in the plant; their activity exhausts itself in the administration of cafeterias or of other welfare institutions . . . This last group of councillors rarely finds a real contact with the local [union] office although most members of these works councils are organized in the unions; they fail to understand their function as well as the possibilities of the unions to aid and assist them in their work.

In the case of a strike, the distance between the effective wage rate and that which the union aims at may be such that the relevance of the union demand for the improvement of the worker's standard is far from being clear to him. Attempts to use the "effectiveness clauses,"[5] in order to enhance the relevance of collective bargaining for the effective wage rates, have so far not met with much success. Strikes have also become rather infrequent in Germany. Undeniably, the workers' primary loyalty does not always belong to a union whose main operations, as far as they are visible to the rank and file, occur at what the Germans call the "level above the plant."

In the development of modern industrial relations the consequences of the problems created by the existence of the works councils are serious indeed. Once the councils have come into being and taken over the wide range of functions assigned to them by law and circumstances, the unions are forced out of their "natural" sphere of activity, even though the political divisions, which may originally have called forth the councils, have ceased to exist.

A summary of council functions is presented in Table 4. As the table indicates, German works councils are the only ones in the four countries concerned which engage in substantial collective bargaining activity.* As to grievance handling, both Germany and France offer a bewildering variety of procedures. The shop stewards in France and the councils in Germany are only one of several avenues available to the worker. It is perhaps not more than a mild overstatement that the effectiveness of grievance handling is in reverse proportion to the number of available grievance procedures. As is the case in collective bargaining, rivalry between plant representation and the union is less likely to occur in France than in Germany in the area of grievance handling. The emergence of union shop committees in Germany and their desire to be involved in grievance handling are clear indications of union-council rivalry in this field.

It has been said that the councils opened the doors for the unions to many firms which otherwise might have remained closed.[6] This might have

* The Italian trade unions have been complaining more and more about plantwide agreements concluded by the *Commissioni Interne*.

applied to the complaint commissions during World War I, the precursors of the councils. Immediately after both world wars, however, few firms would have dared close their doors to the unions which in those days of storm were often the protectors of the enterprise against radical moves on one hand, dismantling and deterioration on the other. The cases in which the councils facilitated unionization can at most have been few and far between.

The Future of German Unionism

The implications of the rebirth of the councils after World War II for the development and the future of German trade unionism are tremendous. The original driving force of the German labor movement — the struggle for equality and union recognition — which inspired the movement during its heroic age, is spent. Dedication to a distant Socialist objective holds out little appeal to the German worker, judging by the unanimous reports of observers as well as by the abandonment of most of the traditional Socialist slogans by the German Social Democratic Party at its congress in 1959.[7] Wholehearted concern with the everyday needs of their members in the plant might have served as a new focus of union activity. In effect, this would have been the long-delayed adjustment of the German unions to the conditions confronting them in the middle of the twentieth century. This solution, however, was blocked by the existence of the works councils which had pre-empted this function. The conservative trend of the West German federal government under Chancellor Konrad Adenauer did not give the Socialist union leaders many openings for exerting their influence on high-level policies. With limited functions in the plant and little power to influence government decisions, German unions have been seeking status and function in the system of industrial relations. The lack of a present-day focus of activity and the longing for the relatively simple tasks and objectives of the past are evident in the fact that German labor is a strongly tradition-bound social group. A glance at many labor and Socialist journals will confirm this observation.

Some of the industrial unions, particularly the metalworkers, seem to have realized the problem or at least some aspects of it. The establishment of union groups in the plants, attempts to inject these groups into the process of grievance handling, efforts to subject the councils to union control, the slogan of "collective bargaining close to the plant" (*betriebsnahe*) — all these are symptoms of a growing realization that the councils deprive the unions of a vital sphere of action. But an existing, functioning institution such as

TABLE 4. Council functions in the four countries

Issues	France	Germany	Poland	Yugoslavia
Bargaining	Union; council not involved.	Council (supplementary to collective agreement)	[a]	[a]
Grievance handling	Shop stewards and labor courts. Plant committee sometimes (in fact, not under the law).	Council and labor courts, often with assistance of local union. Staff council in federal government service.	Union branch[b]	Management boards as court of appeal against the director's decision[b]
Social issues	Councils administer social works	Full codetermination; often in fact administration of social works.	"Conference on workers' self-government" decides	Council and management board decide
Technical issues	Councils suggest and advise	Councils suggest and advise	Highly limited influence	Limited influence, though council and board have power to decide
Economic and financial issues	Councils have the right to be informed and to make suggestions. Not effective. In nationalized enterprises union represented on supervisory board. Two members on board of private share companies, with consultative status.	Economic committee has right to be informed. In codetermination industries employees and union represented on supervisory board.	Responsibility in law; not effective in fact.	Full responsibility in law; highly limited effectiveness in fact.
Personnel management	Consultative	Part veto, part consultative on hiring and firing. Consultative on dismissals (except for managerial personnel).	Conference on workers' self-government has varying degrees of effective influence.	Considerable, though varying, influence on discipline; less influence, varying from region to region and plant to plant, on other matters.

[a] Under the law the union is supposed to engage in bargaining and grievance handling; in fact, it does so only rarely; to the extent to which there is bargaining it is carried on within the council or between council and director.

[b] Various alternative means of grievance handling are available; no data exist as to the frequency with which each is being used.

the council is not easily induced to commit suicide; nor are the employers likely to assist the union in its efforts to substitute itself for the council. The council is "indigenous" to the plant, while the union is an "outsider." Concessions made to the councils are revocable; those embodied in collective agreements with the unions are legally binding. The prospects are that the unions will have a bitter struggle ahead of them if they wish to revise an entire chapter in the history of German industrial relations.

What is involved is the transfer to the unions of at least some, if not most, of the functions which the councils now perform in the areas of bargaining and grievance handling. This requires a fundamental change of union organization so that union groups in the plant can form the base of union structure. The gap between contract wages and contractually determined working conditions on one hand, and those effective in the plant on the other, would have to be narrowed considerably or preferably eliminated altogether. It is obvious that such changes would be exceedingly difficult to make. Yet, without them the German unions are highly limited.

What functions the councils could perform, were such a reform to be carried out, is a moot question. The transfer of the bargaining functions, including grievance handling, to the union would leave the council the nonbargaining tasks, primarily the administration of the welfare agencies in the plant. It is difficult to judge whether this assignment and other duties of a nonbargaining nature would suffice to keep the councils alive.

An alternative would be to make the council, as it is, part and parcel of the union (that is, turn the council into the plant representation of the union). This would involve the introduction of some selection system such as the majority principle United States style. The workers would choose a council; if the council were elected on a union slate it would represent all the employees whether union members or not, and the union would retain disciplinary powers over the council members representing the union. If the union list were rejected, either no council or a nonunion council would be elected. In that case the union would regard the plant as nonunionized, just as in the parallel case in the United States. (This may be criticized as United States "ethnocentrism," and perhaps rightly so. Yet, I believe that many German unionists would not disagree with the proposals outlined above.)

French Shop Stewards

The objection might be made that French unions, though based upon union sections in the plant, have hardly succeeded in obtaining the place in the life of the worker which the German unions have acquired, even though the councils separate them from the rank and file. Obviously, the existence of union groups in the plant and their readiness to perform the tasks of bargaining and grievance handling are necessary but not sufficient conditions for effective unionism. Union power is an indispensable prerequisite.

In the case of Germany it is only a minor oversimplification to state that the unions are lacking in power because the councils are too influential. For the French shop stewards, the opposite holds true: their significance is impaired by the unions' lack of power. As representatives of the union in the plant, the shop stewards share the fate of the union; the stewards' influence in the plant moves in unison with the strength of the unions.

The very existence of the stewards on a broad scale has its origin in one of the great explosions of union growth which are characteristic of French trade unionism: the rise of the Popular Front government in 1936. It is significant that the institution of the shop stewards that had come into being during World War I — under a Socialist Minister of Munitions, Albert Thomas — "lapsed with the decline of unionism following the war." [8] The rapid weakening of the unions in the last few years prior to World War II was reflected in the decline and finally in the disappearance of the stewards. Officially, elected stewards were to be replaced by stewards appointed by the most representative unions; few such appointments were made in fact. Under the Vichy government new systems of plant representation were to be created. These, too, remained on paper. They were revived by an act of legislation after World War II, again a period of high labor influence. Once again the subsequent decline of the stewards kept pace with the diminishing power of the unions.

Fundamentally, therefore, the problem is that of the inability of French trade unionism to maintain its power. Union membership, union influence, and the status of the stewards — as well as many other institutions of the industrial relations system — rise and fall in rapid fluctuations. The most obvious fact is the violent change in union membership; for instance, membership for 1939 was a small fraction of that for 1936, and the figure for 1959 far below that of either 1945 or 1936. Another index is the drop in the amount of union dues in terms of the average wage: over the last century dues have dropped from the equivalent of 120 working hours to that of eight working hours per year.[9]

To examine the reasons for the lack of stability in French union growth and of union power in general would lead far beyond the limits set for this study. Suffice it to say that in the author's view the main reasons must be sought in the nature of French economic and particularly industrial development. In any case, it is not the system of industrial relations, but rather the weakness of union organization which seems responsible for the ineffectiveness of the shop stewards and for the large number of enterprises without them.

French Plant Committees

As to the plant committees, the key to their fate has been in the political arena. Political divisions continue unabated in the French labor movement and make effective union activity exceedingly difficult.[10] The leading union federation is a political outcast, and its power has been greatly reduced. It has tended to use the committees as its own instrument and as the instrument of the Communist Party which dominates the CGT. Union authority over the shop committees has thus been greatly impaired, and this has been one of the main reasons for the committees' decline.

In the early stages of their life, the CGT devoted a good deal of attention to the committees. They were to serve partly as instruments of economic recovery which the Communists then regarded as one of their prime objectives, to serve partly as power bases for the CGT and the party, which was then represented in the government. Following the party line, Benôit Frachon, one of the outstanding CGT figures, described the committees in 1946 as "motive forces of economic recovery, sometimes against the will of reactionary employers who were sabotaging production for political reasons."[11] At the same time, the CGT metalworkers' union urged the activists of the union to "fortify themselves against the 'legalistic' myopia which, in closing their horizon, would lead them to act only within the closed terrain of the law and obtain only what it grants, exclusively by the means which it envisions." The Communist Party then held various economic ministries in the government. The unions and the committees served to carry out the policies laid down by the ministers in behalf of the party. "To produce first and to raise demands afterwards" was the fundamental party line.

When, in 1947, the Communist Party went into opposition, this policy changed into one of sharp hostility toward the government and radical advocacy of immediate wage improvements. During the major strikes of 1947 and 1948 the plant committees were used by the CGT as strike committees. They also were assigned a new role — "to paralyze the effort of those who are leading the country to ruin, to chaos, to unemployment, to foreign domination and to war for the American expansionists."[12] The former advocacy of higher productivity to which the committees were to devote themselves was abandoned as well: "In a capitalist regime and especially with reactionary governments . . . increasing productivity means increasing the profits of capitalists and the misery of workers . . . Among those who pretend that under present conditions increasing productivity will increase wages, some are themselves fooled. But most of those who say that, the politician-lackeys of the American billionaires and their agents in the labor movement, are fakers trying to fool others."[13]

At the same time the committees served as instruments of the Communist Party's political policies. "Again and again," reports Val Lorwin, "the plant committees have been 'mobilized' against the political enemies of the CGT and the Party. A convention of CGT plant committeemen promised to 'mobilize the committees against the American imperialists' plan of enslavement,' that is, the Marshall Plan. Against the Schuman Plan, the CGT urged its committeemen to 'mobilize themselves for the creation in all enterprises of committees of defense of our industry and of the peace.' The committees were to settle the war in Korea, bring the French army out of Indo-China, and ban the atom bomb."

Such a use of the committees was basically contrary to the purposes for which they had been instituted. It is difficult to be categoric in one's conclusions since many factors contributed to the decline of the committees, including the hostility of large parts of French management and the weakening of French unionism in general. Yet, the misuse of the plant committee by the Communists served as a convenient pretext for those French employers who were eager to get rid of this potential threat to their power. For the Communist Party, however, the committees had become "expendable" after 1947. The party was engaged in a bitter struggle against the regime and no longer was concerned with cooperation within the enterprise. The primary purpose to which the committees were put was to support the political campaigns of the party.

This has remained the main assignment of the committees in the eyes of the Communist Party. As long as the majority of the organized French workers maintains their loyalty to a party which is fundamentally hostile to the regime, no system of cooperation in the plant is likely to be successful. Under these circumstances workers' representation in the plant, insofar as it exists at all, is bound to be an organ of conflict rather than of cooperation.

CHAPTER VIII

Problems of the Managerial Councils

Union-council relationships in either Poland or Yugoslavia present a very different picture from that prevailing in the West. In both countries unions operate under a number of serious handicaps.

The Weakness of Unionism

The fundamental problem the unions of Poland and Yugoslavia face is one they have in common with all relatively poor countries attempting to foster rapid economic growth: the necessity of investing a large portion of their scant economic resources clashes head-on with their mission to increase wages and thereby consumption. The more rapid the economic growth, the sharper is the conflict between its requirements and those of effective unionism. In Poland as well as in Yugoslavia this conflict is apparent in every aspect of social and political life. It is at the bottom of the "dictatorship over the proletariat" as well as of the uncertain role which the unions play in the industrial relations systems of the two countries. Instead of being advocates of labor demands toward the economy, the unions have been turned into instruments of the government in its search for as large a volume of capital formation as possible.[1]

A Socialist regime creates additional problems for the union. Classic Socialist theory has been at a loss to determine the place of unions in a collectivized economy. Presented in conventional Marxian terms the problem was simply that unions were instruments of the workers' resistance to capitalistic exploitation; with the transfer of the ownership of the means of production to the community, exploitation was bound to disappear and with it the main *raison d'être* of the unions. This may have been fallacious reasoning even accepting the premises: unions perform many functions — grievance handling, for one — which need not disappear with the end of capitalism. Nor is it inconceivable that the majority in a collectivized economy "exploits" or "oppresses" a minority. Yet as long as exploitation was by definition excluded from a Socialist society, Socialist theory found no easy solution for the problem of union functions beyond the decline of capitalism.

In actual practice the democratic Socialist movement has found an escape from this dilemma: in the British and French nationalized enterprises collective bargaining has not been abandoned but proceeds undisturbed by the change from private to public ownership — apart from relatively minor adjustments in the form of bargaining. Indeed in the British legislation instituting the nationalized enterprises, the nationalized enterprises are given the legal obligation to bargain collectively with their employees' unions, while no such obligation exists under the law in Great Britain for any other enterprise. The orthodox reply has been that while there are some Socialist elements in Britain and France, these countries are still predominantly capitalistic. Yet none of the Communist-controlled countries has dared dissolve the unions; instead they have put them under government control.

Unionism does not seem to be necessarily the product of capitalism, but rather a concomitant of modern industry.[2] It is thus not difficult to conceive of unions operating effectively in a Socialist society. In fact, this may well be one test by which the degree (or absence) of totalitarian control in a Socialist society might be determined.

In Yugoslavia and for a short period in Poland, another element affected the problem — namely, the system of workers' management of the enterprise. To the extent to which the unions and the councils both represent the workers in the plant, union-management negotiations on the plant level would mean bargaining between two sets of representatives of the same group. This seems often to be regarded as a decisive argument against the existence of unions in a system of workers' management. The Yugoslavs themselves seem to think so. "In a certain sense, at the present time," says a report of the Information Service Yugoslavia, "it is still difficult to delineate the tasks of Trade Unions and activities of Workers' Councils in enterprises." And later in the same report: "Trade Unions are no longer protectors of the interests of individual workers or working collectives against a certain organized power, since in this sense in the Yugoslav factories there is nothing workers should be protected against." Yet, this need not necessarily be a decisive argument. It is quite conceivable that a group of people can elect two sets of representatives for different purposes — for example, a school board and a municipal council. The two may engage in effective bargaining, get into conflicts with each other as a result of the different assignments they have, and solve their problems by a compromise. It is perhaps more difficult to imagine serious strikes occurring under such a system, but even this is not impossible: internal cleavages of the constituency may cause one part to strike against the other. Such a strike may have peculiar aspects that distinguish it from other strikes, but it would not be altogether unique. A recent subway strike in New York had as its base this kind of conflict between two (or several) groups of employees, and there have been many other similar experiences in this country and elsewhere.

It is less the Socialist character of the economy or the system of workers' management which gives Polish and Yugoslav unionism its peculiar characteristics (though these elements may contribute to them) and more the desire for hothouse industrialization.[3] The restraint on effective representation of the workers' immediate interests originates primarily in the desire of the regime to keep down current consumption for the purpose of rapid capital formation.[4] As a result, unions in Poland and Yugoslavia have lost the confidence of their members. The workers' council movement in Poland was, to a considerable extent, the result of the workers' disappointment with the unions and an attempt to create new institutions to perform the neglected functions. Even in Yugoslavia where the councils were created by the regime and intended to be merely managerial devices, many employees and council members endeavored to use them essentially for union functions. Only gradually and imperfectly did the managerial functions of the councils take precedence over their (unintended) activity as grievance and bargaining agencies.

Unions and managerial councils thus became competitive. It was partly to avoid this competition — in which the unions did not fare too well — that the Gomulka regime forced the councils into a "merger" with union branch and party cell in the plant, a combination in which the council was submerged by the other two. In Yugoslavia, where the councils are government-sponsored, the Polish "remedy" was not available. Instead an attempt was made to re-establish the foundering unions by renewing their leading personnel. One of the best men of the regime, Vukmanovitch-Tempo, was put at the head of the trade union federation. This has tended to revitalize the unions to some extent; but as long as the fundamental problems of the "take-off" period of economic development are not solved, no real or permanent solution to the problem of trade unionism is likely to be found. Conceivably, however, economic progress may produce a situation in which the pressures on the unions can be somewhat relaxed, and thus some degree of real trade union activity may in due course be admitted.[5]

In the meantime, the regimes in both countries are eager to preserve at least the outward forms of conventional trade union activity. But this is not easy. Collective bargaining in any real sense of the word does not exist. The wage scales, established by the workers' council and reviewed by it after comments by the employees have been received, are submitted for approval to the union as well as the municipality. There may be some semblance of bargaining in this process, with the council and the union being the bargaining partners, but it is not at all unlikely that in this particular arrangement the conventional roles will be reversed: The councils, though representing management, favor higher wage rates; the unions, though officially the spokesman of the employees, advocate restraint. This may be so particularly in those cases in which wage rates in one plant may be threatening to get "out of line" and produce upward movements in other plants in the same area or the same industry.[6] In the process of wage determination the councils and the unions may thus appear as opponents, with the council most often closer to the employees and their interests than the unions.

Grievance handling is primarily in the hands of the managerial hierarchy of the enterprise, including the managing board and the director. Employees may take up grievances with the union branch, and the latter is entitled to take to arbitration grievances of significance beyond the scope of a single enterprise. This, however, is rarely done.

> Workers can also appeal to the trade union for assistance. According to a recent survey, trade union committees in 57 districts received nearly 32,000 complaints and applications from workers in 1958 and 1959, while the Central Council of Trade Unions received more than 9000. Nevertheless, intervention by trade union bodies in individual disputes is still somewhat exceptional and according to some sources not always very vigorous. For example, the report of the labor inspectorate of Slovenia for 1956 . . . states that out of 5407 dismissal proposals submitted to the trade union committees for approval (in accordance with the legislation in force at the time) only 869 (or 16 per cent) were turned down. According to the same report, the reasons behind these dismissals would have been far more closely scrutinised by the commune arbitration boards which, under the earlier regulations, dealt with workers' appeals.[7]

In the field of discipline—where the director is the highest authority "while work is in progress"—a disciplinary committee is the first appeal instance. One of its three members is appointed by the union branch, while the other two, including the chairman, are appointed by the council. A further appeal may be taken to a disciplinary court of the local people's committee consisting of two members of the committee and one union representative. The union may then defend the worker. Few cases seem to reach this court. At the most, the union role in grievance handling and in cases of discipline may be said to be subsidiary. Professor John T. Dunlop thus describes the activity of the local union branches: "[It] seek[s] to get a larger proportion of the employees interested in the enterprise and in workers' council activities; it may initiate meetings of particular departments to discuss the problems of the enterprise, increased productivity, and the achievement of the enterprise's output goals. It seeks to emphasize the interests of workers in one plant in common with those of other workers and the local community. It will emphasize the need for new equipment, community housing, and other community social needs in the disbursement of funds."[8] It is understandable, then, that handling of discipline in Yugoslav plants has been described as too severe.[9]

The councils are, therefore, likely to be closer to the union rank and file than the unions themselves, and closer even than the local union branches. In many, if not most, instances the councils are better unions than the unions themselves. Syndicalistic tendencies are thus a constant, often latent, problem for economic growth. The role of the party, under the circumstances, becomes paramount for the successful functioning of the system.

The Party

In Poland and Yugoslavia, the party (that is, the Communist Party) is the ultimate source of all power, even if its role is sometimes not apparent to the uninitiated observer. The control by the Communist Party of the trade unions and all other organizations of the working class is a fundamental principle of communism. The literature on this is voluminous. It may be sufficient, however, to point out that during the early phases of the international labor movement the primary role of the party was universally accepted by the Marxians. Unions and parties met together in the international Socialist congresses, and the unions were affiliated to the International Workingmen's Association (First International). The fourth congress of that international (Basel, 1869) adopted a resolution requesting the general council of the international to "bring about an international association of the trade unions." The First International failed to carry out this resolution, and even the Second International did not fully implement it until shortly before World War I. The Communist International then returned at least for some time to the spirit embodied in the organizational system of the First International. The statutes adopted by the Second Congress of the Communist International read: "The trade unions who have accepted the Communist platform and are united on an international scale under the control of the Executive Committee of the Communist International form Trade Union Sections of the Communist International." [10] The revised program (1958) of the "Union of Communists of Yugoslavia" (the official name of the Yugoslav Communist Party) uses such terms as these: "The Communists are not giving up their leading social role. On the contrary, the socialist consciousness is in the long run playing a decisive role in the settlement of differences in the socialist development . . . the Communists will continue to struggle to ensure that the key positions of state authority, upon which the further development of the socialist society and the protection of that society against the attacks of various, internal and external, anti-Socialist forces is depending, will be in firm revolutionary hands." Indeed, the Communist Party is the only source of power even when other parties are permitted to exist and participate in the elections to state office as in the case of Poland. For these tolerated quasi-parties do not really aspire to power — which must be the ultimate aim of any genuine political party — but rather to public confirmation of that share in the minor appurtenances of influence which the Communist Party is willing to allot to them.

The party cell in the plant thus represents the only openly organized, genuine political organization of the country, and therefore of the state as well. Since the party also controls the unions which most frequently propose the list of candidates for the council elections, party members are in most circumstances likely to hold the leading roles in the union branch and council. When, during the council elections in Poland, it appeared that the party might not be able to control the councils, the political leadership of the country set a rapid end to the movement.

Control of the councils is in most cases obtained by the simple fact that only the Communists in the plant are capable of concerted action, while the opponents disperse their votes making them ineffective. More important is the general feeling of futility that pervades the potential opposition in any totalitarian regime once the powers that be are firmly established. Anti- or non-Communist workers normally do not regard council elections as an occasion to demonstrate their hostility toward the regime, simply because no anti-Communist consequence of practical significance would follow from even the most glorious election victory of their side. The fact that the Polish council elections for a brief moment threatened to take on the characteristics of an anti-Communist plebiscite among the workers indicates that the regime just emerging from the great shakeup of the Communist world was not then regarded by the workers as irresistibly powerful.

The main concern of the workers in the council elections is commonly practical rather than political. They want council members who are capable of increasing the income of the plant and of defending their interests and thus raising employee incomes. This objective is in immediate conflict with the desire of the party cell to control the council politically under two conditions — insofar as party representatives happen to be technically incompetent council members, and the party wishes to curtail current consumption in favor of investment. These conflicts do exist, but the number of Communists on the councils is hardly the key to party influence. Even a numerically small party representation speaks with great authority, far greater than the numbers would warrant because the party and the state ultimately enforce the will of the party group on the council.[11]

Yet, though the power of the party and of the state is ready to back up the authority of the party members on the council, the issue involved would have to be serious indeed to warrant open intervention of party or government agencies beyond the liberal limits which the law sets for such action. For every act of this kind invalidates the very meaning of the entire system of workers' self-government and casts doubt upon the seriousness of the party's intentions in establishing the system. Open, outside intervention, therefore, is a weapon to be used sparingly, and even concealed forms of party intervention — for instance, by way of the union which in turn is controlled by the party — must be applied with caution if the workers are not to be distrustful of the regime's intentions.

To go too far in the other direction and withdraw party control altogether may be no less consequential. In the absence of guidance and supervision from central or regional party headquarters, the restraints upon consumption built into the system might easily prove ineffective against the powerful urge for higher living standards among the workers. This force may be so strong that the party and union groups in the plant might be swept along in a common drive for higher wages as was the case in the miners' sit-down strike in Slovenia. In such a situation higher party levels may have to intervene.

At any given time, therefore, a balance has to be struck between the necessity (from the regime's point of view) to maintain party control of the plant and in particular of the workers' representation in the plant, and on the other hand the wish to give some real meaning to workers' self-government and, consequently, to the workers' councils. The greater the moral authority of the party, the further it can afford to go in the direction of real workers' self-government. The Polish Communist Party, a small minority in an overwhelmingly anti-Communist country, is compelled to exert closer supervision over the party branches and the council in the plant. With much larger popular support, the Yugoslav Communists have dared to go further toward a more decentralized decision-making system while, of course, still retaining potential or real control of the essentials. As a result, the council experiment was rapidly terminated in Poland, while it continued to develop, although with occasional setbacks, in Yugoslavia.

This issue is closely bound up with that of the relative degree of autonomy given to the plant within the framework of the economic system. Of necessity, the workers' council cannot have more self-determination than the plant enjoys. Given all other circumstances, plant autonomy will be the greater the more rapidly the gap between the aspirations of the workers and reality closes, which means, primarily, the more rapidly per capita incomes are growing. On this score, too, the lack of success of the council experiment in Poland and the relative progress in Yugoslavia become comprehensible. On the opposite side, the greater autonomy of the plant in Yugoslavia may have contributed to the economic progress of the country since the council experiment got under way in the period 1950–52.

Can party control over the councils ever be completely abandoned? In the strict sense of the word, this seems inconceivable. Since the party is the state, to abandon party control would imply withdrawing the state from influence upon the operations of the enterprise, that is, of the councils. In a meaningful way such a withdrawal seems beyond the range of possibility for the predictable future. The forms and the degree of party intervention, however, may change; indeed, it is safe to predict that they will change just as they have undergone alterations over the last few years. The direction of this evolution will depend on many circumstances — domestic and international. One possibility is that acts of intervention may become less frequent, less sharp, and less harsh as time goes on if achievements narrow the gap between expectations and reality. In other words, the totalitarian dictatorship would become less totalitarian, the rules more general, intervention less brutal and unpredictable as the economy progresses and the need decreases to keep consumption at or near starvation levels for the sake of releasing resources for capital formation. But such a prediction rests on pure speculation as well as on the assumption that the dictatorship serves an outside purpose, that of rapid industrialization, and is not simply maintained for its own sake. In any case, for the present, tension between the council system and absolute party control, between the objective of establishing self-government in the plant and dictatorial rule of social life, is built into the fabric of Yugoslavia.

Workers' Participation in Management

In the four countries considered in this study attempts have been made in different degrees to provide for some means by which the workers may have a share in the management of the enterprise. Only in a limited sense, however, can these attempts be described as experiments in industrial democracy. They do not envisage the direct participation of all the workers in business management as the early advocates of the workers' control proposed, but rather participation by delegation (by the election of councils and other representative bodies to participate in managerial decision-making). Direct industrial democracy — comparable to the direct political democracy of some Swiss cantons — may be said to exist, at least in theory, in some small Yugoslav enterprises where all employees function as members of the council. In a modern, fair-sized industrial plant, such a form of management is of course impossible, given the size of the labor force and the complexities of administering a larger enterprise.

Industrial democracy by delegation is less easily distinguished from collective bargaining than direct democracy. The differences are mainly twofold: collective bargaining is a pressure-group activity, while the council shares in the formal processes of decision-making; the range of issues covered specifically by collective agreement is usually narrower than those in whose resolution the managerial councils are supposed to participate (although there is great variety in the latter respect). Perhaps somewhat more important than these formal distinctions — which, anyhow, are often blurred in practice — is the fact that collective bargaining is not intended to give the union responsibility for the management of the firm, while council participation in management does constitute the open assumption of some measure of responsibility. However, this distinction, too, is often lacking in clarity: "irresponsible" unions and "irresponsible" councils may find themselves on different sides of the dividing line in a formal sense, and on the same side as far as the facts are concerned. The formal distinction, nevertheless, has some meaning.

As managerial devices, councils are subject to a number of restrictions: some of these are provided for in the design of the council's managerial role; some arise in fact rather than according to plan.

A fundamental restriction results from limitations of the autonomy of the enterprise which the councils are to manage or comanage. In a system of administrative planning with highly centralized decision-making, the management of the enterprise has authority only over the narrow range of executory decisions which the planning body leaves to the enterprise. These limitations apply to whatever body assumes the responsibility for the management of the enterprise and consequently to a council in charge of management. Only when a substantial measure of decentralization in decision-making occurs can the workers' council assume significant managerial authority. In Poland, the experimental firms can be said to have had such authority in some areas. It is only since 1952 that Yugoslav enterprises have obtained a significant measure of authority which gave the councils at least the statutory possibility to perform managerial functions. The Polish experiment, halfheartedly undertaken, has come to an abrupt end. In Yugoslavia, the degree of autonomy accorded to the firm has undergone a great many variations, and it is too early to attempt to discern a long-run trend.

The councils' authority, subject to many other influences apart from the varying measures of freedom of decision granted the firm, has also undergone considerable fluctuations. In both countries, Poland and Yugoslavia, the enterprise is subject not only to open controls and restrictions but also to concealed influences. The ever-present and, at least in theory, ever-vigilant political party often operates through its branches in the enterprise and through other organizations such as the union more effectively though less visibly than the governmental control systems. Real self-government is impossible as long as the "invisible hand" of the monopoly party controls the councils.

The authority of the councils as managerial devices varies in the four countries considered according to the subject matter involved. In France and Germany councils are given the power to participate in the making of decisions on matters of personnel management. By contrast, their power is highly limited by law and close to zero, in fact, as far as the economic and financial administration of the firm is concerned. Moreover, observers agree that the interest of the councils — as well as of the constituents whom they represent — is highest in those matters that are conventionally subject to collective bargaining, while their concern is least active in the financial and economic areas of management. Some observers claim that it is difficult to decide in this chicken–egg problem whether the lack of interest results from the lack of the councils' authority or, vice versa, whether workers' pressure for effective participation in decision-making was less powerful in financial and economic matters. However, the intricacies of financial and economic problems in a modern enterprise are such that few councillors are qualified to discuss them, while matters of wages and working conditions are by nature closer to the workers' experience and understanding.

The Yugoslav system does not make a simple distinction by subject matter of various degrees of council authority. Yet in practice the councils' active interest seems to have followed about the same pattern as in Germany or France — with considerable regional variations corresponding to the workers' industrial experience and educational level. In any case, it should be noted that on some fundamental questions, such as its investment plans, the enterprise had little, if any, authority most of the time; that its wage schedule requires the approval of the local community as well as of the union; and that the director has an overriding authority to suspend any council decision which in his view runs counter to the law or governmental regulation.

The councils are thus rarely the real decision-making body of the enterprise. They are not intended to perform that function in either Germany or France, while in Yugoslavia whatever the intentions or the ultimate design of the experiment, they have been permitted to be the main decision-maker in the enterprise for a short period only; they have recently been superseded in that capacity by various outside controls.

A sustained experiment in the system of workers' self-government does not yet exist. The "venture into the unknown," the "voyage of discovery" of which Hugh Clegg has been speaking, has not yet reached shore. As a grandiose experiment of workers' education in business management, however, the Yugoslav system may have considerable merit. It applies the principles of American "progressive education" on a large scale by making the council members "learn by doing," and by confronting them with real issues rather than textbook examples. The system spreads business education among a large percentage of the industrial labor force since re-election of councillors is subject to restrictions and the turnover of council personnel is consequently great. The council is therefore, a powerful educational device to facilitate the transition of Yugoslavia from a rural agricultural country to a modern urban and industrial society.

All these are major achievements of the council system, but they have only an indirect and somewhat distant bearing upon the functions of the councils as instruments of workers' self-government.

CHAPTER IX

The Councils in Perspective

In the history of modern industrial society the labor movement has served many different purposes. At different times and in different countries it has been an instrument for the achievement of the most varied objectives, ranging from broad social and political aims, such as the establishment of democratic constitutions, to narrow interest-group demands in the area of wages, hours and working conditions. As a general proposition, the hypothesis may be advanced that in the early stages of industrial development, or even in the pre-industrial era, labor movements tend to pursue a wide range of broad objectives, and that with progressive industrialization this range tends to shrink. If the term "political movement" is reserved for groups concerned with a broad spectrum of social, political, economic, and cultural issues, and a pressure group is defined as a grouping with a narrow scope of interests, then it may be said that in the early stages of industrialization, labor is a political movement. Advancing industrialization tends to transform it into a pressure group.[1]

There are some indications that at an even more advanced stage of industrialization a new trend toward broader interests on the part of labor may arise. This may be the result simply of growth, which makes a larger number of events significant to some parts of the organization; against this, the same evolution permits the large organization to disregard events that may be of interest to small groups only. Possibly, the incredible speedup in the rate of change of fundamentals — population, technology, and power relationships — compels labor to be concerned with the framework of its action rather than to take it for granted and to regard it as stable. In any case, whatever the explanation, a trend turning labor away from a narrow pressure group seems to exist, but the affluent society provides many incentives for labor's continued operations as an interest group.

Some observers have introduced a normative element into what is basically an evolutionary process. One or the other type of labor action — the political or the pressure group — has been described as the proper, correct, or mature form. To some extent this view may be simply ethnocentric: the forms of labor action in one's own nation appear universally applicable and proper. Whatever recent changes in the usage of words may attempt to indicate to the contrary, international uniformity of action was the principle upon which the Communist International was founded. The forms of organization, the party-union relationship, the internal party structure of the Bolshevik Party, and the slogans employed in 1917 were the models to be observed everywhere. "Democratic centralism," the term which described the Bolshevik system, was transferred to the international stage. Of late, the term "poly-centrism" has made its appearance in certain organs of the Communist press — representing a demand rather than a fact, except perhaps by reference to the Sino-Soviet conflict.

While this form of enforced uniformity has been recognized and criticized by observers and participants, another form of uniformity in thinking has been hardly identified as such: the refusal to realize that labor movements at different stages of the industrialization process have different functions to perform. There is still a widespread belief that later forms of labor action are superior, that there evolves a progressively revealed truth. The belief in progress — or some form of social Darwinism — is so ingrained that what comes later is readily assumed to be better; similarly the survival of an organization is accepted as evidence of its superiority, while the extinction of another is proof of its failure. It does not seem to occur to these critics that a less industrialized society may simply require patterns of social action in general and labor action in particular which are different from those of a more advanced industrial era. The disappearance of an organization may indicate that the special tasks which it was designed to perform have been carried out or are no longer relevant. At most, the organization may then be criticized for not having had the flexibility necessary for the performance of new functions. The present may be more important to us than the past, but this does not mean that the past was "wrong."

This relativism of the objectives of the labor movement extends also to its forms or patterns of organization. They, too, evolve with changes in the objectives of the movement or, more accurately, with changes in the priorities given by labor to its various aims. A rearrangement in the hierarchy of objectives will often be reflected in changes in the organizational structure or, more subtly, in the role various layers of organization are, in fact, playing.

As a general proposition, labor in most countries in the West, in the early stages of industrialization, has tended to operate as a class movement. It has emphasized the common class objectives of recognition of the manual worker as a citizen in the community and in the plant; this implied giving him equal political rights as well as the right to form unions and to withhold his labor in collective action. The labor movement was anxious to break down some of the barriers in the way of upward social mobility, to open the door to higher education for its children, to remove the social stigma attached to manual labor, and so forth. (This is at least one meaning of the Socialist "classless society" when the utopian element is removed.) This did not exclude the struggle for higher wages or, frequently more urgent at the time, for the maintenance of the workplace in the face of superior competition by the machine. In the hierarchy of objectives — in the early history of the labor movement — these aims often ranked below the broader political, social, and cultural ones, perhaps because attaining the latter appeared to be a condition for an advance toward the immediate economic goals, or perhaps because the leaders of the movement, coming from outside the laboring class, placed primary emphasis on the broader objectives. This explanation accompanied by contradictory value judgments is the essence of the Lenin-Perlman thesis about the respective roles of intellectuals and manual workers in the labor movement.

Given these objectives, the labor organizations put heavy emphasis on what workers of different crafts and skill levels had in common rather than what divided them. Corresponding to the class goals of the movement was a class organization. Even though unions — when they arose — were organized according to craft, their leadership was typically subordinated to that of the party which represented the class aims of the movement.

At the other end of the pole, unions had little or no status in the plant. They were organized outside the industrial establishment,[2] and employers for a long time refused to have any dealings with them. To the extent to which union representatives existed in the plants, they acted "underground." Their functions were primarily those of membership stewards, carrying on propaganda for the labor organizations, collecting dues, and so forth. When industrial action was engaged in, it was predominantly local. Since both the labor and the product markets were of a local nature, the economic incentive for the development of a national labor organization was lacking (though on the political level the need for it was great). Having modest means at their disposal, workers could only rarely engage in long drawn-out economic battles. Sudden decisions were needed to take the opponent by surprise and obtain a rapid victory. The center of gravity of the economic labor organization was, consequently, in the local section. The combination of this fact with the overriding feeling of class solidarity turned the French "Bourse du Travail," the city central United States style, into the principal battle instrument of the worker at that relatively early stage of industrial development. The membership steward, secret representative of the union in the plant, is a symbol of this phase. As B. C. Roberts says, "Of course, in a sense there had always been a spokesman of the unions inside an establishment, once organization had started, but these were not official representatives and had no place in the constitutions of the unions. The printing industry was an exception to this, for the unions there have long been organized on the basis of 'chapels' in each printing shop, and the 'father' of the chapel has always performed the functions of a modern shop steward." Counterparts in other countries (like the "localist" movement in Germany) are not difficult to find.

Common class objectives find their main expression in the political party of the workers. Where the party is weak, the political council may be used as a substitute or auxiliary — usually temporarily. It is a device to draw larger unorganized and often poorly educated working-class groups into action under the leadership of well-organized and disciplined minorities, taking advantage of a state of popular rebellion during a political or economic crisis. This is at the foundation of the Soviets in Russia as well as of the councils in Hungary in 1956. Even the protagonists of the political councils did not always understand the particular conditions under which these organizations enabled the Bolsheviks to come to power. As a result, the political councils often produced unexpected results when the attempt was made to use them in countries where the political party of the worker was strong, disciplined, and included most of the politically active workers, as was the case in Austria and Germany after World War I. In the circumstances the introduction of a substitute or auxiliary for the party could only lead to a dispersion of efforts and reduced effectiveness of the working-class party rather than to a victorious revolution.

A decisive step in the evolution of the councils occurred when they were put in the service of collective bargaining. A developed system of collective bargaining arose normally in the West at a fairly well-advanced stage of industrial development. Collective bargaining requires not only legislation and administration permitting (or possibly favoring) the growth of representative trade unions but also the emergence of a reasonably well-functioning labor market. For genuine collective bargaining to exist, there must also be a long-run situation on the labor market for at least certain kinds of labor that gives unions bargaining power in the contest with the employer. At given wage rates and over longer periods, substantial excess supplies of labor must occur only rarely. In the West, this combination of circumstances has prevailed most often at a time when industrialization was already well under way. The United States is of course one of the outstanding exceptions: industrialization proceeded almost from the beginning under conditions of long-run labor shortage. In the newly emerging nations, attempts are being made to fit unions into the industrial relations system before industrial development has made much progress in absorbing excess supplies of labor.

To be fully effective, collective bargaining must of course extend into the plant. Grievance handling on one hand and the application of agreed principles of incentive pay or of piece rates on the other require what is, in effect, bargaining at the plant level. Employers in the West directed their last-ditch resistance against this interference of outsiders in the plant, and in some countries continue to do so. France is the outstanding example of such resistance at this time. The British evolution is well described in the following terms:

> Because trade unions were organized outside their establishments, many employers, in the nineteenth century, refused for a long time to recognize the representatives of the unions in their workshops. They refused to have what they called "outside interference," and would negotiate only with their employees as individuals. Gradually this attitude broke down, and collective bargaining became widespread, but with the exception of certain cases, the unions did not make provision for the regular appointment of accredited spokesmen as part of the union machinery inside industry until during and immediately after the first world war.
>
> Shop stewards began to appear in the engineering industry in the eighteen-nineties — they are first mentioned by the Amalgamated Society of Engineers in 1897 — when changes in industrial techniques and workshop management, particularly the adoption of piece-rate and incentive systems, and the introduction of high-speed machine tools, made it essential for the men in the workshop to have someone who knew their problems intimately to represent them on the spot. The national officials of the union could negotiate basic agreements, but were not in a position to understand immediately the details of every dispute that arose in a workshop as a result of the new methods; moreover, the disputes were too frequent to call in a union officer every time they occurred.[3]

The struggle for the admission of the unions into the plant is one of the central issues of an industrial relations system. In the view of many employers, the "autonomy of the enterprise" must be protected not only against the state, but also against the unions and even the employers' association.[4] This is why in so many countries (France and Germany being outstanding examples) the collective agreement is normally an agreement between an employers' association and a union; this keeps the latter at a safe distance from the individual enterprise. Even more important, the agreement typically sets up a minimum wage schedule on which rests the effective wage structure, thus leaving to the enterprise the ultimate decision on actual wage rates. The strongest resistance is directed against the functioning of the union within the enterprise.

In 1949, a number of French trade union centers (the CGT, the Christian CFTC, the white-collar organization CGC — with Force Ouvrière, then in the process of being organized, supporting the demands) submitted to the employers proposals for a collective agreement. These dealt extensively with the rights to be granted to union delegates chosen by the employees or appointed by the union and accredited with plant management. The union delegates — who were to be set up in addition to the shop stewards and the members of the plant committee elected according to the law — were to be given free time at company expense to perform their union functions. They were to have the right to be accompanied by union representatives from outside the enterprise. They were to be able to attend union congresses on company time, and so forth. They were to be given the right to post union announcements in the plant, distribute union publications, collect union dues, and hold union meetings in the plant. In general, their status was to be similar to that of shop stewards elected according to the law, but they were to be union representatives and appointed by the union.

Interestingly, the employers were willing to grant leaves of absence for the performance of union functions *outside* the plant, such as attendance at union congresses. But they opposed with a categoric no all demands relating to union activity within the plant. "Carrying on union activities within the plant would obviously deprive the latter of the character which it must preserve — namely, that of being exclusively a workplace where neutrality is essential."

Undoubtedly, the political divisions of the French unions gave force to the employers' argument. But, as French observers point out, employers' resistance to union activity in the plant antedated the splits within the labor movement. Moreover, the history of trade unionism elsewhere shows that nowhere have unions obtained a base of operations in the plant without a battle.

The unions themselves are quite aware of this. As will be remembered, at the time of the enactment of the original works council legislation in

Germany, union leaders expressed their doubts as to the desirability of the institution. A council was a poor substitute, in their view, for a union shop organization. French unions have expressed their opinion in these terms:

Trade unionism is first of all action in the workplace. The enterprise is the natural locale of union action. All activities outside the workplace have an artificial character even though they are necessary: general assemblies, information gatherings, union officials, etc. . . . The enterprise is the base where unionists obtain experience and practice in trade unionism . . . The shop organization, the shop stewards, the dues collectors in the plant are the indispensable support of all unions.[5]

The bargaining council is thus a substitute for the union shop organization in performing the functions which must be carried out in the plant if bargaining is to be effective. Given the organizational conditions and power relationships that call forth the creation of councils, the bargaining council arrives at that stage of development when collective bargaining moves toward the center of the industrial relations scene.

It is at this stage of industrial development, too, that union reform councils arise, usually in response to a prolonged failure of the union itself to perform the functions its members have entrusted to it. Such a failure may occur for good and persuasive reasons. During World War I the British unions accepted an "armistice" in order to support their country during the war.

[The shop steward movement] which first brought stewards into prominence started in the early days of the war among stewards in engineering works on the Clyde, who formed a committee. Their example was rapidly followed by stewards in other works, and soon there existed a nationally-linked movement, which pursued an independent and militant policy, and was a thorn in the flesh of the union leaders during the rest of the war, even proving strong enough to compel both them and the government to change their policies on occasions. After the war the shop stewards' movement lost much of its influence, and not a few of those who had been its leaders subsequently joined the newly-formed Communist Party, which continued to embarrass union officers through the unofficial actions of shop stewards.[6]

While in Britain the independent shop stewards disappeared after World War I, their German counterpart became, as we have seen, a permanent institution in the form of the bargaining council. The German councils, too, arose as an aftermath of the policy of *Burgfrieden* (self-imposed social peace), which the German unions pursued during World War I. The councils embodied the spirit of rebellion which this policy aroused among many militant trade unionists. This, however, does not mean that this was the only important cause for the rise of the councils. To be permanent, the councils had to become bargaining instruments.

A new era in the history of the councils opens when they are designed to become managerial organizations. The Syndicalist roots of this idea are obvious, but, apart from the most extreme versions of Syndicalist theory, there have been few social reform plans which have given the councils full and sole authority to manage the enterprise. Enterprises do not exist primarily to provide employment and income for the employees, but rather to produce goods and services for the community. Therefore, enterprises must be administered not simply for the benefit of the employees, but in such a way that they perform their function for society. A reconciliation between the group interest of the employees and the interest of society at large is necessary at every stage of the economic process. It is desirable that neither of the two interests becomes overwhelmingly powerful. If the interests of society were all-powerful, the employees of any particular enterprise might be exploited for the benefit of the community at large. This is one element in the justification for maintaining unions in nationalized enterprises, in the Democratic-Socialist approach. Predominant group interests, on the other hand, might lead to competitive scarcities and the exploitation of society by small strategically located groups. Logically, therefore, the councils of each individual enterprise can be given full authority in bargaining, producing, selling, hiring, and firing, only if in none of the input or output markets monopolistic power situations can arise. Since this condition is unlikely to be adequately and universally fulfilled, completely autonomous enterprises and all-powerful councils are unlikely to exist. Indeed, the less developed a country is, the more frequent are in all probability monopolistic market situations outside of agriculture, and the greater must be the restrictions on the autonomy of the enterprise if monopolistic exploitation is to be avoided.

If this reasoning is correct, it would follow that in the early stages of industrial development, rather sharp restrictions on the power of councils as managerial devices are likely to be imposed. A wider autonomy of the firms and of the councils becomes possible when, and to the extent that, economic progress leads to higher degrees of interfirm competition.

The Yugoslav experiment is too brief to permit testing our second hypothesis. As to the first, it clearly applies to the situation as described in the earlier chapter. (The Polish experiment hardly reached a stage in which any but political conclusions could be drawn from it.)

Yet, even within these limits, the system of management by workers' councils raises fundamental issues. Management of a modern industrial enterprise is a profession requiring training — of a somewhat vaguely defined nature — and experience. Can workers and white-collar employees without management training or experience be reasonably expected to perform the managerial function effectively?

The experience in France and Yugoslavia seems to suggest that the answer to this question is in the negative. But is this perhaps merely a temporary failing? Could it not be that with the rise in general educational levels and prolonged industrial experience the necessary talents and knowledge for the performance of managerial functions will be found among blue- and white-collar workers as frequently (or about as frequently) as among members of other social groups? Could the growth of the often better educated white-collar groups within the labor force create conditions in which employees more frequently than in the past have the qualifications required for managerial functions?

The studies in this volume would seem to provide some suggestive support for this assumption. The fact that workers' self-government appears to perform better in the more advanced industrial regions of Yugoslavia than in those first entering the era of industrialization lends some plausibility to this thesis as does the election of large numbers of white-collar employees to the councils in Poland by blue-collar workers who are obviously aware of the need for technical competence in management. The argument is sometimes heard that workers do not have any real interest in managerial problems, and that even when they are given opportunities to share in managerial decision-making their concern is limited to the problems of most immediate import upon their own lives — essentially the problems usually covered by collective bargaining. Workers' participation in management then becomes not much more than a peculiar form of collective bargaining. The French experience with plant committees and the early phase of Yugoslav workers' self-government would lend support to this argument. Yet it is difficult to accept the view that there is some innate lack of managerial talent among the workers *qua* workers, a kind of "manualist" mentality which makes them unfit or unwilling to accept managerial responsibilities. It is prima facie more than unlikely that any of the societies we know so far has found foolproof ways of assuring perfect social mobility so that any person willing to accept management functions, and capable of performing them after the necessary training, would be certain to be given that training and to be assigned management tasks. Quite conceivably workers' self-government might prove to be one of the avenues by which increased numbers of people of working-class background might rise into the ranks of the managerial hierarchy.

This, however, is not workers' self-government. It is not intended to act as recruiting ground and training center for prospective worker-managers — although this may be a highly desirable task, particularly in the countries of early industrialization in which managerial talent is in extremely short supply. Nor is workers' self-government intended to be merely an organization for the general education of employees in the economic, financial, and technical problems of the enterprise and the economy at large, indispensable as such education undoubtedly is in a system of workers' self-government. Council members are to remain workers and not to become permanent managers of the enterprise, and the councils are intended to be managerial rather than educational institutions. Can they perform this function?

It is obvious that many management decisions are to a very large extent technical. Competent decision-making on such issues requires knowledge of a kind which few workers — whether blue- or white-collar — can be expected to have. Such technical decisions must be left to experts. Indeed, few corporation managers make such decisions themselves unless they happen to have the technical knowledge involved — but possessing this kind of knowledge is not ordinarily a requirement for a candidate for managerial positions. Workers' councils should not be expected to have competencies in these areas. Only the most general issues need be brought before the councils. With advancing education and experience the range of such issues might be increasing, but it will hardly be extended beyond a few fundamentals — in much the same way in which boards of supervision perform in French or German corporations. Management has a different function from executory work, and with the progressive complication of the work of the enterprises and the increase in their size the requirements for the successful performance of the task of business administration are bound to increase. An enhanced division of labor rather than a system in which everyone does everyone else's work corresponds to the general laws of economic development. In most areas council-managers can, therefore, be expected only to set the guidelines of policy.

There are, however, areas in the work process itself — depending on the technology of the industry — in which the councils, or a smaller council group such as the Yugoslav management board, may gradually assume wider responsibilities. Work scheduling, the setting of norms and speed, physical arrangements of the workplace and surrounding it, and the scheduling of holidays and vacations are examples of this kind of issue. Perhaps the most important area in which workers' self-government may prove to be effective is that of discipline in the workplace. The self-governing work group — realizing the extent to which the success of the enterprise depends upon the establishment and maintenance of discipline in the workplace — setting and enforcing its own rules against the members of the group may sound utopian. Yet not only some of the results of human relations research, but also some of the experiences of Yugoslav workers' councils would seem to indicate that germs of such an evolution exist. This may lead to far less than Syndicalists and Guild Socialists expected and advocated, but it may be more than critics have been willing to allow for so far.

This prospect creates, then, new issues. What is the place of the union in this system? As was pointed out previously, no solution for this problem seems yet to have been found in Yugoslavia, and the Polish regime has "solved" the problem by suppressing the councils in fact, if not in name and essence. Solutions may not be impossible to find, but there is no hint yet that serious attempts are being made to tackle the issue.

Clearly, unions cannot be protectors of working-class interests and members of management as well without having to face problems of conflicting loyalties. They cannot, as the British laborites put it, sit on both sides of the bargaining table without impairing their effectiveness. The councils, however, are not part of the unions. If the councils act in a managerial capacity — as distinguished from other councils, especially the bargaining councils — they must be independent from the union. The managerial council, then, would represent the interests of the workers as producers or part-owners and the long-run interests of the firm; the union would act in behalf of the workers as employees and defend their short-run interests. The key is the independence of the managerial council from the union. This is far from being a solution to the problem, but perhaps the point of departure for a solution.

More serious still and even more difficult because it is more fundamental is the issue presented by the party. Workers' self-government beyond the most modest forms is incompatible with a totalitarian system. No attempts to "humanize" totalitarianism — sincere and commendable as such attempts may be — can bridge the gap that separates self-government from an unlimited dictatorship. In the case of Poland this contradiction appeared almost the moment the councils were introduced. The much more powerful Yugoslav Communist Party has been able to cover up to some extent the contradictions and to limit their outward appearance. Economic progress may further reduce the sharpness of the conflicts inherent in the contradiction. Yet it is difficult to see how in the long run a fundamental choice between self-government in industry and dictatorship can be avoided. If the workers were indeed to administer the enterprise freely, would they not insist upon their right to determine the economic and financial policies of the government which so vitally influence the fate of the individual enterprise? Only when this choice has been made in favor of self-government can it be said that the experiment of workers' councils as managerial devices is being undertaken in earnest. This does not mean that ideology can ever be eliminated from the area of industrial relations just as it cannot be done away with in any other area of social activity. Without spiritual ties of any kind and reasonably reliable expectations about human behavior, no social organization can function effectively, if at all. But freedom of discussion for all sides in issues arising in the life of the organs of self-government, fair chances of success for either side, absence of police interference, and the refusal to use governmental power for the benefit of one side — these are characteristics of self-government which a dictatorship is unlikely to tolerate. In the end a fundamental decision will have to be made, even though it will perhaps be made gradually and imperceptibly.

Finally, assuming that workers' self-government performs effectively within a reasonably democratic society, will such a society be "classless"? Will councils perform as democratic supervisors of managerial authority to prevent its abuse, or will they share in such authority and in the prerogatives and prerequisites that traditionally go with power, authority, and prestige?

It may well be that the law of supply and demand applies to the solution of this problem as to that of so many others. With managerial talent in scarce supply, power and prestige of managers run high. Aren't they likely to decline when higher and more general education, which progressive industrialization tends to bring about, increases the supply of managerial talent? Quite conceivably managerial income and power differentials will go the same way as have skill differentials under the impact of rising educational levels in the West. In this perspective, workers' self-government and increasing social equality would become realistic objectives when industrialization — the greatest of the contemporary revolutions — has made considerable advances. In the meantime workers' councils as managerial devices may lead to a kind of "meritocracy" which may prove an even stronger system of social inequality the more effectively it provides for upward social mobility of the talented and leaves the opposition without capable leaders.

This attempt to determine the role which councils in their various functions perform in different contexts enables us to formulate some hypotheses about the role councils may play in countries now in the early stage of industrialization. Most of these countries have only recently emerged from colonial status, and if the latter term is defined in a wider economic sense, this statement applies to almost all of them.

In this situation, industrialization is typically a primary national objective. It symbolizes national independence, modernization, destruction of pre-industrial, frequently feudal, social forms. Emotionally, it may thereby take the place that democracy held in the life of European labor in the nineteenth and early twentieth centuries. In other words, general objectives of wide scope may take precedence over narrower group aims.[7] The labor unions are often integrated into a larger movement; their pressure group aims are subordinated to the political objective of this movement, at least in the short run. In the longer run, it may be rationalized that the attainment of these wider objectives is the precondition for the realization of the narrower union aims.

At this stage bargaining councils are likely to play only a minor role if they exist at all since collective bargaining itself is practiced only on a small scale at best. However, plant organizations may nevertheless arise in the form of managerial councils, perhaps after the fashion of the Yugoslav councils. This is especially likely in countries in which Socialist forms of industrial organization prevail. But even if the emphasis on Socialist developments is less pronounced, some degree of worker participation in management is not improbable. This might occur in the countries where organized labor is the strongest single factor among the forces making for modernization and exerts considerable influence. In other countries, managerial councils might originate in the need to recruit managerial talents wherever they can be found.

Gradually, as industrialization progresses, but even before collective bargaining becomes a significant feature of social life, bargaining councils may arise. They may serve as channels for grievances; they may assist workers in their personal troubles. In addition, they tend to be devices by which prospective labor leaders acquire status and draw attention to themselves. In a situation in which the center of gravity of the labor movement is of necessity at a high level of the union hierarchy — where negotiations with an all-powerful government are carried on and most decisions are made by a small elite — the councils may be a useful element of decentralization offsetting to some extent the exceedingly strong trend toward centralized authority in the union.

Whether the bargaining councils will be set up as independent organizations or develop as the lowest level in the union structure is difficult to predict. Exogenous factors — like the Auxiliary Service Law in Germany — may play a decisive role. The stronger the unions, the more likely it is that they may wish to perform the functions which the councils would have to carry out where the unions do not have the strength required. At the same time, performance of these functions in the plant would tend to strengthen the unions and anchor them deeply to the daily life of the workers.

Finally, it is necessary to consider the likelihood of political councils developing in newly industrializing nations. Such councils may serve as tools of any group that is incapable of dominating the unions or — if in control of the unions — of using them to control labor itself. This may be any political group including of course the Communists. Indeed, the possibility that councils will be organized, perhaps rather suddenly, by Communists in order to wrest control of labor from unions and non-Communist political parties exists at all times. The chances of success for such an operation vary in inverse proportion with the growth and the discipline of organized labor.

Notes

INTRODUCTION

1. G. D. H. Cole, *Workshop Organization* (Oxford, 1923).

2. The union referred to is a craft union. G. D. H. Cole, *An Introduction to Trade Unionism* (London, 1953), pp. 51–2. See also Flanders and Clegg, eds., *The System of Industrial Relations in Great Britain* (Oxford, 1954), particularly the essay of J. D. M. Bell, "Trade Unions," pp. 167–8.

3. For a discussion of the relationships among these and related ideologies, see Branko Pribicevic, *The Shop Stewards Movement and Workers Control 1910–1922* (Oxford, 1959).

4. Neil Chamberlain, *The Union Challenge to Management Control* (New York, 1948).

CHAPTER I

1. G. D. H. Cole, *Workshop Organization* (Oxford, 1923), p. 5. Sidney and Beatrice Webb, *Industrial Democracy* (London, 1897), vol. I, p. 90.

2. W. Milne-Bailey, *Trade Unions and the State* (London, 1934), p. 93.

3. Cole, *Workshop Organization,* pp. 6–7.

4. Allen Flanders, "Great Britain," in *Contemporary Collective Bargaining in Seven Countries,* Adolf Sturmthal, ed. (Ithaca, 1957), p. 28.

5. Cole, *Workshop Organization,* pp. 51–2.

6. J. D. M. Bell, "Trade Unions," in Flanders and Clegg, eds., *The System of Industrial Relations in Great Britain* (Oxford, 1954), pp. 167–8.

7. See International Labour Office, *The Trade Union Situation in the United Kingdom* (Geneva, 1961), p. 80.

8. B. C. Roberts, *Trade Union Government and Administration in Great Britain* (Cambridge, Mass., 1956), p. 80.

9. Otto Neuloh, *Die deutsche Betriebsverfassung und ihre Sozialformen bis zur Mitbestimmung* (Tübingen, 1956). Otto Neuloh, *Der neue Betriebsstil* (Tübingen, 1959). In British history where legal wage-fixing lasted until late in the eighteenth century, the "abandonment of the operatives by the law . . . was . . . carried out on principle, with unflinching determination" in the early nineteenth century. Sidney and Beatrice Webb, *The History of Trade Unionism* (London, 1920), pp. 48–63. Quotes from p. 55.

10. In 1856 Alfred Krupp provided in his plant rules that a worker on vacation had to obtain an attestation from the police of his vacation place verifying the duration of his stay. Neuloh, *Der neue Betriebsstil.*

11. A parallel development in Austria-Hungary was the creation by imperial decree on March 18, 1917, of a comprehensive system of complaint commissions. A previous attempt at setting up complaint offices (July 1915) had proved abortive. Charles A. Gulick, *Austria from Habsburg to Hitler*, vol. I, *Labor's Workshop of Democracy* (Berkeley and Los Angeles, 1948), pp. 37–9. Also Fritz Klenner, *Die Österreichischen Gewerkschaften — Vergangenheit und Gegenwartsprobleme*, vol. I (Vienna, 1951). The author quotes a number of documents indicating that the unions had for a long time been demanding legal protection for their representatives in the plants. See pp. 445, 447.

12. C. W. Guillebaud, *The Works Council: a German Experiment in Industrial Democracy* (Cambridge, 1928), pp. 8–9, 12, 41, 44–5.

13. See Adolf Sturmthal, "Nationalization and Workers' Control in Britain and France," *Journal of Political Economy*, LXI. 1 (February 1953).

14. See Henry Ehrmann, *French Labor: From Popular Front to Liberation* (New York, 1947).

15. Pierre Chambelland, *Les Comités d'entreprise: Fonctionnement et Résultats Practiques* (Paris, 1949). Philippe Bayart, *Comités d'entreprise: experiences étrangères, legislation française* (Paris, 1947). Emil James, *Les Comités d'entreprises: Étude de l'ordonnance du 22 février* (Paris, 1945). Val R. Lorwin, *The French Labor Movement* (Cambridge, Mass., 1954). Adolf Sturmthal, "Collective Bargaining in France," in *Contemporary Collective Bargaining in Seven Countries* (Ithaca, 1957).

16. Paul Durand, "La Réprésentation des Travailleurs sur le Plan de l'Entreprise dans le Droit Français" (mimeographed document of the European Coal and Steel Community), p. 2. Also published in German (in printed form): Europaeische Gemeinschaft für Kohle und Stahl — Hohe Behörde, *Die Vertretung der Arbeitnehmer auf Betriebsebene nach dem Recht der Mitgliedstaaten der EGKS* (Luxemburg, 1959). The Durand essay is on pp. 187–240.

17. The first and third of the reform demands were enacted in due course in the legislation on the nationalization of industrial enterprises and by the establishment of the "Conseil Economique" in 1925, and its reorganization in 1936. See Sturmthal, "Nationalization and Workers' Control in Britain and France," and "The Structure of Nationalized Enterprises in France," *Political Science Quarterly*, LXVII.3 (September 1952).

18. Henry W. Ehrmann, *French Labor*, chapter III, presents an excellent discussion of the atmosphere in which the famous agreement was concluded.

19. On "extension" of collective agreements see Flanders, *Contemporary Collective Bargaining*, pp. 327–36. See Ehrmann, *French Labor*, pp. 127–67, for a discussion of collective bargaining in France. See also Lorwin, *The French Labor Movement.*

20. On syndicalism itself, see, for instance, Lewis L. Lorwin, *Syndicalism in France* (New York, 1914). Of the Guild-Socialist literature, I mention only G. D. H. Cole, *The World of Labour* (London, 1913), and Cole's *Self-Government in Industry* (London, 1918).

21. Sturmthal, "Nationalization and Workers' Control in Britain and France."

22. Otto Bauer, *The Austrian Revolution* (London, 1925).

23. Georg von Rauch, *A History of Soviet Russia* (New York, 1957), pp. 21–2.

24. See also Edward Hallett Carr, *The Bolshevik Revolution, 1917–1923* (London, 1950), vol. I, pp. 46 ff. Popov's official "Outline History of the Communist Party of the Soviet Union" (Moscow-Leningrad, 1934), p. 163, presents these facts characteristically: "Certain Bolsheviks, particularly in St. Petersburg (Bogdanov, for instance), failed at first to grasp the full importance of the revolutionary role of the Soviets as

transmission belts from the Party to the masses, and we inclined to look upon them as competitors of the Party."

25. In a speech in Switzerland in January, 1917. Lenin, *Sochineniya* (Moscow, 1938), vol. V. p. 18.

26. On October 27, 1956. See the documents in *National Communism and Popular Revolt in Eastern Europe: A Selection of Documents on Events in Poland and Hungary, February–November, 1956,* Paul E. Zinner, ed. (New York, 1956). The document referred to is on p. 422.

27. The document collection quoted above contains (p. 433) an appeal of the workers' council and student parliament of Borvod County whose first point is: "We demand the formation of a new provisional government fighting for a truly democratic, free and Socialist Hungary, excluding all ministers who have served under the Rakosi System." The remaining six points of the program are of a similarly general and political nature.

28. In *Freie Ungarische Gewerkschaften,* April 1957.

29. See also the document collection, *National Communism and Popular Revolt in Eastern Europe,* p. 481.

CHAPTER II

1. Bureau International du Travail, *La participation des Organisations Professionelles à la vie économique et sociale en France* (Geneva, 1948), pp. 165–6; "Les Comités d'Entreprise, Législation, Réglémentation, Jurisprudence," *Liaisons Sociales,* no. 382, March 31, 1959.

2. Philippe Bayart, *Comités d'entreprise: expérience étrangères, législation française* (Paris, 1947), pp. 228 ff.

3. May 16, 1946. *Journal Officiel,* May 17, 1946. Jacques Michollin, *Les Comités d'Entreprise Mise à Jour 1960* (Paris, n.d.).

4. See Adolf Sturmthal, "Nationalization and Workers' Control in Britain and France" *Journal of Political Economy,* LXLI.1 (February 1953). However, the state court (Conseil d'État) recently decided that the plant committee legislation applied also to the nationalized enterprises. *Le Monde,* May 5, 1959.

5. Bayart, *Comités d'entreprise,* pp. 123–4 note, 284–5 note.

6. *Journal Officiel,* February 17, 1946.

7. Law of July 7, 1947.

8. Paul Durand, "La Représentation des Travailleurs sur le Plan de l'Entreprise dans le Droit Français" (mimeographed document of the European Coal and Steel Community), p. 33.

9. André Rouast and Paul Durand, "Précis de législation industrielle (Droit du travail)," 3rd ed., p. 223, quoted by Val Lorwin, *The French Labor Movement* (Cambridge, Mass., 1954), p. 258, note 9.

10. M. J. Brèthe de le Gressaye, "La détermination des attributions des représentants du personnel en vue du contrôle du temps consacré par eux à leurs fonctions," *Droit Social,* 24. 7–8: 417–19 (July–August 1961).

11. This is a device designed to provide a "more rapid and less costly procedure" than that of the ordinary courts. Michel Vasseur, "La compétence des juges de paix en matière de contrat de travail," *Droit Social,* 15.2: 106–9 (February 1952). William H. McPherson, "Les Conseils de Prud'hommes: Une Analyse de leur Fonctionnement." *Droit Social,* 25.1 (January, 1962).

12. Val Lorwin, *The French Labor Movement,* p. 256.

13. This and some other items quoted below are drawn from a large-scale investigation of the functioning of the plant committees undertaken by the journal *Droit Social* and published by it under the title "L'expérience des Comités d'entreprise. Bilan d'une Enquête," 15.1, 2, 3 (January–March 1952). This will be quoted "L'expérience" hereafter. This has been supplemented by my own field work and other literature quoted below. See "L'expérience," p. 23.

14. Law of April 16, 1946.

15. There have been numerous complaints about the absence of effective protection of shop stewards against discrimination. Lorwin, *The French Labor Movement,* p. 260, note 16. Also Paul Durand, "Les problèmes posés par la protection des délégués du personnel et des membres des comités d'entreprise," *Droit Social,* 13.10 (December 1950). A decree of January 7, 1959, has extended to the candidates the same protection against dismissal which the elected shop stewards and committee members enjoy. This refers, however, only to the candidates offered by the "most representative" unions.

16. Lorwin, *The French Labor Movement,* pp. 260–1. This applies only in the case of a "serious fault" of the employee.

17. For a differing appreciation see Paul Durand, "La Réprésentation des Travailleurs," p. 22. On the other hand Lorwin, *The French Labor Movement,* p. 262, states: "In short, it may cost an employer a modest money payment and considerable effort to fire a shop steward . . . But if he is sufficiently determined, he can get rid of him. The relief for the individual is incomplete. The protection for the function of representation, while much greater than under the Popular Front legislation, is still minimal."

18. CFTC, Fédération de la Métalurgie, *Rapport moral présenté par le bureau fédéral, 1950,* p. 85, quoted in Lorwin, *The French Labor Movement,* p. 267.

19. Durand, *La Représentation,* pp. 36–7.

20. "Le rôle du comité d'entreprise en matière de logement," *Droit Social,* 15.7 (July–August 1952). *Revue des Comités d'entreprises,* no. 37 (April 1950).

21. Litigation on this issue has been considerable. "Les Comités d'Entreprise," *Liaisons Sociales,* pp. 72–3.

22. "L'expérience," p. 15; Durand, *La Représentation,* pp. 50–1. For the evaluation of the committees I have drawn upon interviews and the literature. In addition to the sources quoted so far, this includes, ASHE, "Les Comités d'entreprise. Un Echec? Un Succes? Leur Avenir: Resultat d'une enquête dans la région lyonnaise," *Chronique Sociale de France,* Cahier 8, 63rd year (December 30, 1955). Maurice Montuclard is engaged in a study of "successful" plant committees. For a preliminary report see Maurice Montuclard, "Pour une sociologie de la participation ouvrière dans les Comités d'Entreprise," *Sociologie du Travail,* 2nd year, no. 4 (October–December 1960).

23. "L'expérience," p. 16.

24. "Christianisme Social," 1950. nos. 3–4, pp. 150–1.

25. "L'expérience," p. 164.

26. The range of the welfare budgets as a percentage of the payroll runs from 0.75 to 8, with the average estimated at 4 per cent. Georges Lasserre, *French Experiments in Workers' Participation* (Paris, 1958), p. 13.

27. *Droit Social,* 15.7:13, 166 (July–August 1952).

28. Durand, *La Représentation,* p. 53.

29. They are made "deliberately technical and difficult," Lasserre, *French Experiments in Workers' Participation,* p. 14.

30. Compared with the British nationalized enterprises, the French publish meager reports. Sturmthal, *The Structure of Nationalized Enterprises in France,* p. 377.

31. Lasserre, *French Experiments,* p. 15. ASHE, *Chronique Sociale de France,* p. 641.

32. *Ordonnance* of January 7, 1959, decree of August 29, 1959.

33. See, in particular, André Bergeron, "Intéressement," *Force Ouvrière,* September 10, 1959, p. 8.

34. Lorwin, *The French Labor Movement.*

35. Lasserre, *French Experiments,* p. 13; Durand, *La Représentation,* p. 53, expresses slightly more negative views of the committees' work in the technical field. See also pp. 12–3.

36. *Droit Social,* p. 23. The labor inspectors reported to the minister that in "80 percent of the enterprises one cannot find any more candidates for the committees or the shop stewards." "To hunt delegates" (*la chasse aux délégués*) is a frequently heard expression indicating the opposition of employers to shop stewards.

37. The term is Paul Durand's.

38. Pierre Waline, "Le Patronat Français et les Conventions Collectives," *Revue Economique,* 2.1:29 (February 1951), quoted in Lorwin, *The French Labor Movement,* p. 273.

39. *Droit Social,* p. 24.

40. Durand, *La Réprésentation,* pp. 54, 272.

41. Lorwin, *The French Labor Movement,* pp. 205–6. Sturmthal, "France," in *Contemporary Collective Bargaining in Seven Countries.*

42. H. Lesire-Ogrel, "Au Sujet de la représentativité des Syndicats indépendants," *Droit Social,* 22.5:286–7 (May 1959).

43. Sturmthal, *Unity and Diversity in European Labor,* pp. 66–70.

44. Bayart, *Comités d'entreprise,* pp. 261–2.

45. On the more dubious aftermath of the Renault agreements, see F. Sellier, "Stratégie de la lutte sociale: France 1936–1960," Collection "Relations Sociales," *Economie et Humanisme* (Paris, 1961), pp. 200–3.

46. Sellier, "Stratégie de la lutte sociale," Chapter X.

47. Durand, *La Réprésentation,* p. 26. I am drawing freely in this section upon the late Professor Durand's report.

48. Decree of August 1, 1947.

49. Banque de France, Comptoir National d'Escompte. Banque Nationale pour le Commerce et l'Industrie, Société Générale, Crédit Lyonnais among the banks; La Séquanaise, l'Union, L'Urbaine, l'Aigle, le Soleil, la Nationale, le Phénix among the insurance companies.

50. Sturmthal, "The Structure of Nationalized Enterprises in France," pp. 363–4; also Sturmthal, *Unity and Diversity in European Labor,* p. 193.

CHAPTER III

1. See Kurt Brigl-Matthiass, *Das Betriebsräteproblem* (Berlin and Leipzig, 1926), pp. 2–3.

2. Paul Fisher, *Works Councils in Germany,* Visiting Expert Series no. 18 (Frankfurt, 1951). For the councils of the interwar period, see Brigl-Matthiass, *Das Betriebsräteproblem;* C. W. Guillebaud, *The Works Council, A German Experiment in Industrial Democracy* (Cambridge, 1928); Boris Stern, *Works Council Movement in Germany* (Washington, 1925).

3. An abridged English translation of the 1951 codetermination act and of the works constitution law edited by John P. Windmuller, was published in *Industrial and Labor Relations Review,* 6.3 (April 1953). A brief survey of the large American litera-

ture on codetermination is contained in Adolf Sturmthal, "The Labor Movement Abroad," in Neil W. Chamberlain, Frank C. Pierson, Theresa Wolfson, eds., *A Decade of Industrial Relations Research 1946–56: an Appraisal of the Literature in the Field* (New York, 1958), pp. 178–81, and note 22, pp. 198–99.

4. For a very interesting discussion of the background of the codetermination law, see Herbert J. Spiro, *The Politics of German Codetermination* (Cambridge, Massachusetts, 1958), particularly chapter 2; and Abraham Shuchman, *Codetermination: Labor's Middle Way in Germany* (Washington, 1958).

5. Moreover, the latter law was supplemented by laws of January 8 and March 20, 1953, and a decree of March 18, 1953.

6. Marcel David, *La Participation des Travailleurs à la gestion des Entreprises Privées dans les Principaux Pays d'Europe Occidentale* (Paris, 1954), pp. 137–8.

7. Henry C. Wallich, *Mainsprings of the German Revival* (New Haven, 1955).

8. The law makes a distinction between "hearing" and "consulting" (*hören und beraten*). No consequence of substance follows from this distinction.

9. H. C. Nipperdey, "The Development of Labour Law in the Federal Republic of Germany since 1945," *International Labour Review,* LXX. 2:154 (August 1954).

10. Specifically by the law of February 15, 1922; similar legislation was enacted in Austria on May 15, 1919. Charles A. Gulick, *Austria from Habsburg to Hitler,* vol. 1, *Labor's Workshop of Democracy* (Berkeley and Los Angeles, 1948), p. 203; Fritz Klenner, *Die Österreichischen Gewerkschaften* (Vienna, 1951), vol. 1, pp. 560–2.

11. Spiro, *Politics of German Codetermination,* pp. 89–90.

12. Carl Jantke, in Bergmann and Zeche, *Die sozialen Arbeitsverhältnisse einer Schachtanlage des nördlichen Ruhrgebiets in der Sicht der Bergleute* (Tübingen, 1953), p. 140.

13. *Ibid.,* p. 140.

14. The concern with private advancement keeps many of the younger men among the workers and particularly among the white-collar employees from accepting council nominations. Spiro, *Politics of German Codetermination,* pp. 90, 91, 94.

15. The workers are used to paternalism from the employers, generally seek paternalism, and probably prefer getting it from members of their own class, in whose election they can participate. Spiro, *Politics of German Codetermination,* p. 152, and similar observations, *passim.* Also the observations of Clark Kerr in "Collective Bargaining in Postwar Germany," *Contemporary Collective Bargaining,* Adolf Sturmthal, ed. (Ithaca, 1957), and in "The Trade Union Movement and the Redistribution of Power in Postwar Germany," *Quarterly Journal of Economics,* LXVII (November 1954).

16. Otto Kirchheimer, "West German Trade Unions: Their Domestic and Foreign Policies," in *West German Leaderships and Foreign Policy,* Hans Speier and W. Phillips Davison, eds. (Evanston, Ill., 1957), pp. 163–4.

17. This scheme of organization may be superseded by agreement, either at the industry or at the plant level. Shuchman, *Codetermination,* p. 162.

18. Spiro, *Politics of German Codetermination,* p. 95. In one coal mine five council committees were established: social committee; youth, new miners and culture; housing; group team rates; safety. See Jantke, p. 139.

19. Data from interviews and a study on grievance handling by the Rationalisierungs-Kuratorium der deutschen Wirtschaft, Frankfurt am Main, 1958 (mimeo.).

20. There were differences in the relative emphasis on council and shop committee in the different plants investigated. See Theodor W. Adorno and Walter Dirks, *Betriebsklima: eine industriesoziologische Untersuchung aus dem Ruhrgebiet* (Frankfurt, 1955), pp. 50–51. Neuloh, *Die Deutsche Betriebsverfassung,* pp. 61, 63, shows the shop committee member on various organization charts.

21. For examples, see the printed report of the Second Federal Works Council Conference of the I. G. Metall, held in February 1958.

22. Theo Pirker, Siegfried Braun, Burkart Lutz, Fro Hammelrath, *Arbeiter, Management, Mitbestimmung* (Stuttgart and Düsseldorf, 1955), p. 239.

23. Adapted with a minor modification from Spiro, *Politics of German Codetermination,* p. 86. The German text can found in Neuloh, *Die deutsche Betriebsverfassung,* pp. 286–7, or in the *Bundesgesetzblatt.*

24. Even when the *Mantel-Tarif* is supplemented by special wage contracts concluded for shorter periods — a year or two — and covering smaller areas than the general agreement, the rates set in the wage contracts are not regarded as effective rates, but only as minima to be exceeded in most cases. See Friedrich Fürstenberg, *Probleme der Lohnstruktur, Die wirtschaftliche und soziale Bedeutung der Lohnunterschiede* (Tübingen, 1958), and the sources mentioned in note 25.

25. "Betriebsnahe Tarifpolitik tut not," *Der Gewerkschafter,* 6.8:8 (1958). For a report on the investigation mentioned above, see "Der Unterschied zwischen den Tariflöhnen und den Effektivverdiensten in der Metallindustrie der Bundesrepublik; Ergebnisse einer Untersuchung," *Schriftenreihe der Industriegewerkschaft Metall für die Bundesrepublik Deutschland,* no. 24 (Frankfurt, 1956). A semi-official study indicates that the index of average hourly earnings for industrial workers (including construction) rose from 1950 to 1961 by 130 per cent; that of negotiated hourly wages rates for male workers in industry, trade and services, by 93 per cent. Although the coverage of the two series is not the same, the figures give some indication of the increase in the spread between contract and effective rates.

26. William Fellner et al., *The Problem of Rising Prices, Organization for European Economic Cooperation* (Paris, 1961), pp. 320–1.

27. Nathan Reich, "Collective Bargaining: The United States and Germany," *Labor Law Journal,* May 1957, p. 346. During 1960 and 1961 German unions became quite aggressive in their wage demands.

28. These data are given in a report by Fritz Strothmann to the Fourth Works Councillor Conference of the I. G. Metall held in October 1961 (mimeo.).

29. Art. 54, Ib, c; 56, 60, of the Works Constitution Law.

30. Frieda Wunderlich, *German Labor Courts* (Chapel Hill, 1946); W. H. McPherson, "Basic Issues in German Labor Court Structure," *Labor Law Journal,* 5.6 (June 1954).

31. Art. 61, 3, of the Works Constitution Law.

32. But the extent to which the works council is known among the workers is primarily dependent on its grievance handling. See Jantke, *Die Sozialen Arbeitsverhältnisse,* pp. 142–3. In the investigation of the atmosphere of a plant, one third of the employees referred to their works council as their main grievance authority, one quarter to the shop steward, but one quarter designated the superior in the plant. The latter was particularly often mentioned in a mine.

33. Good examples of the diversity of welfare activities are given in Spiro, *Politics of German Codetermination,* pp. 95–6.

34. "Der Arbeitnehmer als Partner im Betrieb," *Neue Zürcher Zeitung,* Jan. 5, 1963.

35. See W. M. Blumenthal, *Codetermination in the German Steel Industry* (Princeton, 1956); W. H. McPherson, "Codetermination in Practice," *Industrial and Labor Relations Review,* 8.4 (July 1955); W. H. McPherson and others, "German experience with Codetermination," *Proceedings* of the Eighth Annual Meeting, Industrial Relations Research Association, 1955; Herbert J. Spiro, *Politics of German Codetermination;*

Abraham Shuchman, *Codetermination;* as well as the German literature referred to in previous notes.

36. For the following, see Spiro, *Politics of German Codetermination,* pp. 100–2.

37. The reason given according to Spiro, *Politics of German Codetermination,* p. 101, is that some council chairmen have little confidence in their colleagues' sense of proportion about economic matters. If told "that the company was planning to invest several million marks in expansion of plant, their colleagues would at once demand a pay raise for the workers." Quite clearly, this reasoning expresses the chairman's paternalistic attitude towards his colleagues.

38. Pirker et al., *Arbeiter.*

39. I am not aware of an empirical study of this problem having been made in France. There are, however, interesting implications in Michel Collinet, "L'Ouvrier Français; Essai sur la Condition Ouvrière 1900–1950." Collection *Masses et Militants* (Paris, 1951), and in *Esprit du Syndicalisme* (Paris, 1952), by the same author.

40. Pirker, et al., *Arbeiter,* p. 435.

CHAPTER IV

1. André Philip, *La Démocratie Industrielle* (Paris, 1955), pp. 120 ff; George W. Hoffman and Fred W. Neal, *Yugoslavia and the New Communism* (New York, 1962).

2. Rudolf Bicanic, "Economic Growth under Centralized and Decentralized Planning, Yugoslavia — a Case Study," *Economic Development and Cultural Change,* VI.1:64 (October 1957).

3. Information Service Yugoslavia, "The Development of Workers' Self-Government; Management of Enterprises before the Introduction of Workers' Self-Government" (mimeo). Also printed in French: "Évolution du Système d'Auto-gestion Ouvrière," *Questions Actuelles du Socialisme,* no. 41 (March–April 1957).

4. An excellent source for these early developments is Ch. Bobrowski, *La Yugoslavie Socialiste* (Paris, 1956).

5. See for instance a statement of Boris Kidric in 1951, quoted in Information Service Yugoslavia, "The Development of Workers' Self-Government," p. 4. Edward Kardelj, "Le problème de la Répartition," *Questions Actuelles du Socialisme,* 41:88 (March–April 1957).

6. All figures from Federal Statistical Offices, *Statistical Pocket-Book of Yugoslavia, 1958* (Belgrade, April 1958), pp. 49–50.

7. See Rudolf Bicanic, "Economic Growth," p. 65, "Every detail of supply, production and distribution was planned centrally and directly from above. This led to arbitrariness and to interruption in the continuity of production, to "stoppage" of commercial services, etc. (i.e., when prices were not calculated in time, or orders signed by the minister) and to lack of interest, responsibility, and initiative among the working people." See also Jan Marczewski, *Planification et Croissance Économique des Democraties Populaires* (Paris, 1956), pp. 286 ff.

8. In *Questions Actuelles du Socialisme,* 15:77 (1952), quoted in Marczewski, *Planification et Croissance,* where there is a detailed list of discrepancies between plan and achievement. In particular, in agriculture almost all results were below prewar even though the plan had provided for an advance of 52 per cent above the 1939 levels.

9. Information Service Yugoslavia, *The Development of Workers' Self-Government* pp. 4–6.

10. There is ample descriptive literature on the Yugoslav council system. A semi-official description is in A. Deleon, *33 Questions — 33 Answers on Workers' Self-Government in Yugoslavia* (Belgrade, 1956). See also International Labour Organization, "Workers' Management and Labour Relations in Yugoslavia," record of an informal discussion held on June 16, 1958 in connection with the 42nd Session of the International Labour Conference. Labour-Management Relations Series, no. 5 (Geneva, 1958). See also ILO, *Workers' Management in Yugoslavia* (Geneva, 1962). This is based partly on field investigations. William N. Loucks, "Workers' Self-Government in Yugoslav Industry," *World Politics,* XI.1 (October 1958). John T. Dunlop, *Industrial Relations Systems* (New York, 1958), chapter 7.

11. "The earlier plans were heavy tomes weighing more than three pounds, the new ones were small booklets of some 40 pages," Bicanic, "Economic Growth," p. 66.

12. Bobrowski, *La Yugoslavie Socialiste,* p. 162.

13. *New York Times,* April 20, 25, and May 7, 1962.

14. For further description of this system, see Bobrowski, *La Yugoslavie Socialiste,* pp. 158 ff.

15. United Nations, "Economic Planning and Management in Yugoslavia," *Economic Bulletin for Europe,* 10.3:49 (Geneva, 1958).

16. Dr. Lado Vavpetic, Professor at the Faculty of Law, Ljubljana: "On some questions of the relations between the organizations of the State Administration and the organs of Workers' self-government," in "The New Yugoslav Law," *Bulletin on Law and Legislation in the Federal People's Republic of Yugoslavia,* VIII.2–4:85–102 (April-December 1957). The return of extensive price controls in early 1962 has greatly reduced the area within which the Yugoslav firm can operate by its own decisions.

17. Food prices at retail stores were reported to have increased by 25 per cent between December 1961 and April 1962. *New York Times,* April 25, 1962.

18. In Poland this issue was discussed as well. See Chapter V, note 26.

19. R. Stagner, *Distribution of Income in Enterprises* (Belgrade, 1961).

20. Janez Stanovnik, "Planning through the Market. The Yugoslav Experience," *Foreign Affairs,* XL.2:257–8 (January 1962).

21. Stanovnik, in "Planning through the Market," claims that Yugoslav enterprises retain a larger portion of their earnings than — on the average — their United States counterparts. *Yugoslav Trade Unions,* I:68 (July–September 1960), estimates the "free" funds of the enterprise for 1961 — perhaps a bit generously — at 46 per cent of the net income. In 1954 federal profits tax and district tax absorbed 78.2 per cent of gross profits. Rudolf Bicanic, "Interaction of Macro- and Micro-economic Decisions in Yugoslavia, 1954–1957," in Gregory Grossman, ed., *Value and Plan; Economic Calculation and Organization in Eastern Europe* (Berkeley and Los Angeles, 1960), p. 356.

22. Stanovnik, "Planning through the Market"; Paul Landz, "Reforms in Yugoslavia," *Problems of Communism,* X.6 (November–December 1961).

23. Henry C. Simons, "Some Reflections on Syndicalism," In *Economic Policy for a Free Society* (Chicago, 1948).

24. The present tense has been used in the text since most of the discussion refers to the system as it existed between 1952 and 1961. The reader should keep in mind, however, that new control measures were introduced in 1962. It is too early to judge their scope.

25. Shoes and some types of textiles are somewhat more subject to competition than most other consumer goods. In a sense it may perhaps be said that the Yugoslav experiment would have greater chances of success in a developed industrial country such as the United States than in the area in which it is taking place. For a recogni-

tion of the problem of monopolies see the report by Svetozar Vukmanovic-Tempo in *Yugoslav Trade Unions Under New Conditions* (Belgrade, 1959), pp. 49–54.

26. See note 29 below.

27. United Nations, "Economic Planning and Management in Yugoslavia," p. 46.

28. A brief history of the early system of income distribution is in Svetozar Vukmanovic-Tempo, "A Decade of Workers' Management," *Yugoslav Trade Unions*, Belgrade, I.1:4–9 (July–September 1960).

29. Bobrowski, *La Yugoslavie Socialiste*, passim. The two pillars of the system used in 1952 were a compulsory coefficient for the utilization of equipment — referred to above — and different coefficients for different enterprises in determining the wages fund. The first proved impossible to implement; no techniques were available for an objective measurement of plant capacity, nor was it possible to enforce the utilization ratios. In the measurement of the wages fund of the different plants, the regime used the formula: $w = r/(1 + x)$, w = wages fund, r = receipts minus material costs, x = a coefficient set by administrative action for each branch of economic activity. The average x for 1952 was 113. This method raised the issue of labor productivity and led to the dismissal of unnecessary workers in order to divide w among fewer heads, but at the same time confused the issue. Sales prices proved at least as important for the wages fund as physical productivity; a high x reduced the relationship between effort and wage increases. No objective basis for setting the different coefficients was established so that administrative action once again was the key to the distribution of the national income. Thus in 1952 the coefficient x was 582 for manufacturing, 19 for agriculture, 146 for construction, 215 for transportation, 82 for trade, 76 for artisans.

30. Freedom of the enterprise had reached its peak to that date in 1961. See "Yugoslav Economic Experiments" in *The Economist*, June 17, 1961. Although a drought must bear the main responsibility for the poor harvest of that year, it is probable that the freedom somewhat abruptly given to the councils to decide on the allocation of the surplus between personal incomes and the various funds (housing, general reserve, depreciation, investment, training, health program, vacation camps) added to the troubles.

31. Harry Schleicher, "Jugoslawien zwischen Planwirtschaft und Selbstverwaltung," *Europa Archiv*, 15.2 (June 20, 1962).

32. William N. Loucks, "Workers' Self-Government."

33. United Nations, "Economic Planning and Management in Yugoslavia," p. 49.

34. "Regulation on salaries of workers of Economic Organizations" of April 27, 1957, reprinted in "The New Yugoslav Law."

35. Federal Statistical Office, *Workers' Councils and Managing Boards of Economic Enterprises in 1956*, Statistical Bulletin No. 77 (English version). Unless otherwise stated, all figures refer to enterprises with 30 employees or more.

36. From the point of view of effectiveness of the councils this has been criticized, and the proposal has been made to extend the period of service to two years, with half the council members to be elected each year. Marko Krjichnik, "Organisation et méthodes de Travail des organes d'autogestion ouvrière," *Questions Actuelles du Socialisme*, 43–4:110 (July–October 1957). In fact, as was mentioned before, decrees in 1955 and 1958 have extended the term of office of council and board members to two years.

37. *New York Times*, May 7, 1962.

38. Krjichnik, "Organisation et Méthodes de Travail," pp. 115–6.

39. Krjichnik, "Organisation et Méthodes de Travail," p. 116, favors abandoning the managing board.

40. Benjamin Ward, "Workers' Management in Yugoslavia," *Journal of Political Economy,* LXV.5 (October, 1957). Branko Horvat and Vlado Rašcović, "Workers' Management in Yugoslavia, A Comment," *Journal of Political Economy,* LXVII.2 (April 1959).

41. "Evolution du Système d'autogestion ouvrière," *Questions Actuelles du Socialisme,* pp. 110–1.

42. "Évolution du Système d'autogestion ouvrière," p. 112. Krjichnik, "Organization et Méthodes de Travail," p. 115, rejects categorically proposals to pay the council members. Statisticki Bilten Broj 77, tables 2–34, p. 48, and English text, p. 22, give data on the compensation of council members.

43. Krjichnik, "Organisation et Méthodes de Travail," pp. 112–5.

44. Horvat and Rašcović, "Workers' Management in Yugoslavia," p. 197.

45. *New York Times,* January 31, 1958.

46. Horvat and Rašcović, "Workers' Management in Yugoslavia," pp. 197–8.

47. Of 2935 industrial enterprises (including mining and construction) only 43 were reported to have introduced piecework systems of payment, 112 were completing plans, and 129 were just beginning to draw up plans. U.S. Department of Labor, *Labor Developments Abroad,* October 1959, p. 5.

48. Hassan Brkitch, "La place des Conseils Ouvriers dans notre système," *Questions Actuelles du Socialisme,* 43–44:80 (July–October 1957).

CHAPTER V

1. This chapter is reprinted with some modifications from *Industrial and Labor Relations Review,* 14.3:379–96 (April 1961).

2. General surveys of the economic evolution for this period can be found in Thad Paul Alton, *Polish Postwar Economy* (New York, 1955); Institut National de la Statistique et des Études Économiques, *Memento Économique, La Pologne* (Paris, 1953); R. P. Rochlin, *Die Wirtschaft Polens von 1945 bis 1952* (Berlin, n.d.); Jan Marczewski, *Planification et Croissance Économique des Democraties Populaires,* 2 vols. (Paris, 1956); W. J. Standiewicz and J. M. Montias, *Institutional Changes in the Postwar Economy of Poland* (New York, 1955). A penetrating analysis can be found in John M. Montias, *Central Planning in Poland* (New Haven, 1962).

3. Standiewicz and Montias, *Institutional Changes,* pp. 18–19.

4. Alton, *Polish Postwar Economy,* pp. 40, 58.

5. "Observations on Workers' Self Government," by a Polish Observer, report (mimeo.) submitted to an international seminar on "Workers' Participation in Management" (Vienna, September 1958).

6. United Nations, *Economic Bulletin for Europe,* 9.3:21–48 (November 1957). The rise of industrial output "reflected an extraordinary concentration . . . of all possible resources, including both import capacity and investment means, on fostering the growth of industry — and especially of heavy industry. Building and construction were practically limited to what was necessary to provide the essential facilities for the industrial development, including the housing needed for workers in new and expanding enterprises, and the development of transport lagged behind the rate of industrial growth to such an extent as constantly to hamper the general industrial expansion."

7. "The main disproportion, as everyone knows," said the periodical *Zycie*

Gospodarcze, no. 13, 1959, "was connected with the inadequate development of agriculture. This prevented any rise in the standard of living of the population."

8. Marczewski, *Planification et Croissance Économique,* vol. 1, p. 249.

9. United Nations, *Economic Bulletin,* p. 23.

10. The Central Statistical Office succeeded in showing an increase of 27.6 per cent in real wages from 1949 to 1955. This estimate is based upon a faulty index of retail prices and has been sharply criticized in Poland itself. John Michael Montias, "Unbinding the Polish Economy," *Foreign Affairs,* 35.3:474 (April 1957). The author comes to the conclusion that urban real wages suffered "sharp setbacks" in 1951 and 1952 and "never fully recovered" from them.

11. "Observations . . . ," p. 2; also Szymon Jakubowicz, "New Forms of Industrial Management," *Polish Perspectives,* no. 2, June 1958.

12. It is reported that costs per automobile were found to be more than twice the price at which automobiles sold (64,000 *zlotys* versus 31,000). "La Courte Expérience des Conseils Ouvriers en Pologne," *La Documentation Française,* no. 2453, August 26, 1958, p. 4; Andre Babeau, *Les Conseils Ouvriers en Pologne* (Paris, 1960).

13. *Nowa Kultura,* Oct. 20, 1957, under the title "Tell the Truth! This is how everything started!" Quoted in "La Courte Experience," p. 4, note.

14. Montias, "Unbinding the Polish Economy," p. 478.

15. See "La Courte Expérience," p. 4, note 3. There is no doubt, however, about Yugoslav influence after October. The Russian-Yugoslav dispute may have made it appear unwise to refer to the Yugoslav precedent in Poland. This is almost painfully obvious in some publications such as Szymon Jakubowicz, "New Forms of Industrial Management," *Polish Perspectives,* no. 2, June 1958. The author refers to the "U.S.S.R., Czechoslovakia, East Germany and Poland [where] various systems of organization and management of industry are being established to replace the previous, almost identical, systems." The omission of Yugoslavia in this listing cannot be accidental.

16. "Observations . . . ," p. 3.

17. Urban, "Magna Carta Libertatum," *Po Prostu,* September 30, 1956. Similarly, at a later stage, the review *Nowe Drogi* said: "The unions, exclusively concerned with carrying out the production plan, have more and more ceased to represent the working class and to defend its interests," February 1958, p. 84.

18. W. Brus, "Pazdziernik, Model Pazdziernikowy" (October, the October Model), *Zycie Gospodarcze,* no. 42, 1957. "Economic reforms," he said, "were not only fundamental from the economic point of view but [provided] also the basis of lasting political changes, as the essential condition of Socialist democracy." Quoted in J. M. Montias, "The Polish 'Economic Model,'" *Problems of Communism,* 9.2:18 (March–April 1960).

19. "La Courte Expérience," p. 6.

20. Decree of Feb. 18, 1955 regarding the "fund of the enterprise."

21. Polish discussion on the problems of economic management are commonly designated as debates on the "model." Montias, "The Polish 'Economic Model,'" p. 20.

22. "Teze Rady Ekonomicznay" (Theses of the Economic Council), *Zycie Gospodarcze,* no. 22, 1957, p. 2.

23. Montias, "Unbinding the Polish Economy," p. 23. For a criticism of the narrow scope of the price reform, see Juliusz Gordon, "Towards a Better Organized Price Structure," *Gospodarcze Planova,* no. 3, 1960.

24. See, for instance, the discussion in the Twelfth Plenum of the Central Committee of the United Workers' party in November 1958.

25. The irrationality of the price system seems to have been one of the main factors responsible for the meat crisis of 1959. Gomulka himself referred to the encouragement given to meat consumption by the "unfavorable relationship of meat prices to

the prices of other foodstuffs." See his report to the Third Plenum of the Central Committee of the United Workers' Party, *Trybuna Ludu*, no. 18, Warsaw, 1959.

26. Thus Prof. Bronislaw Minc in *Polityka*, no. 45, Nov. 8, 1958, says: "There are various ways of getting higher profits. One way is the difficult road of technical progress, reduction of costs and a real increase in output. There is also a much easier way, that of pushing up prices by changing the pattern of the range of products manufactured. And this latter road has not been blocked." See, however, the critical comments of Grzegorz Pisarski in *Zycie Gospodarcze*, no. 47, Nov. 23, 1958, who points out that changes in product patterns may "well be the result of an initially incorrect evaluation by trade of the influence of rises in the income of the population on shifts in the pattern of demand." The discussion is summarized in "Discussion on Prices," *Polish Perspectives*, nos. 1–2 (9–10), January–February 1959.

27. Jozef Gajda, "Management of Industrial Enterprises under Central Economic Planning in Poland." Paper presented to the Seventh Annual International Meeting of the Institute of Management Sciences, in October 1960.

28. Urszula Wojciechowska, "Enterprise Fund Problems," *Nowe Drogi*, no. 4, 1960.

29. Montias, "The Polish 'Economic Model,'" p. 17, note 2.

30. Wojciechowska, "Enterprise Fund Problems."

31. Montias, "Unbinding the Polish Economy," p. 17. The consequent overpayments have contributed to the inflationary pressures. "Poland's Economic Overhaul," *The Economist*, CXCVII 6115 (London, 1960).

32. "La Courte Expérience," p. 10.

33. Contrary to figures of the trade union federation, which spoke of 2824 councils, Gomulka used the figure "some 5600 workers' councils" in the spring of 1958. *Trybuna Ludu*, Warsaw, April 15, 1958.

34. The president of the works council of the Czeladz Coal Mine quotes a list of similar complaints in the Weekly Council Supplement of *Glos Pracy*, September 13, 1957. "La Courte Expérience," pp. 22, 24, note 5.

35. In a textile plant investigated by J. Kolaja, *A Polish Factory: a Case Study in Workers Participation in Industry* (Lexington, 1960), p. 33, the union secretary described the union tasks: "We look out for the welfare of the workers, we take care of their housing problems, tram and railway reduction tickets, organization of excursions, and so on." All these, significantly, are welfare problems of the workers arising outside the plant.

36. *Nowa Kultura*, April 4, 1957.

37. According to a member of the economic council, R. Fidelski, *Nowe Drogi*, April 1957. Systematic body search of workers leaving the plant is reported in a case study of a textile plant in Lodz. Kojala, *A Polish Factory*.

38. *Polish Perspectives*, 3.1 (January 1960).

39. *New York Times*, November 12, 1960.

40. The phrase coined was "labor parliament," *Po Prostu*, January 6, 1957.

41. Gomulka's speech of April 14, 1958 made before the Fourth Congress of the Trade Union Federation was published in *Trybuna Ludu*, 10.12:403–407 (June 6, 1958); see also "La Courte Expérience," pp. 29–30.

42. Italics added.

43. "The New Law on Workers' Controls," *Polish Perspectives*, no. 3 (11), March 1959.

44. In connection with the Third Congress of the party (March 1959), an interesting debate took place in various Polish periodicals. An attempt was made to take advantage of the disappointment brought about by the failure of the council experiment

to advocate a return to the system of management of the pre-October era (Prof. Bronislaw Minc, "Changes in the Direction of the National Economy," *Zycie Gospodarcze,* February 27, 1959). The response seems to indicate that the prevailing opinion among the economists at least rejected this "conservative leaning which we have to call the dogmatic tendency." "Industrial Management," *Polish Perspectives,* no. 6 (14), June 1959.

CHAPTER VI

1. Adolf Sturmthal, *Unity and Diversity in European Labor* (Glencoe, 1953), pp. 37–70.

2. See F. Meyers, *European Coal Miners Unions: Structure and Function* (Los Angeles, 1961).

3. Val Lorwin, *The French Labor Movement* (Cambridge, Mass., 1954), p. 149.

4. See Meyers, *European Coal Miners Unions,* p. 23.

5. *Yugoslav Trade Unions,* Belgrade, June 1955, pp. 20–23.

6. "Fur die Praxis des Betriebsrats," *Der Gewerkschafter,* 6.12:30 (Frankfurt, 1958).

7. A. Deleon, *33 Questions — 33 Answers on Workers' Self-Government in Yugoslavia* (Belgrade, 1956), p. 47, cites one example of attempted interference with the drawing up of lists of candidates; in this case the director was the guilty party.

8. See Sturmthal, *Unity and Diversity in European Labor,* particularly pp. 53–62; Lorwin, *The French Labor Movement.*

9. Otto Stolz, *Die Gewerkschaften in der Sackgasse. Ein Kritisches Porträt* (Munich, 1959), pp. 43–50.

CHAPTER VII

1. Adolf Sturmthal, *Unity and Diversity in European Labor* (Glencoe, 1953), pp. 45–6.

2. *Soziale Praxis,* no. 27, April 3, 1919; quoted in Kurt Brigl-Matthiass, *Das Betriebsräteproblem* (Berlin and Leipzig, 1926), p. 30. For recent complaints about "plant egoism," see Fritz Klenner, *Das Unbehagen in der Demokratie* (Vienna, 1956), pp. 35–6.

3. For Germany, see Brigl-Matthiass, *Das Betriebsräteproblem,* pp. 36–75. For Austria, Charles A. Gulick, *Austria — From Habsburg to Hitler,* vol. I, *Labor's Workshop of Democracy* (Berkeley and Los Angeles, 1948), pp. 205–14.

4. Klenner, *Das Unbehagen,* pp. 33–40, devotes one central section of his study to "the problem of alienation from the trade union." Benedict Kautsky, "Betriebsrat und Gewerkschaft," *Die Zukunft,* January, 1954, refers to "the elimination of the unions from the consciousness of their members." Sharp comments are also made by Otto Stolz, *Die Gewerkschaften in der Sackgasse. Ein kritisches Porträt* (Munich 1959). See also Henry C. Wallich, *Mainsprings of the German Revival* (New Haven, 1955), pp. 306–11).

5. Described in Chapter III.

6. Thus Hugh Clegg in *A New Approach to Industrial Democracy* (Oxford, 1960), p. 54, says, "both in the Weimar Republic and since the War, German unions have been able to make use of the legal powers of the Work Councils to penetrate many firms that would otherwise have refused their entry. On balance, Work Councils may have done more to strengthen the unions than to undermine them."

7. See, for instance, F. R. Allemann, "German Socialists Abandon Marxism," *The New Leader,* January 15, 1960.

8. Val Lorwin, *The French Labor Movement* (Cambridge, Mass., 1954), p. 258.

9. Georges Lefranc, *Les Expériences Syndicales en France de 1939 à 1950* (Paris, 1950), pp. 359–60.

10. A very good discussion of this is in F. Meyers, *European Coal Miners Unions: Structure and Function* (Los Angeles, 1961), pp. 58–61. The de Gaulle era may have brought about a change in the relations among the competitive union federations. Cooperation among them, including the Communist-led CGT seems not only possible, but also effective. Whether this is a permanent change in interunion relations remains to be seen. Politically, the Communists are likely to profit most from such cooperation.

11. Quoted in Lorwin, *The French Labor Movement,* p. 267.

12. Benoît Frachon in *Revue des Comités d'Entreprise,* 1948, quoted in Lorwin, *The French Labor Movement,* p. 268.

13. Frachon, speaking to the CGT convention in 1951; Lorwin, *The French Labor Movement,* pp. 268–269.

CHAPTER VIII

1. A report of the Information Service Yugoslavia on the "Trade Union Branch in the System of Workers' Self-Government" states: "In the first phase of their post-war activities in Yugoslavia trade unions were concerned chiefly with the questions of production. Apart from the protection of workers' personal rights in labor relations, development of cultural life in factory collectives, etc., trade unions were engaged in the field of enterprises' production as well." An article in *Yugoslav Trade Unions,* Belgrade, November 1954, reproducing in English articles from *Rad,* the organ of the central council of the trade union federation of Yugoslavia, has the title: "The Trade Unions — One of the Organizations of Management."

2. Clark Kerr and Abraham Siegel, "The Structuring of the Labor Force in Industrial Society: New Dimensions and New Questions," *Industrial and Labor Relations Review,* 8.2 (January 1955). Clark Kerr, Frederick H. Harbison, John T. Dunlop, and Charles A. Myers, "The Labor Problem in Economic Development: A Framework for a Reappraisal," *International Labour Review,* LXXI.3 (March 1955), and *Industrialism and Industrial Man* (New York, 1961).

3. For a discussion of these problems and some of the literature on the subject see Adolf Sturmthal, "Unions and Economic Development" in *Economic Development and Cultural Change,* VIII.2 (January 1960).

4. The first task assigned to the unions in the constitution of the Trade Union Federation of Yugoslavia is: "To educate the working class in the spirit of scientific Socialism and to work to educate it politically, culturally, and in economic and technical matters." Dunlop, *Industrial Relations Systems* (New York, 1959), p. 293.

5. See Emily Clark Brown, "The Local Union in Soviet Industry: Its Relations with Members, Party, and Management," *Industrial and Labor Relations Review,* 13.2 (January 1960). The impressions reported by the author may perhaps be regarded as tentative validation of the hypothesis advanced above: Gradually rising living standards and a self-propelling process of economic growth advanced beyond the take-off stage may make possible gradually more effective union activities.

6. Milovan Djilas, *The New Class, An Analysis of the Communist System* (New York, 1957), p. 110, says: "Workers' organizations under the Communist System are really 'company' or 'yellow' organizations of a special kind. The expression 'of a

special kind' is used here because the employer is at the same time the government and the exponent of the predominant ideology."

7. The ILO report, "Workers' Management in Yugoslavia" (Geneva, 1962), in discussing grievance handling refers to the unions literally in a footnote, p. 199, note 2.

8. Dunlop, *Industrial Relations Systems,* p. 293–4, "Party control via the trade union Sindikat has been a more significant factor . . . The sindikat has played an increasingly important role more in protecting the 'national interest' than in protecting the interests of workers as such," George W. Hoffman and Fred W. Neal, *Yugoslavia and the New Communism* (New York, 1962), p. 245.

9. The ILO report, p. 197.

10. A. Lozovsky, *Marx and the Trade Unions* (New York, 1935).

11. Benjamin Ward, "Workers' Management in Yugoslavia," *Journal of Political Economy,* October 1957, pp. 107, 373–386.

CHAPTER IX

1. See Adolf Sturmthal, *Tragedy of European Labor, 1918–1939* (New York, 1951).

2. B. C. Roberts, *Trade Union Government and Administration in Great Britain* (Cambridge, Mass., 1956), p. 57.

3. The source for the reference to the engineers is T. B. Jeffreys, *The Story of the Engineers* quoted in Roberts.

4. F. Sellier, *Stratégie de la lutte sociale; France 1936–1960* (Paris, 1961), pp. 159, 162.

5. *Bulletin of the Militant CFTC,* November 1956, p. 24, quoted in Sellier, *Stratégie,* p. 160 (author's translation).

6. Roberts, *Trade Union Government.*

7. John T. Dunlop, *Industrial Relations Systems* (New York, 1959), pp. 294–96, and the study of Hugh Clegg, *A New Approach to Industrial Democracy* (Oxford, 1960). Although I would rather sharply disagree with some of Clegg's ideas, the experiences of self-government in industry quoted by him (pp. 119–28) and the considerations with which he accompanies his report are much in line with the suggestions made above. It may also be appropriate to refer to R. H. Tawney's foreword to Carter L. Goodrich, *The Frontier of Control: A Study in British Workshop Politics* (New York, 1921). According to Tawney the Goodrich study suggests that the sharp division ordinarily drawn between the sphere of "management" and that of "labor" is an abstraction which does less than justice to the complexity of the facts. If it is broadly true that in modern industry the function of the former is direction and of the latter the execution of orders transmitted to it, the line between them, nevertheless, fluctuates widely from industry to industry. "It varies, for one thing . . . with the nature of the work which is being carried on . . . It is also, of course, the result of conscious effort" (pp. xi–xiii). The view expressed in the text differs from that of David Riesman, for example, who is looking for "freedom in play" and speaks of the "fallacy of misplaced participation." See, however, Daniel Bell, *Work and Its Discontents. The Cult of Efficiency in America* (Boston, 1956).

8. Though frequent, this situation is not inevitable. In various parts of sub-Saharan Africa organized labor has been weak and has demonstrated little inclination to play a significant political role. See Elliot F. Berg and Jeffrey Butler, "Trade Unions and Politics in Middle Africa," in *Political Groups in Middle Africa,* James S. Coleman and Carl Rosberg, eds. (forthcoming).

Index

Adenauer, Konrad, 59, 61, 162
ADGB, 15, 157, 158; *see also* DGB
Adler, Friedrich, 23
Adorno, Theodore W., 201
AFA, 15
Agricultural cooperatives, 88
Ahlener program, 59, 61
Algeria, 25
Allemann, F. R., 209
Alton, Thad Paul, 205
André, Philip, 202
Association Capital-Travail, 42
Association des Cadres Direigeants de l'Industrie, 39
Austria: partisan politics and councils, 23, 154
Austria-Hungary: grievance commissions, 196
Auxiliary Service Law, 13, 53, 158, 193

Babeau, André, 206
Bargaining, *see* Collective bargaining
Bargaining councils: 2, 3, 5; follow union representation in plants, 11; functions of, 10; in newly industrialized countries, 192; problems of, 156–167; a substitute for union shops, 186; *see also* Collective bargaining
Bauer, Otto, 20
Bayart, Phillippe, 196, 197, 199
Bell, Daniel, 210
Bell, J. D. M., 195
Berg, Elliot F., 210
Bergeron, André, 199
Bezirk, 80, 144
Bicanic, Rudolf, 202, 203
Bismarck, Otto von, 12
Bizerba case, 79
Blum, Leon, 158
Blumenthal, W. M., 201
Board meeting attendance (France), 41
Bobrowski, Ch., 202, 203, 204
Böckler, Hans, 59, 60
Bourse du Travail, 183
Braun, Siegfreid, 201
Brèthe de le Gressaye, M. J., 197
Brigl-Matthiass, Kurt, 199, 208
Brkitch, Hassan, 205
Brown, Emily Clark, 209
Brus, W., 206
Builders' Guild, 20
Burgfrieden, 186
Business or financial reports (France), 40
Butler, Jeffrey, 210

Canadian unions, 10, 11
Card stewards, 2, 10
Carr, Edward H., 196
Catholic Center Party, 60, 158
Catholic Labor Federation, 152
CDU, 59, 61, 62, 66, 67, 141, 152, 153
CFTC, 34, 45, 46, 49n, 141, 144, 151, 156, 158, 185
CGC, 45, 143, 185
CGT, 35, 38, 40, 41, 43, 44, 45, 46, 49n, 51, 140, 144, 151, 156, 157, 158, 166, 167, 185
Chambelland, Pierre, 196
Chamberlain, Neil, 195
Charbonnages de France, 49n
Charter of Amiens, 151
"Charter of Labor," 19, 25
Checkweigh man, 1, 10
Christian Democratic Party, 61
Christian Democratic Union, *see* CDU
Christian Trade Union Federation, *see* CFTC
Class objectives, 182, 183, 184, 191
Clegg, Hugh, 178, 195, 208, 210
Coal mining industry: checkweigh man, 1, 10; council committees (Germany), 200; dismissals in (France), 34; Miners' Statute (France), 34, 49, 50; plant committees (France), 27; plant directors (Germany), 144; safety delegates (France), 18, 27, 49, 50; syndicats (France), 143
Codetermination enterprises: 55–57; and governing boards, 21, 51, 82; and industrial democracy, 61; and new stratum of functionaries, 69; literature on, 200; Social Democrats and, 59

Cole, G. D. H., 1, 6–7, 8, 9, 196
Collective bargaining: a management technique, 21; and grievance handling, 11; definition of, 3; development of, 183–184; in American unions, 6; in France, 17, 19, 45, 46, 47–49, 161; in Germany, 76–79, 161; in nationalized industries, 169; in Poland and Yugoslavia, 171; syndicalist attitude toward, 17; task of workshop organization, 2, 9; *see also* Bargaining councils
Collector, 2, 10
Collinet, Michel, 202
Commissione Interne, 1
Committees, *see* Plant committees, Shop committees
Communes in Yugoslavia, 95, 111
Communist influence: in managerial councils, 22–23; in newly industrialized nations, 193; opposition to in Poland, 137–138; *see also* Poland; Yugoslavia
in Austria, 23
in France: 17, 28, 151, 152; changes in policy, 49n; economic policies, 43; plant committees, 166–167; "workers' control," 18; workers' housing, 35
in Germany: trade unions, 60, 62, 145, 149; Westfalenhütte Dormund Council, 75; West Germany today, 152, 154; works counsellors, 66, 157
Communist International, 172–173, 181
Communist Party Central Committee (Poland), 125, 126
Confédération Générale des Cadres, *see* CGC
Confédération Général des Syndicats Independants, 46
Confédération Générale du Travail, *see* CGT
Conseil des Prud'hommes, 30
Constitutional Assembly (1848–49), 53
Control Council Law (No. 22), 54
Cooperatives: in France, 38; in Poland, 120; in Yugoslavia, 88
Council-administrated economy, *see* Poland; Yugoslavia
Councils, *see* Workers' councils
Cour de Cassation, 148
Currency reform (Germany), 61

DAG, 66, 149
DASP, 89
Dassault contract, 48
David, Marcel, 200
Davison, W. Phillips, 200
de Gaulle, Charles, 25, 209; capital-labor association, 42; educational programs of, 45; role of communists in policies of, 43
Deleon, A., 203, 208
De Leon, Daniel, 20
Deutscher Gewerkschäftsbund, 60; *see also* DGB
DGB, 13, 60, 61, 141, 145, 149, 152, 153, 158; *see also* ADGB
Disciplinary councils (France), 50
Directors of plants: in Germany, 82, 144; in Poland, 132; in Yugoslavia, 96–97, 112–115
Dirks, Walter, 201
Dismissals: in France, 33–34, 49; in Germany, 63, 71; in Yugoslavia, 113, 117
Djilas, Milovan, 209
Djilas trial, 99
Domino, W., 124
Dunlop, John T., 172, 203, 209, 210
Durand, Paul, 196, 197, 198, 199

Earnings, *see* Wages
Economic committees (Germany), 64–65, 82
Economic disputes (Germany), 64
Economic rationality: in Poland, 128, 129, 139; in Yugoslavia, 100
Education of workers: for committeemen in France, 44–45; councils as training devices, 178–179, 188–189
Egalitarian distribution, 131
Ehrmann, Henry, 196
Elections: workers' councils in the four countries, 147
France: stewards and plant committees, 28–29, 46; workers' councils, 147–148
Germany: shop stewards, 71; workers' councils, 62, 65–69, 147, 148–150
Poland: workers' councils, 147, 150
Yugoslavia: workers' councils, 96, 110–111, 147, 150–151
Enterprise committees (France), 36, 41
Erhard, Ludwig, 61
Ethnocentrism, 164, 181
Evolution of councils: 6–24; changing objectives, 180–181; in France, 17–19, 25–28; in Germany, 11–16, 53–62; in Poland, 21–23, 119–139; in Yugoslavia, 21–23, 86–118; political councils, 23–24

Fair Labor Standards Act, 76
Father of the chapel, 1, 8, 10, 183
FDGB, 152
Fellnor, William, 201
Fidelski, R., 207
Financial reports of companies (France), 40
Fisher, Paul, 199
Flanders, Allen, 195, 196
Force Ouvrière (FO), 45, 141, 143, 151, 156, 185

Frachon, Benôit, 166, 209
France: 25–52; board meeting attendance, 41; business financial reports, 40; Charter of Labor, 19, 25; collective bargaining, 17, 19, 45, 46, 47–49, 161; council elections, 147–148; council functions, 163; councils and political parties, 151–152; dismissals, 33–34, 49; economic activities, 40–42; evolution of labor movement, 17–19, 25–28; incentive pay, 39; management participation, 19–20; minority representation, 156–158; "most representative unions," 45–46, 148, 157, 165; nationalization laws, 20; section, 143; shop stewards, 27, 28–32, 161, 164–166; syndicats, 142–144; union membership, 165; union pluralism, 45; union structure, 142–144; unions and political parties, 140, 142, 151–152; welfare activities, 33–38; *see also* Communist influence
  plant committees: 1, 4, 17–19, 32–45, 138, 157; failure of, 44–45; legalized, 25–26; political connections of, 166–167
Freier Deutscher Gewerkschäftsbund, 152
Friedrich Wilhelm IV, 12
Furstenberg, Friedrich, 201

Gajda, Jozef, 207
German Salaried Employees' Union, 66, 149
Germany: 55–85; coal and steel industries, 55, 56; codetermination enterprises, 21, 51, 55–57, 59, 61, 69, 82, 200; collective bargaining, 76–79, 161; currency reform (1948), 61; directors of plants, 82, 144; dismissals in, 63, 71; fear of unemployment, 74–75, 160; grievance handling, 13, 53, 63, 71–72, 79–81, 161, 163; hiring practices, 63, 64, 81; labor and political parties, 141, 152–153; labor force structure, 83–85; minority representation, 157, 158; Nazi period, 16; occupation period, 55, 58; plant egoism, 159; political councils, 23; refugee groups, 84; überbetrieblich, 4; West Germany's industrial problems, 16; works constitution law, 57–65, 73–76, 149; *see also* Communist influence
  councils: 61, 62–70; bargaining, 186; election of, 147, 148–150; evolution of, 11–16, 53–62; functions of, 63–65, 163; managerial activity of, 21, 82–83; older men predominant in, 67–68, 83, 154; political parties and, 66–67, 152–153; rivalry with unions, 13–16, 159–162, 165
  unions: council-union rivalry, 13–16, 159–162, 165; future of, 162–164; geographic organization of, 7; postwar union movement, 59–61; structure of, 144–145
Geschäftsstelle, 80, 144
Gomulka, Wladyslaw, 120, 123, 126, 129, 135–136, 138, 170, 207
Goodrich, Carter L., 210
Gozdzik, L., 123
Great Britain: checkweigh man, 1; collective bargaining, 169, 184; nationalization measures, 20; nationalized industries, boards of, 56–57; reform councils, 4; shop stewards, 9–10, 186; syndicalism, 20; trade unions, 6, 10, 11
Grievance handling: in France, 18–19, 29–31, 161, 163; in Germany, 13, 53, 63, 71–72, 79–81, 161, 163; in Poland, 137, 163, 171; in the United States, 11; in Yugoslavia, 118, 163, 171
Grossman, Gregory, 203
Guild socialists, 2
Guillebaud, C. W., 196, 199
Gulick, Charles, 196, 200, 208

Hammelrath, Fro, 201
Harbison, Frederick H., 209
Hari, Bela, 24
Harmel, Léon, 18
Hiring practices: in Germany, 63, 64, 81; in Yugoslavia, 116–117
Hirsch-Duncker, 60, 157, 159
Hitler, Adolph, 56
HOAG, 79
Hoffman, George W., 202, 210
Horvat, Branko, 205
Hothouse industrialization, 129, 170
Housing for workers: in France, 35; in Germany, 70; in Poland, 130–131
Hungarian rebellion, 2, 22, 23–24
Hüttenwerk Oberhausen, A. G., 79

I. G. Metall, 148, 150
Incentive pay: in France, 39; in Poland, 130, 131; in Yugoslavia, 103, 104, 106–107, 115; settlement by local bargaining, 9
Incentives for enterprises: in Poland, 129–130; in Yugoslavia, 101
Incentives for workers: in Poland, 130–131; in Yugoslavia, 103, 104, 106–107
Industrial democracy, 61, 176; *see also* Managerial functions
Inflation: from "hot-house industrialization," 129; in Poland, 129; in Yugoslavia, 106, 114, 116
International Business Machines Co., 149

Jakubowicz, Szyman, 206
James, Emil, 196
Jantke, Carl, 200, 201
Jeffreys, T. B., 210

KAB, 152
Kardelj, Edvard, 93, 202
Kautsky, Benedict, 208
Kautsky, Karl, 20
Kerr, Clark, 200, 209
Kidric, Boris, 202
Kirchheimer, Otto, 200
Klenner, Fritz, 159, 196, 200, 208
Kolaja, J., 207
Kolkhozes, 88
Krjichnik, Marko, 204, 205
Krupp, Alfred, 12, 195

Labor courts: in France, 30, 34; in Germany, 64, 80–81
Labor inspector (France), 31, 33, 34, 50, 51
Labor movement: admission of unions into plants, 184–186; and political parties, 140–142, 151–155; as a class movement, 182, 183, 184, 191; collective bargaining development, 183–184; in newly industrialized nations, 192; in totalitarian systems, 190–191; meaning of the term, 140; range of objectives, 180
Labor unions, *see* Trade unions
Lange, Oskar, 120
Lasserre, Georges, 40, 41, 44, 198, 199
Le Creusot, 18
Lefranc, Georges, 209
Legien, Karl, 159
Lenin, Nikolai, 22
Leontieff's Input-Output Analysis, 99
Lesire-Ogrel, H., 199
Liebknecht, Karl, 23
Lipinski, Edward, 134
Loga-Sowinski, Ignacy, 137
Lorwin, Lewis L., 196
Lorwin, Val, 30, 45, 167, 196, 198, 199, 208, 209
Loucks, William N., 203, 204
Lozavsky, A., 210
Lublin Committee, 119
Lutz, Burkart, 201
Luxemburg, Rosa, 23

McPherson, William H., 197, 201
Majority principle, 156–158
Management councils: functions of, 3–4; independence from union, 190; in newly industrialized nations, 192; in France, 25–28; in Germany, 15; in Poland, 21–23; in Yugoslavia, 21–23, 110, 111–112; problems of, 168–179; *see also* Codetermination enterprises; Managerial functions
Managerial functions: growth of, 187–189; in France, 19–21; in Germany, 82–83, 177–179; in Poland, 132–133, 169–172, 176–177; in Yugoslavia, 96–104, 169–172, 176–179; social mobility and, 191–192; syndicalist programs for, 19–21; training for, 188; *see also* Management councils
Managing boards (Yugoslavia), 96–97, 110–112, 188, 189
Mannesmann Company, 73
Marczewski, Jan, 202, 205, 206
Marinko, Miha, 114
Marshall Plan, 167
Matignon agreement, 19
Medical service (France), 34
Mensheviks, 22
Metalworkers: in France, 143, 166; in Germany, 77, 79, 144
Meyers, F., 208, 209
Michailovic, General, 88
Milne-Bailey, W., 7, 195
Minc, Bronislaw, 207, 208
Minc, Hilary, 122
Miners' Statute (France), 49, 50
Mining industry, *see* Coal mining industry
Monopolies: in less developed countries, 187; in Yugoslavia, 103–104
Montias, J. M., 205, 206, 207
Montuclard, Maurice, 198
Moonlighting (Yugoslavia), 107, 114
Morris, William, 20
Mouvement Republicain Populaire (MRP), 45, 141, 151
Myers, Charles A., 209

Nagy, Imre, 24
National Congress of Works Councils, 15
Nationalized industries: boards of in Great Britain, 56–57; collective bargaining in, 169; disciplinary committees (France), 31; in Yugoslavia, 88–89, 95–104; justification for unions in, 187; plant committees (France), 20, 26–28; syndicalism and, 17; workers' council (Poland), 127; workers' representation (France), 51; workers' suggestions (France), 43; *see also* Poland; Yugoslavia
Nazism: industrial relations under, 16, 54, 58
Neal, Fred W., 202, 210
Neuloh, Otto, 195, 201
Neumann, Siggi, 153
Nipperdey, H. C., 200

Objectives of councils, 180–181
Organizing stewards, 2, 5
Owen, Robert, 20

Paternalism: in French welfare services, 39;

in German welfare services, 81; in German council system, 68
Piece rates: favor local bargaining, 9; in Germany, 77; in Poland, 134, 139; in Yugoslavia, 101, 105
Pirker, Theo, 201, 202
Pisarski, Grzegorz, 207
Plant assemblies (Germany), 64, 69
Plant autonomy: and interfirm competition, 187
Plant committees in France: 32–45; economic activities, 40–42, 138; education for committeemen, 44–45; effectiveness in action, 36–37; election of, 28–29, 46, 157; failure, reasons for, 44–45; financing, 36; functions, 33–38; grievance handling, 31; in nationalized industries, 26–28; legislation creating, 25–26; number of, 44; plant *vs.* enterprise committees, 36; political ties of, 166–167; production problems, 43; welfare services, 33–38, 138; *see also* Shop committees
Plant egoism, 159
Poland: 119–139; Communist Party, 119, 120, 123, 136–138, 141–142; collective bargaining, 171; decentralization in decision making, 126; de-Stalinization, 120, 122, 123, 126; directors, 132; economic and social background, 119–122; economic growth, 121; economic rationality, 128, 129; experimental enterprises, 124, 133; housing provisions, 130–131; incentives for enterprises, 129–130; incentives for workers, 130–131; managerial councils, 21–23; observance of central authority's framework, 128; party cell committees, 136–137; strikes, 136; trade unions, 125, 126, 133, 136, 145–146; wage structure, 134; workers' autonomy, 123
  councils: conflicting objectives of, 133; decline of the, 135–139; election of, 147–150; functions of, 126–127, 163; implications of the system of, 127–130; operation problems of, 131–135; origin of, 125; political parties and, 152; presidiums of, 132, 136
Political councils: 2, 4–5; effectiveness of, 183; evolution of, 23–24
Political parties: influence of and the labor movement, 140–142, 151–155, 180; in French labor movement, 166–167; *see also* Communist influence; Poland; Political councils; Yugoslavia
Poly-centrism, 181
Popular Front (France): 25, 27, 45, 165; industrial relations legislation, 17–18, 19
Poznan strike, 120, 123, 124
Pressure groups, 180
Pribicevic, Branko, 195
Price system: in Poland, 128–129; Yugoslavia, 98, 100, 103
Printing industry: father of the chapel, 1, 8, 10, 183; union shop units, 10
Production bonuses (France), 39
Production programs: workers' role in (France), 43
Profit sharing: incentive *vs.* egalitarian systems, 131; in Poland, 127, 130–131; in Yugoslavia, 102, 104
Proportional representation, 157–158

Rascovic, Vlado, 205
Rauch, Georg von, 196
Reform councils, 4, 5, 186
Refugee groups in Germany, 84
Reich, Nathan, 201
Renault automobile plant, 47, 51
Riesman, David, 210
Roberts, B. C., 10, 11, 183, 210
Rochlin, R. P., 205
Russia: inequality policy, 107; managerial councils, 22; Revolution of 1905, 22; Soviets, 1, 4; Twentieth Party Congress, 122

Safety and health committees (France), 49, 50–51
Safety delegates (France), 18, 27, 49, 50
Salm, Fritz, 77
Schleicher, Harry, 204
Schuman Plan, 167
Sellier, F., 199, 210
Shop committees: de facto committees, 2; *see also* Plant committees in France
  in Germany: and council elections, 148; election of, 72–73; grievance handling, 79; members, 145; only union representative in shop, 145; strike involvement of, 74
  in Poland, 125, 145–146
  in Yugoslavia, 145–146
Shop stewards: 1, 5; descriptions of, 2, 10; in craft unions, 9–10
  in France: 28–32, 164–166; dismissal of, 33; election of, 14, 28–29, 46, 157; finding candidates for, 31–32, 44; future of, 45; grievance handling, 29–31, 161; revived after World War II, 27; union strength and, 164–166; welfare activities, 35
  in Germany: 70–72; grievance handling, 71–72, 80
  in Great Britain: 184, 186
Shuchman, Abraham, 200, 202
Siegel, Abraham, 209
Simons, Henry, 102

Social Darwinism, 181
Social Democratic Party, 7, 59, 60, 62, 66, 67, 141, 152–153, 154, 159, 162
Socialist Labor Party (France), 20
Social mobility, 191
Social security benefits (Yugoslavia), 107
Social welfare, *see* Welfare services
Soldiers' and Workers' Councils, 22
Soviet of Workers' Deputies, 22
Soviets, 1, 4, 22, 183
Soviet Union, *see* Russia
SPD, *see* Social Democratic Party
Speier, Hans, 200
Spiro, Herbert J., 200, 201, 202
Stagner, R., 203
Stalin, Joseph, 22; de-Stalinism in Poland, 120, 122, 123, 126
Standard of living (Yugoslavia), 116
Stanovnik, Janez, 203
State Bus Transport Enterprise, 89
State Commission of Economic Planning, 120–121
State Goods and Textiles Trading Enterprise, 89
State Trading Enterprise, 89
Stern, Boris, 199
Steward, *see* Shop stewards
Stolz, Otto, 208
Strike benefits (Germany), 75
Strikes: in France, 166; in Germany, 62–63, 74, 75, 79–81, 161; in Poland, 120, 123, 124, 136; in Yugoslavia, 114
Strohmenger, Karl, 79
Strothmann, Fritz, 201
Structural problems of labor organizations, 140–155
Syndicalism: and managerial authority, 2, 23, 187; in France, 17, 19–21, 42, 51; problem for economic growth, 172
Syndicats, 142–144

Tawney, R. H., 210
Tax benefits in France, 42
Taxes in Yugoslavia, 101, 104, 107
Technical decision making, 189
Tendenzbetriebe, 159
Thomas, Albert, 18, 165
Ticket steward, 2, 10
Time-and-motion studies (France), 39
Tito, Marshal, 88, 91, 94, 110
Totalitarian system: and economic progress, 175–176; and workers' self-government, 190–191
Trade unions: a concomitant of modern industry, 169; admission into plants, 184–186; and council elections, 146–151; and political parties, 140–142, 151–155; as social communities, 7; communist control of, 172–176; place in collectivized economy, 168–169; structure of, 142–146; union-council relations, 156–162; *see also* Labor movement
  earliest British, 6–7
  in France: 25–26, 45–49; and committee failures, 44; grievance handling, 29; pluralism in, 45; weakening of, 31
  in Germany: at council meetings, 69; future of, 162–164; grievance handling, 79, 80; in postwar Germany, 59–60; shop committees, 72–73, 74; united union movement, 66–67; *vs.* councils, 13–16; wage agreements, 76–77
  in Poland, 125, 126, 133, 136, 168–179
  in Yugoslavia, 105, 117, 118, 168–179
Twentieth Party Congress, 122

Überbetrieblich, 13
Underdeveloped nations, 193
Unemployment: fear of in Germany, 74–75, 160; in Yugoslavia, 116
Union pluralism, 45
Unions, *see* Trade unions
United Polish Workers' Party, 123
United States unions: and political parties, 142; majority principle, 156, 164; organization of, 10–11
U.S.S.R., *see* Russia

Vasseur, Michel, 197
Vavpetic, Lado, 203
Verein für Soziale Betriebspraxis, 57
Volksdeutsche, 84, 88
Vukmanovitch-Tempo Svetozar, 170, 204

Wages: committees' influence on (France), 39; contract rate *vs.* effective rate (Germany), 76–77, 161, 164; function of works councils (Germany), 63; increases (Germany), 78; in Poland, 134, 171; in Yugoslavia, 101, 105–111, 171; *see also* Incentive pay; Piece rates; Profit sharing
Wagner Act, 11, 156, 158
Waldeck-Rousseau, 18
Waline, Pierre, 199
Wallich, Henry C., 200, 208
Ward, Benjamin, 205, 210
Webb, Sidney and Beatrice, 8
Wehner, Herbert, 153
Weimar Republic: 54, 55–56, 60, 61, 74, 82, 157, 158; councils *vs.* trade unions, 13–16
Welfare services: in France, 4, 33–38, 39; in Germany, 63, 81

West German Republic: union federation (DGB), 60; workers' representatives, 16; *see also* Germany; Works constitution law
Wilhelm I, 12
Windmuller, John P., 200
Wojciechuwska, Urszula, 207
Workers' and Soldiers' Councils, 22, 23, 53
Workers' autonomy, 123
Workers' councils: changing objectives, 180–181; collective bargaining development, 183–184; educational or training bodies, 178–179, 188–189; election of in the four countries, 147; evolution of, 6–24; functions in the four countries, 163; managerial councils, 168–179; managerial functions, 176–177, 187–190; political parties and, 2, 151–155; problems in a council-administrated economy, 97–102; technical decisions, 189; types of, 2–5; union-council relations, 146–151, 156–162; *see also* France; Germany; Poland; Yugoslavia
Workers' housing, *see* Housing for workers
Workers' Party (Poland), 120
Working conditions: committees' role in (France), 39; councils' role in (Germany), 63, 64
Workplace organization, *see* Workers' councils
Works Constitution Law: and grievance handling, 71–72; background of, 57–62; joint voting lists, 149; law and practice, 73–76; operation of, 65–67; summary of, 62–65, 73–74
Works Council Law, 53–54

Yugoslavia: 86–118; benefits of the new system, 115–118; break with Soviet Union, 91–92; business management, 95–104; communist influence, 141–142; competency, recognition of, 116; council and political parties, 152; council functions, 163; councillors, 108–111; decentralized decision making, 98, 116, 175, 177; deviations from established schemes, 113–114; differential controls, 114; directors, 96–97, 112–115; dismissals, 113, 117; economic growth, 90–93; economic planning, 89–91; economic rationality, 100; elections, 110–111, 147, 150–151; federal system of government, 93–95; hiring practices, 116–117; incentives for enterprises, 101; industrial development, 87–88; inflationary pressure, 106, 114, 116; internal divisions, 86–88; investment plans, 99; managerial functions, 21–23, 96-97, 110, 111–112, 169, 188, 189; monopolies, 103–104; multiplicity of controls, 115; nationalized industries, 88–89, 95–104; observance of central authority's framework, 97–100; plant autonomy, 187; problems in a council-administrated economy, 97–104; standard of living, 116; taxes, 101, 104, 107; unemployment, 116; unions, 117, 118, 145–146, 168–179; wage system, 101, 103, 104, 105-111, 115

WERTHEIM PUBLICATIONS IN INDUSTRIAL RELATIONS

J. D. Houser, *What the Employer Thinks*, 1927

Wertheim Lectures on Industrial Relations, 1929

William Haber, *Industrial Relations in the Building Industry*, 1930

Johnson O'Connor, *Psychometrics*, 1934

Paul H. Norgren, *The Swedish Collective Bargaining System*, 1941

Leo C. Brown, S.J., *Union Policies in the Leather Industry*, 1947

Walter Galenson, *Labor in Norway*, 1949

Dorothea de Schweinitz, *Labor and Management in a Common Enterprise*, 1949

Ralph Altman, *Availability for Work: A Study in Unemployment Compensation*, 1950

John T. Dunlop and Arthur D. Hill, *The Wage Adjustment Board: Wartime Stabilization in the Building and Construction Industry*, 1950

Walter Galenson, *The Danish System of Labor Relations: A Study in Industrial Peace*, 1952

Lloyd H. Fisher, *The Harvest Labor Market in California*, 1953

Theodore V. Purcell, S.J., *The Worker Speaks His Mind on Company and Union*, 1953

Donald J. White, *The New England Fishing Industry*, 1954

Val R. Lorwin, *The French Labor Movement*, 1954

Philip Taft, *The Structure and Government of Labor Unions*, 1954

George B. Baldwin, *Beyond Nationalization: The Labor Problems of British Coal*, 1955

Kenneth F. Walker, *Industrial Relations in Australia*, 1956

Charles A. Myers, *Labor Problems in the Industrialization of India*, 1958

Herbert J. Spiro, *The Politics of German Codetermination*, 1958

Mark W. Leiserson, *Wages and Economic Control in Norway, 1945–1957*, 1959

J. Pen, *The Wage Rate under Collective Bargaining*, 1959

Jack Stieber, *The Steel Industry Wage Structure*, 1959

Theodore V. Purcell, S.J., *Blue Collar Man: Patterns of Dual Allegiance in Industry,* 1960

Carl Erik Knoellinger, *Labor in Finland,* 1960

Sumner H. Slichter, *Potentials of the American Economy: Selected Essays,* edited by John T. Dunlop, 1961

C. L. Christenson, *Economic Redevelopment in Bituminous Coal: The Special Case of Technological Advance in United States Coal Mines, 1930–1960,* 1962

Daniel L. Horowitz, *The Italian Labor Movement,* 1963

Adolf Sturmthal, *Workers Councils: A Study of Workplace Organization on Both Sides of the Iron Curtain,* 1964

STUDIES IN LABOR-MANAGEMENT HISTORY

Lloyd Ulman, *The Rise of the National Trade Union: The Development and Significance of its Structure, Governing Institutions, and Economic Policies,* 1955

Joseph P. Goldberg, *The Maritime Story: A Study in Labor-Management Relations, 1957,* 1958

Walter Galenson, *The CIO Challenge to the AFL: A History of the American Labor Movement, 1935–1941,* 1960

Morris A. Horowitz, *The New York Hotel Industry: A Labor Relations Study,* 1960

Mark Perlman, *The Machinists: A New Study in Trade Unionism,* 1961

Fred C. Munson, *Labor Relations in the Lithographic Industry,* 1953

Garth L. Mangum, *The Operating Engineers: The Economic History of a Trade Union,* 1964

PUBLISHED BY McGRAW-HILL BOOK CO., INC

Robert J. Alexander, *Labor Relations in Argentina, Brazil, and Chile,* 1961

Carl M. Stevens, *Strategy and Collective Bargaining Negotiation,* 1963

Bei Fragen zur Produktsicherheit wenden Sie sich bitte an:
If you have any questions regarding product safety,
please contact:

Walter de Gruyter GmbH
Genthiner Straße 13
10785 Berlin
productsafety@degruyterbrill.com